LIFE OF TUKARAM

LIFE OF TUKARAM

TRANSLATION

from Mahipati's Bhaktalilamrita, Chapters 25 to 40

BY

JUSTIN E. ABBOTT

MOTILAL BANARSIDASS

Delhi Varanasi Patna Madras

First Edition Poona 1930, Reprint Delhi 1980, 1986

MOTILAL BANARSIDASS
Bungalow Road, Jawahar Nagar, Delhi 110 007
Branches
Chowk, Varanasi 221 001
Ashok Rajpath, Patna 800 004
6 Appar Swamy Koil Street, Mylapore, Madras 600 004

ISBN: 81–208–0169–5 (Cloth)
ISBN: 81–208–0170–9 (Paper)

PRINTED IN INDIA
BY JAINENDRA PRAKASH JAIN AT SHRI JAINENDRA PRESS, A-45 NARAINA INDUSTRIAL AREA, PHASE I, NEW DELHI 110 028 AND PUBLISHED BY NARENDRA PRAKASH JAIN FOR MOTILAL BANARSIDASS, DELHI 110 007

PREFACE

The life of Tukaram, as portrayed by Mahipati in the Bhaktalilamrita chapters 25 to 40, presents many difficult problems for the historian, but for one who can lay aside these problems, and can let his imagination accept the vivid picture Mahipati gives us, undisturbed by questions of fact or legend, the life of Tukaram is full of human interest, full of food for the moralist, full of suggestions for the idealist, and to every one an inspiration to a better and nobler life.

Historical problems.—As generally accepted Tukaram was born in 1608, and ascended bodily into heaven in 1649. Mahipati wrote his account of Tukaram in 1774, or 125 years after Tukaram's disappearance. Now Mahipati does not give the slightest hint either in the Bhaktalilamrita, or in the Bhaktavijaya, written 12 years earlier, as to where he obtained his information regarding Tukaram's life. It is easy enough to make conjectures, as many do, but for the true historian all evidence is lacking. One hundred and twenty-five years give ample time for legends to grow around an honoured name, but whether fact or legend, we do not know Mahipati's source of information. Did he have access to books that have disappeared? Did he visit Dehu, where Tukaram's descendants were living, and gather local traditions? Did he to some extent draw on his own imagination to supply a natural setting to some of Tukaram's autobiographical *abhangs?* [Verses]. These questionings are partially answered by the fact that books were produced by the laborious efforts of copying by hand.

There were not many copies of any book. We know that some have entirely disappeared. We can conjecture that Mahipati's original source has been lost. We do know that Mahipati had a considerable library, and that he used books that contained the lives of saints, as for example, his use of Keshavsvami's life of Eknath, and of Namdev's account of Dnyanadev, and other saints, but we do not know, whether Mahipati had before him some written, but now lost, source. The account of Tukaram in the Bhaktavijaya, written in 1762, has suggestive similarities and dissimilarities from his Bhaktalilamrita account. Did he depend on his memory? That might explain minor discrepancies, but it also contains incidents not found in the Bhaktalilamrita. In conclusion, we do not know Mahipati's sources of information, nor their historical value.

The *abhangs* of Tukaram contain some of an autobiographical nature, and correspond with Mahipati's account. It has been conjectured, therefore, that some of Mahipati's stories may have been imaginary, so as to provide a natural setting to the contents of those *abhangs,* the general fact being supplied by Tukaram and the details by Mahipati. But the historian meets with a very serious difficulty here, arising from uncertainties connected with the text of Tukaram's *abhangs.* Tukaram did not sit down, and write a book of poems, and issue it under his signature. If tradition can be trusted, he spent much of his time, day and night, in the performance of *kirtans,* or services of song, in the praise of God, or on any theme which he wished to impress on his hearers. His thoughts flowed in words that took the form of a metre called the *abhang,* and as they were spoken, they were recorded by his close companions, Santaji Teli Jaganade, Gangadhar

Maval, and Rameshvar Bhat. A very old manuscript still exists among the descendants of Santaji Teli at Chakan, which claims to be in Santaji's handwriting, and bears every evidence of an age that makes this claim quite probable. In this manuscript there are 1323 *abhangs,* and it is to be presumed that this collection would contain all the *abhangs* that in Santaji's life time were considered the *abhangs* of Tukaram. But there are other and later collections of *abhangs* that bear Tukaram's name, that number more than four thousand, and the suspicion has weight that many of these are by other authors, who by adding the characteristic words, "Tuka mhane," (Tuka says), at the end of their *abhangs,* have been able to find a place for them among the real *abhangs* of Tukaram. There are many such collections, all differing more or less; and the printed texts, of which there have been many, have followed whims of the publishers, and not the laws of textual criticism. The result is a confusion of texts, which destroys the historic value of the *abhangs.* We cannot know what *abhangs* are really Tukaram's, and what belong to later times. No *abhang* can be depended upon absolutely as words that fell from Tukaram's lips. If Mahipati used any of these *abhangs* that are not Tukaram's, their authority is of little value. If these additions are late, and founded on Mahipati's account, they have no historic value. But the text and its problems, give the historian much darkness and very little light.

Tuka's life as portrayed.—Divesting ourselves of the troublesome questions of historicity, and not caring whether Mahipati gives us facts or legends, we become prepared to enjoy the portrayal of life that appeals to our sympathy, because so human, that calls us to moral and spiritual ideals, to some of which we may take exception, but which takes us out of the realm of the low and the mean, and into the realm of the pure and the noble, and for which his final end seems so fitting, a chariot of light from Heaven taking him bodily away, as belonging more to Heaven than to earth.

A word to the reader.—To the Western reader, unfamiliar with Indian life, thought, and literature, this translation may contain much that will not be understood. There are allusions to social customs, religious rites, Puranik stories and the like that need explanation to be appreciated. The religious point of view will puzzle many. It would be possible to help the reader by extended footnotes, but it has seemed better to me to confine myself to being a translator, and letting my readers seek elsewhere the answer to their questionings, if their curiosity is sufficiently keen. I may say, however, that the more they read of these translations, and the more they use the Glossary in the Appendix, the more familiar they will become with Indian life and thought, history and legends.

Naturally a translation has less attraction than the original. But unfortunately Mahipati's readers are few. Western readers of my translation will meet with much they cannot understand. Never having lived in India, they cannot picture the scenes so vividly told by Mahipati. They cannot see the life in the little village of Dehu, identical with the life that still exists in the town, and on the bank of the Indrayani that flows by the town, still sacred for the washing away of sins, as well as bodily filth. They cannot see Tuka, the singing Gosavi, with his cymbals in his hands, singing God's names as he walks the streets of the little town, or along the path leading to his retreat in the mountain of Bhamgiri. The temple of Vithoba, the idol within, the nightly *kirtans* in the temple precincts, Tuka leading with his cymbals marking time, and he himself sometimes dancing in ecstasy, are familiar scenes to those whose language is Marathi, but unfamiliar to most of those who read this translation. The danger of misunderstanding Tuka is a real one therefore, and this word of caution will not be in vain, if readers, unfamiliar with Indian life and thought, are careful not to judge too hastily.

Tuka's asceticism may perhaps be misunderstood. Tuka became an ascetic, not because he saw in asceticism a way to some spiritual advantage, but because he made God so central in his thought that he lost all interest in his body. He became a Videhi, that is, one so absorbed in his thought of God, that he had no time or thought or desire to supply bodily needs. He ate when food was given him, he slept when Nature compelled it. His body functioned in its natural way, but he took no interest in it. His thought centered only on God. While this ascetic life seemed ideal for himself, and for those who like him were drawn into it through an inspiration that seemed outside of themselves, it does not appear that Tuka urged it as an ideal life for all. On the contrary, if there is truth in Mahipati's story of King Shivaji's visit to this saint, and his determination to give up the kingly life, and Tuka's reminding him of the teaching of the Bhagavadgita, that every caste had its special duties to be performed, and that it was his duty to remain a king, with his kingly duties. If this story is true, it gives us Tuka's principle, that all men may be called to a higher life, but few only chosen for such a life as he lived, indifferent to bodily needs, and God his central, and only thought.

Another point, which the Western reader may be depended upon to misunderstand, is Tuka's Theology. This misunderstanding arises partly from the fact that some of the most important philosophic terms have no exact equivalents in English, and other important words, have an English word equivalent etymologically but that English word does not have the same content as the Sanskrit or Marathi term. The translation of Maya, as illusion, is an example of confusing inaccuracy. God is spoken of as both *sagun* and *nirgun,* as used by Tukaram.

Another fruitful source of misunderstanding is the Westerners' misconception of Hindu idolatry and polytheism. Vishnu, Krishna, Ram and Vithoba, for example, seem so many separate, independent gods, and the stone images which represent them in their temples seem but little removed from the fetishism of savage people. And yet India's best thinkers, her deeply philosophic minds, and her noblest saints, like Eknath, Tukaram and Ramdas, have been enthusiastic idolators, without a suspicion in their minds, that such worship could be called a sign of mental weakness, or moral degeneracy. It is not necessary to agree with India's best thinkers, her moralists or religious teachers, but these men are worthy of respect, and should be listened to with respect, and without the pride that can see truth only in one's own knowledge.

To understand the Theology of Tukaram or any of the Maratha saints, one should not begin with idolatrous worship and work backward, but should begin with that philosophy that for centuries has dominated Hindu thought. Its basis is an absolute Monism. This whole universe, every thing included, consists of one substance. For convenience of talking about it, it may be called Brahma, or otherwise named, but no human words can be used in describing it, for nothing is known of it. But on this monistic basis Hindu Theology begins. God, a personal being, omniscient, omnipotent, and good, is a form in which the one Substance exists. God is the creator of the forms in which the one Substance exists. There is but one God. Thus the strictest monotheism stands as the basis of Hindu Theology. But God being one of the various forms in which this universe consists, it is assumed that He can be described, and He has been described by philosophers, and poets, and teachers. In the description of Him the most important is that He manifests Himself in different forms, and hence come such manifestations of His personality, as Brahmadev, God functioning as Creator; Vishnu, God functioning as the life of all things; and Shiva, God in the decay and death of all things. But these Manifestations have also appeared in diverse times, and in diverse manners as *avatars* for special purposes, each with a name to distinguish one from another. All these manifestations and *avatars* are thus of God-Supreme. Hinduism stands, therefore, for the strictest Monotheism, but admitting many manifestations and *avatars,* with their special characteristics to suit the occasion for their appearance.

The history of idolatry is not clear, but to God-fearing Hindus it has seemed a way of natural approach to God. It has never been considered the only way. The *manas puja,* or the direct mental worship, has always been given a higher place, and idolatry has been considered a lower step to lead to a higher, but the stone or metal image of some supposed manifestation of an *avatar,* in its setting in a temple sacred to that manifestation, has been and is to-day an inspiration to the worship of God. The rationality of idolatry can be easily attacked, and it can be placed on exhibition with other superstitions, but it cannot be denied that God-fearing Hindus have found spiritual satisfaction in their worship of God through an idol. Eknath, and Tukaram, and Ramdas are typical examples of loving devotion expressed through idolatry. As we have remarked, idolatry is not the only conception or worship that India has evolved, and the future may show a trend to the higher forms, with idolatry left for the most ignorant. Tukaram's *abhangs* belong to the past untouched by any breath of modern criticism. And they must be so understood in all judgments formed concerning them.

Tuka, as he calls himself, and as Mahipati calls him, was not a learned man. He never went to school. His father taught him the little that he knew. He did not know Sanskrit. He must have found great difficulty in understanding the works of Dnyanadev, and Eknath, in their antique Marathi forms, when he retired with his books to his mountain retreat, to read and study them. He was not at first aware that he was a poet by his very nature. His caste, as Shudra, was comparatively low, and no inspiration came to him from that source, nor from the Brahmans of his acquaintance, to whom he was accustomed to bow as Hindu social laws demanded. Tuka's growth was like the growth of a tree, from seed to full stature, on some retired spot, unassisted except by the very laws of his own being. Forced at first by hard necessity he was a petty grocer in a little village, successful, because of his natural ability and honesty, but his heart was not in his business. He wanted God in his soul, and all earthly things, money and property he counted as dung. Naturally he failed in business, and then came a period of adjustment to his now complete indifference to earthly things, and the unsympathetic attitude of his sharp tongued wife, and scorning neighbours. He had no religious teacher. He had no one to guide him in his moral life, or in his relations to men in general. No human teacher taught him not to return evil for evil. No one taught him that a soft answer turneth away wrath, but to what pages can one turn to find such a life elsewhere in his actual ministering to the human needs about him? Mahipati pictures him helping the sick, carrying the burdens of the weary, giving water to the thirsty, food to the hungry, going on errands for the lame. Even animals came in for his kind thought. He watched for such as needed water or food. Even in this he met with no sympathy from his wife, and little from his neighbours. Tuka had to walk alone. His teacher was no other than the Spirit within him. This brings us to the latter half of his life, in which God is his all in all. God was his food and his drink. The world was nothing to him. God was his center. His poetic inspiration came unexpectedly to him, but once in its grasp he thought and spoke only in *abhangs*. No one taught him the art of poetry. His words flowed out of a heart full of overflowing love of God, and good will to men.

It is not surprising that tradition has described his end as different from that of others. A chariot of light from Heaven to take his body as well as his soul has seemed to tradition as the fitting end for such a life. When Tuka was accosted on street or path with the question, "Where are you going?" His invariable answer is said to have been, "I am on my way to the city of Heaven." And tradition has given him the triumphant passage from earth to heaven in a chariot of light, with celestial beings viewing the scene with delight, and showering flowers upon the departing saint.

A word in regard to my translation. While the Marathi of Mahipati yields readily to an English translation on the whole, his abundant use of idioms introduces difficulties of two kinds. One is to understand his idioms, and the other to find an adequate English expression for them. I wish, therefore, to express my sincere thanks to Pandit Narhar R. Godbole for his careful criticisms and suggestions which enable me to overcome these difficulties.

Dr. Wilbur S. Deming of Satara has given of his valuable time in seeing the Stotramala, and this Life of Tukaram through the latter stages of the Press. I owe him my sincere thanks.

JUSTIN E. ABBOTT.

Summit, N.J., U.S.A.
May 10*th*, 1929.

CONTENTS

CHAPTER 25

MAHIPATI'S PREFACE

Obeisance to Shri Ganesh. 1. Victory to Thee, Pandurang [Krishna], Husband-of-Rukmini [Krishna], Immutable, Unalterable, Unchangeable, Voluntarily incarnate, Mine-of-mercy, Lord-of-all, First-Cause* [Purush]. 2. I, in every way helpless, come to Thee as a suppliant, with true devotion, O Shri Hari [Vishnu]. With Thy look of mercy land me on the other side of the ocean of this worldly existence. 3. I am ignorant of how to read the *Vedas* and *Shastras,* as also ignorant of recitations, austerities and religious rites. I do not know Sanskrit, the language divine. I have no knowledge of Philosophy. 4. Although this is so, O Husband-of-Rukmini, [Krishna] yet because of love for Thee a strong desire has arisen in me to describe the honoured lives of Thy servants. Therefore, fulfil my heart's longing. 5. I am not a clever poet,

---

*The poet-saints believed that God-Supreme has manifested himself in diverse times and in diverse ways, and these manifestations and avatars have their distinguishing names. Their writings show that it was immaterial to them whether they used the name God, Vishnu, Ram, Krishna or Vithoba, or the many epithets that are supposed to characterize them. In their conception of the Deity, all, whatever their names, were manifestations of the one God. They were, therefore, the strictest of Monotheists and in that particular, stand with Christianity, Judaism and Muhammadanism, in proclaiming the Oneness of God. The ascribing of polytheism to these poet-saints is a Western misconception founded on ignorance. They believed in one God and his many manifestations. Hence the many names under which God appears, each having some philosophic conception, some history, some Puranic story, or some epithet from experience, as a reason for their names. The Western reader will wonder at many of the epithets used of God, but all have their explanation. Pandurang, Husband-of-Rukmini, Lord-of-Pandhari, Shri Hari, Shripati, Recliner-on-the-Serpent, Brother-of-the-Helpless, Ocean-of-Mercy, etc., all have their explanations and meanings.

highly gifted. I have not the strength of a widely comprehensive intellect. Indeed, I am defective in every way. This Thou well knowest, O Dark-complexioned-One [Krishna]. 6. Through the help of givers, beggars somehow manage to live. And the blind, taking the hand of the seeing, are able even to walk quickly.

7. So, O Lord-of-Pandhari [Krishna], all the burden is now on Thy head. Give me now, who am helpless, the assurance that I need not fear failure, and cause me to relate the story of Thy Bhakta [Worshipper], Tukaram. 8. The Vaishnavas, belonging to the *Bhagavat* cult, sing the marvellous renown of Thy servants. By my hand also, O Husband-of-Rukmini, cause the Bhaktalilamrita [Nectar of the deeds of the Bhaktas] to be written. 9. When a wind storm howls through the ethereal space, even the great trees sway by its force. So Thou, O Dark-complexioned-One, are the giver of thought. I have no power independent of Thee.

10. So now my hearers, give attention, and respectfully incline your ears to listen. The loving *bhakti* [devotion] of Tukaram made the Lord-of-Heaven subject to him. 11. Listen with reverence to the story of the detailed beginnings, O wise *bhaktas*, of this world-guru [religious teacher], this distinguished Vaishnava [Worshipper of Vishnu], who truly descended (from heaven) to this earth-globe. 12. It is a fact that Tukaram was born in the *Shudra* caste, but he was a Vaishnava *bhakta*. He was an actual world-*guru*, and had descended to save the world. 13. To the home of his family line the family deity, Lord-of-Pandhari, had come long ago. The idol of Vithoba [Krishna] itself had come to Dehu, seeing the love (of that family). 14. Perhaps the listeners, with some doubt in their minds, may respectfully

question the speaker, and ask who of Tukaram's ancestors brought the King-of-Pandhari to his home, "Tell us, pray." 15. Hearing this question from the listeners, the speaker is moved with intense joy, and replies, "As to what you have asked me, listen to that story also."

Tukaram's Ancestor Vishvambhar

16. Vishvambhar Bava, a great *bhakta,* was an ancestor of Tukaram's. It was because of his loving devotion that the Eagle-bannered-one [God Pandurang] came (to Dehu), from a love he naturally felt (for Vishvambhar). 17. How it was that Vishvambar showed his loving devotion, and worshipped the Husband-of-Rukmini [Krishna], I request the saints to listen with reverence to the detailed story, describing how it occurred. 18. In carrying on his prosperous trade, Vishvambhar never uttered an untruth. And the wealth of money and grain which he obtained through his store of past good deeds [Prarabdha] he spent in benevolent deeds. 19. *Sadhus,* saints, dwellers at sacred places, Brahmans, and guests, when seen by him, were invited to his house, and lovingly, and reverentially served. 20. While thus carrying on his domestic life, and commercial transactions, he was constant in repeating aloud the names of God. At night time he would collect together the pious minded, and with joyous enthusiasm, perform services in praise of God [*kirtans*]. 21. Loud shouts to the accompaniment of cymbal, *vina,* and drum [mridanga], made a veritable din of deafening sounds which sounded like divine music. Stories, especially of Ram and Krishna, were sung and listened to. 22. Thus in his sincere and kindly feelings towards all creatures, he spent himself in

benevolent deeds. And as his life was passed in acts of worship, all his emotions became absorbed in God.

23. Vishvambhar's mother frequently reminded her son, that it would be well to hasten preparations for going to Pandhari [Pandharpur]. 24. (She reminded him) that from generation to generation in his family line they went on pilgrimages to Pandhari. There should be no interruption to this custom. On it depended the prosperity of their domestic life. 25. Now to begin with, Vishvambhar was a very loving servant of God, and added to that was the exhortation from his mother (so that he acted) as a faithful Brahman would in the sphere of good deeds, and in the recitation of Vedic verses. 26. Or as when one is in a fever from the three forms of affliction, but soon falls in with some saintly person, and listening to his effective philosophic thoughts, finds his fever lessening. 27. Or, to begin with, one is a good disciple, and a pious one, and to such his Sad-Guru had prescribed a service of prayer. Immediately singing and listening to the praise of Shri Hari's goodness, his heart is full of joy. 28. Or as when Madalasa had preached by word of mouth to her son concerning divine knowledge, and there immediately arose in his heart indifference-to-worldly-things, so it happened to Vishvambhar. 29. Vishvambhar replied to his mother, "You have taught me a good lesson." And making her a profound obeisance [*sashtang namaskar*], he started on a pilgrimage (to Pandharpur).

VISHVAMBHAR'S PILGRIMAGE TO PANDHARPUR.

30. As Vishvambhar reached the main road to Pandharpur he saw other pilgrims also on the way. Joining with them at once in their acts of worship, he arrived in

due time at the sacred city of Pandhari [Pandharpur]. 31. He made his mind repentant of sins, and then bathed in the Chandrabhaga river. He went to see the shrine of Pundalik* and reverently worshipped before it. 32. He then circumnambulated the sacred city, and thus brought to his view the whole city. Then finally with prostrate bowings [*Sashtang namaskar*], he approached the main door of the temple. 33. He bowed with love before Garud and Maruti. Vaishnavs were at the time singing the praise of God, and as he listened to them his heart rejoiced. 34. Then as he saw the Supreme-Brahma, the Eternal-Being, the Jewel-in-the-heart-of-His-*bhaktas,* standing with His eyes fixed on the tip of his nose, in apparent contemplation, [i.e., the image of Vithoba] his own mind became one with Him. 35. Seeing the auspicious festivities, his heart was filled with supreme joy. The Lord-of-the-world was standing on a brick, and with his hands akimbo. 36. His whole body was smeared with fragrant powders. Around his neck was a garland of tender *tulsi* sprigs. As Vishvambhar looked upon that dark coloured image, his

---

*The shrine of Pundalik still stands on the bank of the river Chandrabhaga at Pandharpur, and is worshipped by all pilgrims to the sacred city. The story of Pundalik is an old one. He was at first a wicked and cruel son. He treated his parents shamefully. But on a pilgrimage to Benares, he fell in with a saint and was converted. From that day he could not do enough for his aged parents. So unusual was his devotion to his parents that Krishna came down from Heaven to watch him. When told that it was Krishna who had come, he replied, "I am too busy in washing my mother's and father's feet. Here is a brick, stand on it and wait." Krishna was so pleased to see such extraordinary devotion to parents that he told Pundalik to ask of Him whatever he desired. He replied, "All I wish to ask is that you remain here in Pandharpur for ever, standing on that brick as you are now doing." From that day to the present he thus stands in the form of an idol in the temple of Pandharpur, and worshipped by millions of devoted hearts.

heart filled with joy. 37. And when He who is all merciful to His *bhaktas,* and who is the beautiful father of the Yogis, was seen by Vishvambhar, he immediately embraced the God. 38. Seeing that Brahmadeva even cannot adequately describe the union of God and His *bhaktas,* why should a common mind (like my own) make a vain show of ability to do so? 39. And as he saw this *sagun* form of God [God with qualities] he held it in the recesses of his heart. As he saw this pure Brahma-joy revealed in the universe, his heart felt joy. 40. After spending five nights there, and feeling a sense of satisfaction with the services of song, and the repetition of God's names, he obtained the permission of the God to leave, and returned to his village. 41. With his heart placed at the feet of Vitthal, Vishvambhar entered his home, and as he entered the house he bowed to his mother, thus expressing his love.

Vishvambhar Homesick for Pandharpur.

42. Sitting quietly by his mother, he recounted his experiences, and added that having seen the extraordinary glory of that sacred city of Pandharpur his heart was drawn to it. 43. Vishvambhar remained at his home, but his mind turned again and again to Pandhari, where Pandurang unclad stood on the brick, on the bank of the river Bhima. 44. He would exclaim to himself, "Blessed, blessed is the sacred city of Pandharpur." And there would come often to his mind the image of Murlidhar [Krishna] at Venunad, and the great glory of the holy bathing tank, Padmatirtha. 45. "The Chandrabhaga river as his sister, Pundalik the *muni* as his own brother, Rai and Satyabhama as his mother, and Mother Rukmini, all these came to his mind. 46. Vishvambhar would say to himself,

"When shall I meet with the Husband-of-Rukmini [Krishna] ?" Tears flowed from his eyes, and his throat choked with emotion. 47. "Blessed are the noble *bhaktas*, pious and loving, with whom the Dark-complexioned-one [Krishna] plays, and even the smallest living creatures there are blessed." He was all the time thinking of them. 48. Just as a woman lives at her mother-in-law's, but in her heart is always thinking of her own mother, or as a calf, tied by a rope, seeks to go to its mother. 49. Or like a beggar wandering in the markets begging, but has money buried in the ground just as it is his very life. 50. Just so was Vishvambhar's mind. It had its longing for Vitthal's feet, and his constant exclamation was, "O compassionate Pandurang, I feel very sad thinking of Thee."

Vishvambhar goes to Pandharpur.

51. One day on the ninth, arising quickly at early dawn this Vaishnava *bhakta* started with resolute haste. 52. He walked day and night, and finally arrived at the sacred city of Pandurang. He bathed in the Chandrabhaga, and then went to see Vithoba. 53. His parallel feet were on the brick, his arms akimbo, and his unclad bodily features made a sight that was beautiful; and it made him forget all thought of himself. 54. Vishvambhar embraced the image, and tightly clasped its feet. In doing so he lost entirely all his afflictions, and he became one without bodily consciousness. 55. He performed the Tenth-day ceremony, strictly confining himself to one meal. On the Eleventh he fasted with an all-night watch-meeting in praise of Hari, and all through the night he listened to the services of song in praise of God. In doing this his heart was full of love. 56. On the twelfth of the fortnight he stopped

his fasting, and with invited Vaishnava *bhaktas* sat down to dine, for God is close to those who are saints, and lives amongst them with love. 57. Kala [Death and Destruction] is unable even to look at those who are constantly in the company of saints. Vishnu stands beside them, looking on them with love and compassion. 58. For three nights Vishvambhar remained in the sacred city in the company of God and His *bhaktas*, and then he asked of Pandurang permission to return home. 59. When the Life-of-the-World gave him permission his eyes filled with tears, and he exclaimed, "I cannot bear the thought of separation from Thee." 60. His voice choked with emotion; his eyes filled with tears, and he exclaimed, "O Vitthal, my heart is all disturbed at the thought of separation from Thy feet." 61. The Life-of the-World listened to Vishvambhar's words, and then said to him, "There is not the least space anywhere that is without me. 62. Just as the air pervades the great celestial expanse, so I, Krishna, pervade all the animate and the inanimate. 63. And just as the brilliancy of the sun, by its very nature, gives light to the earth, so know in your heart that I, Vishnu, give light to you. 64. Just as various ornaments are beaten out of gold, but the gold itself is but one substance, so although to the ignorant the world appears (a reality), it is really I, O Vishvambhar. 65. If those ornaments are melted, has the gold been destroyed thereby? So at the final destruction of all things, I remain indestructible, unchangeable, eternal. 66. This my divine nature is described in detail in the Vedanta. Carry this conception of me in your mind, and return quickly to Dehu." 67. Vishvambhar replied to Krishna, "Keep that knowledge to Thyself. My love is fixed on that divine form that has qualities [*sagun*]. 68. The conception of formlessness, called *virat*, even the Vedas are unable to grasp. Then what can I do with it, I, a mere mosquito. And where then could I look for the happiness that comes from a conception of God with attributes [*sagun*]. 69. Thy form, with Thy parallel feet is resplendent. As Thou tellest me, then if Thou art without attributes, whom shall I embrace, and of whom shall I sing? O Shripati! 70. How can I worship Thee in a form that has no attraction for me? How, O Krishna, can my ears then take in the praises of Thy goodness? Tell me." 71. Hearing these words of Vishvambhar, the Life-of-the-World smiled, "Your good qualities are of such a nature as to attract the evil eye." 72. Saying this, the Lover-of-his-*bhaktas,* the Helper-of-the-Helpless, placed his hand on Vishvambhar's head, and said to him, "Wherever you repeat my name, there I surely am." 73. Thus speaking, the Husband-of-Rukmini gave him a *mantra,* in which was the name of Hari, and sent him on his way to Dehu still holding resolutely to his idea of love for a God with attributes [*sagun,* a Personal God.]

VISHVAMBHAR PRAISED AND BLAMED BY PEOPLE.

74. Vishvambhar now began to go to Pandhari every fortnight, and to be there on the eleventh day of the month. He made this a regular practice, and enjoyed from it an incomparable happiness. 75. From the month of Kartik [November] until the month of Jyeshth [June] he went back and forth sixteen times, and looked upon the God with attributes [*sagun*]. 76. The people of Dehu were amazed at Vishvambhar's state of mind. Listen, I pray you, to what different people said of him. 77. "He has thrown aside all desires in his domestic life, and given himself to the contemplation of Vithoba. Otherwise why does he go back and forth every fortnight and weary himself? 78.

If he is disgusted with his domestic life, he could yet remain happily at Pandhari, but his love seems to be in two places, and so he goes and then returns to his home." 79. Others said, "Fate has been kind to him. Why do you needlessly insult him? In these days we see no one so devoted to God as he is." 80. Thus people of different opinions expressed themselves variously regarding him. But it was all the same to Vishvambhar. Honour and insult were the same to him. 81. Vishvambhar was a *bhakta* of God-loving nature, and his heart was fixed on God with attributes [*sagun*]. But now a most extraordinary event took place. Listen, you pious *bhaktas*!

Vishvambhar's Dream Becomes True.

82. The eight months quickly rolled by during which Vishvambhar went back and forth from Pandhari every fortnight. The Lord-of-Heaven felt indebted to him for this service, without a doubt. 83. In the ninth month and on the eighth day of the month, at night time, when Vishvambhar was asleep, the Husband-of-Rukmini came to him in a dream and spoke to him. 84. "My dear Vishvambhar," He said, "you have made me your debtor through your service. So I have come to your town. There is no necessity laid on you now of going to Pandhari. 85. You have been very kind to me. Truly I can never repay you. So I have come here to remain, seeing your love for me." 86. Thus speaking, Krishna went to the mango grove, and there went to sleep, so he seemed in the dream. 87. When Vishvambhar awoke he lovingly repeated God's names, and remarked, "How curious are the ways of Fate. I have met with the Husband-of-Rukmini. 88. After meeting with me, the Lord-of-Pandhari went into the Mango grove. He probably is asleep there now. I must

go there at once and see." 89. In the town there were Vaishnavas to whom he told this secret of his heart, for he had seen this in his dream, and believed that God had come hither from Pandhari. 90. "Now let us go at once to the Mango grove and bring into the town the Husband-of-Rukmini," said Vishvambhar. The Vaishnavas, hearing this news, were greatly astonished. 91. They took with them also other people of the town. To those who were not *bhaktas* of Krishna, and whose minds were skeptical, the thing did not seem true. 92. They remarked, "Vishvambhar has so given himself to contemplation of God, that he probably has seen the same image in his dream. That God-with-attributes should be seen directly before one in the form of an image, how can such an impossible idea really take place?" 93. Others replied to this, "Why do you express doubts? One does not need a mirror to see a bracelet. You will soon easily see what his faith brings forth." 94. With such thoughts in their minds the townspeople went along with Vishvambhar, and in this crowd of saints he walked along with great joy. 95. Singing God's praise and dancing, they arrived at the Mango grove. But behold, the Lord-of-Pandhari was not there. Still a very extraordinary fragrance was noticed. 96. And fragrant flowers, fragrant powders and the *tulsi* leaves were lying about in that place. As they saw this rather strange sight, all expressed astonishment. 97. Some one remarked, "Look you, this seems to be the beginning of the dream's becoming true. But our faith is not pure, hence we do not see the God." 98. Just then Vishvambhar remarked, "Let us dig into the ground and see." Suddenly a voice from the sky was heard by every one. 99. It said "He-who-dwells-in-Heaven has come here to Dehu to meet Vishvambhar. Do not touch the earth with a tool, but dig with your hands. 100. A distinguished and noble Vaishnava will descend as an avatar in Vishvambhar's family line, and by the charm of his *kirtans* [services of song] the world will be saved." 101. Hearing this divine voice, the assembled *bhaktas* rejoiced. They clapped their hands to the Name of God, and loud was the outburst of praises to God. 102. Then Vishvambhar put his hand to the work and the other Vaishnava *bhaktas* began to dig. And behold, there came out with the earth a great quantity of fragrant powders, and tulsi leaves. 103. And as they continued looking, an image of Pandurang, of a dark blue colour, came into view. At His left was Mother Rukmini. His beautiful features were remarkable. 104. He wore a yellow robe around His waist. Around His neck was a *tulsi* garland. Seeing this beautiful image all broke out into cries of Victory! Victory! 105. Vishvambhar took up the image, and with love for it in their hearts they approached the village. The *bhaktas* of Vitthal were all shouting Vitthal's name, and dancing as they sang His praises. 106. When they came to the sacred precincts of the town, they installed the image there. Nearby flowed the Indrayani river, a sight of which gives final deliverance to all beings. 107. They called together Vedic Brahmans, and provided all that was needed for the occasion. They worshipped the Husband-of-Rukmini in the act of sprinkling water, while repeating *mantras* from the Vedas. 108. They bathed the image with the five nectars, milk, curds, butter, honey and sugar, to which was added raw cane sugar, and then they sprinkled water over Him. 109. They wiped the god with a towel, and then clothed with a yellow robe. They put ear-rings in His ears and put a crown on His head. Thus they beautifully decorated

Krishna. 110. Then with love they presented to him flowers, *tulsi,* the platter with lights, the waving of lights and incense. They offered him daintily cooked food, and other offerings, all the while the Brahmans were repeating *mantras* with a loud voice. 111. According to his ability Vishvambhar feasted the Brahmans, and the Vaishnavas conducted a service of praise to God. All the inhabitants of the town spent the whole night in the worship of the God. 112. In the middle of the night, when alone by himself, Vishvambhar thus praised God, "Victory! Victory! to Thee Ocean-of-Mercy, Husband-of-Rukmini. Thou who alone pervadest the Three Worlds [Heaven, Earth, and Hell]. 113. Even Indra can hardly see Thee. Thou whom Shiva contemplates. And for my sake, O Vitthal, Thou hast come here to the bank of the Indrayani. 114. I am one who has not rendered Thee service, nor loving devotion. I do not know how to render worship and due reverence. But Thou art the Brother-of-the-helpless, and a Cloud-of-mercy. I know this fully from my experience." 115. Having listened to Vishvambhar's praise, the Husband-of-Rukmini replied, "Tell me whatever wish you may have in your heart." 116. The loving *bhakta* listened and said, "I wish that I may always love Thy worship. I want association with saints. You see what the longing of my heart is, O Vitthal! 117. In future days may my posterity give Thee loving devotion. This is my request, O Husband-of-Rukmini. Fulfil this longing of my heart. 118. Remain here for a *kalpa,* and by the mere sight of Thee save the ignorant. May the Lotus-eyed-one dwell here and make the village of Dehu a sacred place." 119. To this request of the loving *bhakta* the Helper-of-the-Helpless smilingly replied, "That which you hold as the longing of your heart, I, the infinite [Anant], am the provider of it." 120. Such was the promise given at this time (at night and alone), and Vishvambhar prostrated himself at the God's feet. The people of this sacred town also, all of them, gave themselves to worship.

DEATH OF VISHVAMBHAR.

121. Days passed in that loving attitude of mind, but now came the time for Vishvambhar's departure. The chariot-of-light [Viman], called Pushpak, came down for him from Vishnu's Heaven. 122. The angels of Vishnu said to Vishvambhar, "Come now to Vishnu's Heaven." As Vishvambhar heard this call he pleaded as follows with Pandurang. 123. "My two sons and my wife are now on your lap, O Shri Hari. I am on my way to the Heavenly city. That is certain, O Vitthal." 124. Having thus spoken, he repeated aloud the name of Hari, and life left his body. He sat in the heavenly chariot of light (and was taken to Heaven). 125. On the way Heavenly singers sang with their sweet voices, with the loud acclaim of God's name, and shouts of loving words. Thus accompanied, Vishvambhar arrived at the Heavenly City. 126. As a result of his wonderful good deeds, he obtained a place near Vishnu. And this Vaishnava *bhakta* is to-day enjoying the highest form of union with God.

VISHVAMBHAR'S WIFE, AMABAI.

127. After Vishvambhar had reached his heavenly home, certain events took place. I ask you, good people, to listen attentively to the very interesting story. 128. Vishvambhar's wife bore the name of Amabai. With her heart's

loving devotion she also worshipped Vishnu. 129. She had two sons, by name of Hari and Mukund. But Amai was indifferent to worldly affairs and gave herself with love to the worship of God. 130. She had an impartial compassion for all creatures. Her tender love raised no question of mine and thine. And with her heart's devotion to the feet of God she made the Lord-of-Pandhari her own. 131. By reason of her method of loving worship, God-Supreme gave her direct manifestations of Himself. He appeared suddenly to her in a dream, and talked with her. 132. "I, the Eagle-bannered-One, have naturally seen your loving devotion, and I am pleased with you. If, therefore, you have a desire for anything, tell it to me." 133. To this suggestion of Krishna's, Amai replied to the God as follows: "Aside from Thee, O Shri Hari, I truly care for nothing else. 134. I care not for the enjoyment of anything, I care not for the Deliverance [from births and deaths]. I care not for money or wealth. I ask only that I may have a longing for Thy worship. And may my heart lose its identity in Thy essential form. 135. If I have the least wish aside from this, my mother has brought me forth in vain." As Amai thus spoke, the Husband-of-Rukmini smiled and said, 136. "Mother, blessed is your mind. May it ever be so. I, Ocean-of-Mercy, am pleased with you. I will place you at my lotus feet." 137. Amai replied in the joy of her love, "Thou alone art He who makes the mind act. This the *Vedas* and *Shastras* declare, and many poets have said the same." 138. Having said this, Amai prostrated herself on the ground. Vishnu was pleased, and lifting her up pressed her to his heart. 139. All this Amai saw in her dream. In a moment she was awake, and repeating Hari's name she sat in amazement (at what she had dreamed).

Amabai Prospers in Worldly Affairs.

140. While Amai's heart was without desires, and, therefore, asked for no money or riches, still the Husband-of-Lakshmi became her debtor, and all the *Siddhis* began to embrace her. 141. She did nothing of any kind to advance her worldly affairs, but everything in her home worked in her favour. Whatever she at any time wished for, it all came to her.

142. But where the *Siddhis* are favourable, there at once comes to the would-be-seeker (of good) a degeneracy of heart. As worldly prosperity and riches increase, separation from God becomes most certain. 143. Where sensual desires superimpose themselves, repentance has no place in the heart. And where there is no repentance there sin by its very nature enters. 144. Just as when night comes, ghosts come out of cemeteries, or as when Pain and Poverty see a man who lacks good fortune, it is there that they come. 145. Or as when a vile man comes into an assembly, open disgust is naturally manifested, so when one's heart becomes addicted to sensual things, without any effort it embraces evil deeds. 146. Therefore, it is that *sadhus* and saints freeing themselves from encumbrances retire in solitude into the forest, and there worship God (Hari).

Amai's Sons Grow Worldly Minded.

147. But now enough of these reflections. All the *Siddhis* (as I have said) came to their home and embraced them. As a result the sons of Amai forgot God [Hari]. 148. The two sat by themselves one day and thought in their love of such things, that they ought to be in the army,

where they would have horses, palanquins and decorations. 149. "So let us go and meet the king, and faithfully serve him. By following the profession of a Kshatriya there will come the enjoyment of riches." 150. The two then made a reverential bow to their mother, and told her of what was in their minds. "We are going to see the king and take up the Kshatriya's profession." 151. Amai replied to them, "What is there lacking here at home? Vithabai will provide for all our needs." 152. The mother thus pleaded with them, but the sons were not pleased with her answer. So learning what their intention was, she gave them permission to go. 153. Hari and Mukund, the two sons, prostrated themselves before their mother, and immediately started on their way, and went to see the king. 154. The king seeing the bravery and skill of the two sons gave them money. They then laid plans for bringing to where they were, their wives together with their mother. 155. They wrote a letter to their mother, Amai, and with it sent men and horses (to bring them). When the mother saw them she felt distressed. Said she, "Vithoba will be separated far from me." 156. But she made her parting bow to the image of Pandurang, and with eyes filled with tears said, "O God, Thy feet will now be far separated from me." 157. With these words her voice choked with emotion. But gathering all her belongings, she started on her way. 158. She took along with her her two daughters-in-law, and arriving she met her two sons. But her spirit remained with the God. Her heart was pierced by her love. 159. Just as a beggar wanders through a bazaar, but his thoughts are ever on the money he has concealed in the ground. Or, like a calf, fastened with a rope, has its mind on its mother. 160. Or, like the *chakor* bird, conscious of its own body, still is always looking for the moon.

So the heart of Amai was filled with the Husband-of-Rukmini. 161. Through Fate and the Deeds in a former birth, fortune and wealth came to the sons. Seduced by it, they lived in its enjoyment. The Helper-of-the-Helpless understands this.

THE SONS RIDICULE THEIR MOTHER'S DREAMS.

162. After some time had passed, while Amabai was asleep Vithabai appeared to her in her state of dreaming. 163. It was a clear dark blue image. The brilliancy of the yellow robe shed a bright light. Heavenly earrings glistened in its ears, in shape like crocodiles, beautiful to look at. 164. Appearing to Amai in this form in her dream Krishna said to Amai, "Entangled by your affection for your sons, you have cast me aside. 165. Through the assurances given me by Vishvambhar he caused me to come and dwell in the sacred town of Dehu. Now you have forgotten all that, and are seeking for pleasure from worldly things. 166. Put away all your love for money and riches, and at once start for the sacred town of Dehu." When the Lord-of-Pandhari had said this much, Amai awoke. 167. Wondering over the dream, Amai at once called her sons and choking with emotion told them the contents of her dream. 168. "Your father" she said, "made a pact with Krishna through his assurances, and after installing his image went to his heavenly home. 169. God-Supreme came to me in a dream and talking with me directly told me to come back immediately to the bank of the Indrayani." 170. Hearing their mother's account of the dream, the sons broke out into a laugh, and replied, "How can one regard as true the experiences in a dream? 171. We are diligent in our service of the king, and in doing so the Husband-of-Rukmini

is pleased. God does not disregard him who honours the doing of his special duties." 172. Amai listened to what they said, and kept silence. She could not drop her love and affection for her sons, and nothing could stand before them.

AMAI'S DREAM COMES TRUE.

173. After a few days had passed the sons jokingly remarked to their mother, "Well, what did the Lord-of-Pandhari say to you last night? Let us hear it." 174. Amai replied, "I have had two visions of God since then in which He said, "Leave your children and all your property, and come at once to Dehu." 175. They listened to what their mother had to say, but they did not feel the truth of it. The strange events of the future were to be realized, hence the degeneracy of their minds. 176. A few days thus passed, and the Lord-of-Pandhari became supremely angry. He manifested himself to Amai in a dream. Listen to the story, you pious folk. 177. The Lord-of-Pandhari appeared in a dream and said to her, "If you will not listen to me, this very noon there will be a disaster. Let your ears take in this prophecy. 178. All your riches and money will be scattered, and your sons will die." The Life-of-the-World having said these words, Amai began to weep. 179. "You say," she said, "my sons will die, then who will see me on my way to the final good?" Hari replied, "I have assumed the indebtedness to you, and I shall certainly pay my debt." 180. After Amai had seen this vision in her dream she awoke. Her sons came and said to her, "Mother, why do you weep?" 181. "Some time ago I told you my dream," she said, "but you regarded it as untrue. In to-day's dream the Life-of-the-World appeared in a towering rage. 182. He said to me,

'To-day as the noon hour comes, your sons will die; all your riches and money will be scattered in a moment's time.' " 183. Although Amabai told them this, the sons did not believe it true. Just as when Sanjaya prophesied future events Dhritarashtra would not believe him. 184. The moral laws, laid down by Mandodari, Ravan thought as false. That which is to take place has many curious possibilities. One does not know what has been laid up in one's past lives. 185. The two sons, Hari and Mukund, said to one another, "Because our mother has reached the state of old age, she is prophesying adversity." 186. The sons then said to their mother, "As we are going to die to-day, quickly prepare a meal with your own hands and seat us for the feast." 187. The mother gave her orders to the daughters-in-law, and they served two plates. The two seated themselves for the feast, and ate to the full. 188. While eating their *pan supari,* they jokingly remarked, "Mother knows all about the past and the future." Just then a messenger arrived and said, "The king has called you. 189. A great hostile army has appeared. You must go to attack it." When they saw the king's letter of command, they started to go with all haste. 190. They got their troops ready. They said farewell to their mother, drums were beaten, and they hastily started. 191. Suddenly the hostile army came opposite them, and a frightful battle took place. Both those brave men fell wounded on the battle field, and the cry was heard, "Alas! Alas!" 192. The enemy at that moment gained the victory, trumpets proclaimed their victory, and they looted the belongings of the army. 193. Hari and Mukund lay helpless. Bitterly they repented. "We did not listen to our mother," they said, "therefore, this has come upon us." 194. The moment they repented, they cried to Pandurang for help. "O

God-Supreme, Purifier-of-the-sinner, quickly come to us, O Keshava." 195. God heard this cry for mercy and gave them at once a vision of Himself. He seated both them in Pushpak, the chariot of light, [Viman] and took them to His Heaven. 196. Vishvambhar had taken a promise from Him to save his whole family line, and it was because of that promise that the Lord-of-Heaven came down to meet them.

AMAI AND A DAUGHTER-IN-LAW RETURN TO DEHU.

197. As I have said, the two young men fell in the battle. When Amai heard the news it was an ocean of sorrow that was stirred from its depths. How can it be fully described in a book. 198. Just as when Gandhari heard that her family line had been destroyed, she fell in a faint, and then threw herself on the ground, so it happened to Amai. 199. And when the queen of the younger brother, Mukund, saw with her own eyes all this sorrow, she lighted the funeral fire and accompanied her husband. 200. God met her in this close of her life, and accompanied her to Heaven. And there as she saw her husband she joined with him in a whispered conversation.

201. Now turning to other events, the elder of Amai's daughters-in-law was an expectant mother, and, therefore, she remained behind (not following her husband). 202. The enemy had looted the family of all their clothing, ornaments, money, and other property, and Amai, taking her daughter-in-law with her, fled away. 203. Thinking all the time of Hari, she arrived on the holy ground of Dehu. She went immediately to the temple, and saw the Giver-of-final-Bliss. 204. Her throat choked with emotion as she held the idol to her heart. She tightly embraced his feet, and spoke as follows:

Amai Scolds God.

205. "O You, destroyer of my domestic life! How well you have brought about this state of discord! You have caused my dear children to fall on the battle-field. O you destroyer of my home, Shri Hari! 206. Your slaves give themselves to your worship, and then you bring about their destruction in this fashion. When they are separated from you, you make the whole world a desert for them. 207. Shiva worshipped you, and then you carried and seated him in a cemetery. You gave him a spirit of indifference-to-worldly-things, so that he could no longer have a desire for sensual things. 208. I have listened to the story of Sanak and others, how in contemplating you, you made them unconscious of body, though in the body, and seated them in the Heavenly Home. 209. You, Supreme-Lord-of-the-Universe, brought about the quelling of all the evil passions of the Vaishnava Narad, and giving him only a loin cloth sent him wandering over the three worlds of the Universe. 210. On the eleventh of the fortnight you made Rukmangad observe a Hari watch-night service. Then you destroyed his city, but seated him in Heaven. 211. You killed Ravan, the brother of your *bhakta*, Bibhishan, and then showed your generosity by giving to Bibhishan the gift of Ceylon. 212. O Supreme-Lord-of-the-Universe, your *bhakta*. Pralhad, had to suffer much, because he repeated your name, and in the end you killed his father. Your deed was an unworthy one. 213. Well, why dwell on these stories of others. I will speak now from my own experience. You killed my sons, You Infinite-Being, while I was looking on. 214. You, the Controller of the wheel of this earthly existence, You Wearer-of-garlands-of-wild-flowers, you reduced to dust my

domestic life. You took the life of my infants, and brought them to be near yourself, You, yes, You! 215. Now tell me at once who is going to care for me."

God's Soft Answer to Amai

The Soul-of-the-Universe listened to Amai and then replied. 216. But first He drew her to His heart, then said, "What had to happen has in the end happened. But do not now be at all troubled. I, The Supreme-one-in-the-Universe, am with you." 217. Thus, in many ways He, the mine of mercy, soothed her feelings. Listen now you pious folk, with reverence to the events that followed.

218. To carry on her domestic life there was need of money and grain, and there was no one to provide these necessities. The daughter-in-law, who was an expectant mother, had been sent to her own mother's home. 219. She herself dwelt for a time in the sacred city (of Dehu), but her mind was not at ease. And because of her troubles, her eye-sight became badly affected, and finally she became totally blind. 220. At her door there had been a noble Shevaga tree, but due to her grief it had withered away. Then Krishna, in a visible form talked with Amai. 221. "O Mother," said Krishna, "I am ever near you, and why is your heart troubled? How often am I to tell you this? 222. In my *avatar* as Krishna, I caused the dead son of my guru to meet his father. And in the same way I will bring to you your own son, if you will but now say the word. 223. And in the future I shall give you divine eyes." To these words of the Husband-of-Rukmini, Amai replied, "I do not want perishable things. 224. I once gave you my word, O Hari, Have you forgotten it now? That I had no wish for anything, but Thee. Remember this, and keep

it in your mind. 225. Even if you suddenly gave me without asking, I truly will not accept it." The Husband-of-Rukmini listened and then replied, 226. "I am now going to become your own son, and Rukmini will become your loving daughter-in-law. She will serve you with her love, and let you lack in nothing." 227. To this suggestion of Krishna's Amai replied, "Thou art the Father-of-the-Universe, the Saviour-of-the-World. How canst Thou become my son?" 228. To this Krishna replied, "By the power of a loving faith I became the infant child of Yashoda. Are you not at all aware of that?" 229. When Krishna had thus spoken to Amai she prostrated herself on the ground before Him, exclaiming "O Lover-of-thy-*bhaktas,* Giver-of-final-Bliss. Thy acts are truly wonderful."

God in the Form of Amai's Son Cares for her.

230. Because of Amai's loving devotion, Shri Hari assumed the form of her son, and used to take her by the hand, and lead her into the temple. 231. There the Lord-of-the-world Himself with his own hand would provide her with all the things required in rendering worship. Her hunger and thirst He constantly cared for. He allowed her to lack in nothing at all. 232. Blessed indeed was Amai's devotion! Although Krishna was in the form of Buddha, inactive, yet was he always caring for her. 233. He who was the object of contemplation for Sanak and others, and the object of worship by Shiva, He in order to repay the debt He owed to His servant Vishvambhar, took this *sagun* form. 234. Adimaya, Mother Rukmini, became Amai's daughter-in-law. She carried on the household affairs, so that there was nothing whatever lacking. 235 He who is the Supreme-Spirit, Pure Intelligence, Unaffected by Maya, Cloud-of-Joy, He sat beside Amai, and with

love, fed her. 236. Amai used to say to Him, "Vithu, Come and eat with me." "I certainly will," the Lord-of-Pandhari would reply, and then show his love by taking a morsel of food. 237. He, who would not partake of the offerings made by the great *rishis* in their sacrifices, He, with supreme love, dined on the left-over food of this loving *bhakta.* 238. Hari is infatuated by sincere devotion, and pays no regard to the caste or family rank of those who worship him. And according to a man's inner feelings of devotion Krishna adapts Himself.

239. After the two had eaten together, the Life-of-the-World gave her water for cleansing her hands. He would prepare with His own hands the *pan supari* and give it to her. 240. Then taking Amai by the hand, the Eagle-bannered one would gently lead her, where Rukmini had placed a cot, and there on that bed laid her down to sleep. 241. Just as the Soul-of-the-Universe said in the eighth chapter of the Bhagavadgita, namely, "In the hour when a *bhakta* is casting off his body, I, the Infinite One, will care for him," so in this case He was caring for Amai. 242. Shri Hari put aside the greatness of His glory, and sat at her feet, and with his own hands shampooed her feet. That He should do so seems wonderful to me. 243. Rukmini with her own hands bathed her, and combed and braided her hair, and lovingly rubbed her back. And the reason for this was her loving devotion.

244. This continued many days but no one in the town knew of it. They sometimes remarked, "Amai must have some neighbour who is caring for her. 245. Hari's acts are wonderful." To some, Rukmini seemed a daughter-in-law. Others thought her a neighbour. He did not let people know anything about it.

AMAI'S DEATH, AND ASCENSION.

246. After some days had passed the end of Amai's life approached, Krishna brought for her the Heavenly chariot of Light [Viman]. 247. As the day consecrated to Hari (the eleventh) of the bright half of Shravan (August) arrived, at the first watch of the day, lo! what Sharangadhar (Krishna) did as he placed Amai's head on his lap; and then mark what He did. 248. He then drew out her life, and in a moment's time, gave her a celestial body, which He lifted up into the chariot of light and brought to the Heavenly Home. 249. In the form of her son, and together with her relatives and the people of the town, He gave her the last rites on the funeral pyre, the Life-of-the-World Himself giving her the water to drink. 250. Thus the Helper-of-the-Helpless performed her funeral rites with his own hand. On the thirteenth day He gave the funeral feast to those of her own caste. 251. In the meantime, the daughter-in-law of Amai lived in Navalakha Umbare. But when she heard the news of her mother-in-law's death, she felt deep sorrow. 252. I have already mentioned that she was an expectant mother. Now her son was full grown. Bringing him with her, she arrived at Dehu. 253. She expressed her great sorrow to the people that she did not have a hand in those last rites. (Astonished) they replied, "But you were here, and performed all the funeral rites." 254. Hearing this, both son and mother, were dumbfounded.

I now ask my hearers to give close attention to the next most interesting chapter. 255. It is the Brother-of-the-Helpless, Mine-of-Mercy, Dweller-on-the-bank-of-the Bhima, the Husband-of-Rukmini, who dwells in the heart of Mahipati and causes him to write the words that make the contents of this book. 256. Svasti! Listen you loving pious folk, to this book, the Bhaktalilamrita, for through listening alone all one's longings are fulfilled. This is the twenty-fifth interesting chapter.

CHAPTER 26.

Invocation.

Obeisance to Shri Ganesh.

1. Victory! Victory to Him who-dwells-in-the-Ocean-of-Milk, to Him who-reclines-on-the-Serpent, The Husband-of-Lakshmi, to Him who-attracts-the-Hearts, to the Brother-of-the-Helpless, to the Cloud-of-Mercy, to the Life-of-the-World, to Shri Vitthal. 2. The moment Thy compassionate eye falls on any one, the snare that holds him in this worldly-existence is cut. Just as when the touch stone [*paris*] attracts the iron, in the end no dark coloured iron remains. 3. Or as when suddenly the sun appears in the place of the darkness of the night, the darkness turns into brightness, and in all directions a brilliancy lights up every thing. 4. Or as if into a dirty stream there should suddenly come a flood of Ganges water, then its waters become holy. One cannot think otherwise. 5. So by Thy look of compassion, immediately one loses the illusion of this worldly-existence. And those who come to Thee as suppliants, with a sincere heart, their faults no longer remain. 6. Thou, O Shripati, hast saved outcastes, and others of low caste, women, *Shudras*, and those whom the *Vedas* despise. 7. That animal, the elephant Gajendra, and the toad, [Dardur—manduk], called to Thee in

their distress. In a wonderful way Thou, Lord-of-Heaven, came in answer to their cry, and Thou caused them to enjoy the happiness of Final-Union with Thee. 8. Those whom the *Vedas* and *Shastras* regard as worthy of contempt, and yet who have with a sense of love sung of Thy goodness, they become honoured by those who are of high birth. Such is the power of Thy Name. 9. The great and holy Valmiki has related the story of the monkeys. By the compassionate look of Thy lotus-eyes Thou didst make that genus holy. 10. Thou wast aware that the curd drinking cowherds had filthy habits. Dvaipayana had described them in the Bhagavat. But those worthy of contempt become worthy of honour, who with a pure heart come as suppliants to Thee. 11. Endless *bhaktas* have been saved. It is impossible to count their number. It is for this reason that I, Mahipati, with my love have come as a suppliant to Thee.

VISHVAMBHAR AND AMAI'S GRANDSON VITHOBA.

12. In the last chapter it was related how Amai was taken to her home of final bliss. Also how, when her daughter-in-law heard all the news, she was filled with amazement. 13. Vithoba, her son, said to his mother, "Seeing that we had not come here, how could this have happened? 14. If we should say the story is not true, still all the people of the town were at the feast, and all bear witness to its truth." 15. To this question by her son, the mother made reply, "In this quarrel the Husband-of-Rukmini, our enemy, is certainly involved. 16. Your grandfather, Vishvambhar, made the Husband-of-Rukmini the object of his worship. And because of Vishvambhar's devotion, He came here to Dehu in the *sagun* form of an

image. 17. Vishvambhar had two sons by name of Hari and Mukund. They were in the service of the king, and there accumulated money and other property. 18. We three, namely, two sisters-in-law, and Amai, our good-natured mother-in-law, lived here together. But we were then sent for, and escorted (to the place where Hari and Mukund lived). 19. After we had been there for some time the Lord-of-Pandhari appeared to Amai in a dream, and said, "To-day you will suffer a great calamity." 20. No one listened to her, and both brothers fell on the battle-field. Then we, both, my mother-in-law and myself, fled from there, and came here. 21. Amai cried, and scolded Pandurang. Then God took our forms, and paid the debt He owed to her (your grandmother).

Vithoba Scolds God and threatens Suicide.

22. When Vithoba heard his mother's account he was filled with rage. He quickly performed his bath, and then proceeded to the temple. 23. He stood in front of the idol, and said to God: "You brought a great calamity upon us. Was that a good thing for you to do, Vitthal? 24. My Grandfather became your bhakta, but you had my father killed on the battle-field. You have brought dishonour upon us in this world. I am not going to stay here with you. 25. And with that remark he grasped a weapon in his hand, and was about to plunge it into his abdomen, when Krishna seized his hand. 26. Vithoba cried, "Hari, Let go my hand, I will not listen to what you say at least at this moment. I have heard with my ears your reputation in the animate and inanimate world. 27. Prahlad was a Vaishnava *bhakta* of Thine. He worshipped Thee with love. And yet, appearing in that pillar,

you killed his father. 28. You killed that good and innocent Vali, the father of Angada. And then you cast a spell upon him, and made him your servant. 29. In that same way you, Husband-of-Rukmini, killed my father. I have no regard for my life. I have no desire for living." 30. Seeing his determination the heart of the Husband-of-Rukmini melted with pity. He took Vithoba by the hand, and gave him a loving embrace. 31. He wiped Vithoba's tears away with His own hand, and said, "Why do you trouble yourself thus in vain? That which was to happen has already happened. The Maya of Vishnu is a juggler." 32. And then said, "Vishvambhar left, having taken a promise from me, which has made me a debtor to your family. It has been in order to pay that debt that I have remained here in Dehu." 33. I am Krishna, the Advocate-of-my-*bhaktas,* while you call me your enemy. But just as one might call nectar a poison, so you have seemed to do. 34. Or as when the sun just begins to appear, how can darkness be said to exist? Or just as one should not liken the little puddle of water to the Ocean-of-Milk. 35. The *ashvattha* tree is a noble portion of Vishnu. Its very sight destroys sins. But to call it a *hivar* tree seems to be your way of thinking. 36. The Lord-of-all-the-Yogis is the Husband-of Uma, Dweller-in-the-cemetery. Now to call him a ghost shows that the ignorant do not know of his majesty. 37. I am the Advocate-of-the-bhaktas, and the one who wields the club and the disk, and yet, you call me quarrelsome. This seems to me very strange. 38. I am the servant of your family through a debt. Take this assurance from me." As Krishna thus spoke, Vithoba fell at His feet. 39. In His compassion Krishna showed clearly to the family the nine forms of *bhakti,* and mother and son changed to a feeling of love.

Thereafter they devoted themselves constantly to His worship. 40. They ceased to remember their former sorrows, and adopted the habit of going on pilgrimages to Pandhari. And Shri Hari cared for all their necessities.

Vithoba's Descendants.

41. Vithoba's son bore the name of Padaji. He also rendered loving worship, and the Husband-of-Rukmini was the object of his devotion. 42. Padaji's son was Shankar. He also worshipped the Husband-of-Rukmini. Kanhaya was Shankar's son, and Bolhoba was his son. 43. To Bolhoba was born that supreme Vaishnava *bhakta*, Tukaram.

Bolhoba, Father of Tukaram.

Listen you pious loving folk, to the orderly recital of Tukaram's life. 44. (But first as to Bolhoba), he had a desire in his heart and prayed to Pandurang. Said he, "O God-Supreme, Husband-of-Rukmini. Fulfil the longing of my heart." 45. You, listeners, will say to me, "What kind of worship did Bolhoba render? And due to what action did God actually appear to him?" Listen you pious folk, according to your mental capacity, to a detailed account.

46. Bolhoba, with love in his heart, was accustomed to carry on regular worship by himself alone. During the months of Ashadh and Kartik (July and November) he made pilgrimages to Pandhari. 47. He fed the hungry, and gave the thirsty water to drink. He paid worshipful reverence to *Sadhus*, saints, and Vaishnavas. 48. In carrying on his busi-

ness he never spoke untruths. In all creatures he saw his own soul. He never felt any difference whatever. 49. Yet while performing all these good deeds, he had in his heart a deep longing. He cried out, "O Husband-of-Rukmini, Life-of-the-World, Cloud-of-Compassion, O Shri Vitthal. 50. As Helper-of-the-Helpless, Thou didst in former times at once fulfil the longings of the saints. Such praise of Thee is sung all through the Three worlds. The *Purans* acclaim Thy noble deeds. 51. O Life-of-the-world, according as Thy *bhaktas* had desires so Thou didst fulfil them. O Cloud-of-mercy, my mind holds in its recollection those praiseworthy deeds of Thine. 52. There was that Upamanyu, the son of a Brahman, who asked for a cup of milk, but knowing his heart Thou didst place him in the ocean of milk. 53. Then there was the boy Dhruva, exceedingly ignorant, and yet he desired a throne. Seeing the intensity of his desire, Thou, Shri Hari, wast pleased. 54. Assuring him by taking him by the hand, Thou didst place him in his fixed position (in the heavens), [The Polar Star]. And around him revolve the moon, the sun and all the multitude of stars. 55. Our Marathi words are not equal to the task of extolling Thy generosity, O Shri Hari! The six Shastras and the four Vedas tried to describe it, but wearied out in the attempt, and they failed to form an estimate of it."

56. It was in such language that Bolhoba in his constant worship pleaded with the Husband-of-Rukmini; and carried on the Hari watch-night services and the Ekadashi ceremonies with expressions of his deep love. 57. For twenty-four years he made pilgrimages to Pandhari. Shri Hari then manifested to him his favor. Just how He did it, Listen!

58. Bolhoba's wife was a supremely pious and devoted wife. She also used to pray, "O God-Supreme, Husband-of-Rukmini, fulfil our desire." 59. Thus this couple had this one thought (to have a son). Suddenly the three gods appeared in a dream, and gave them a vision of themselves, 60. namely Brahmadeva, Vishnu and Shiva. "We are pleased with you" they said. "If, therefore, you have any particular wish, tell it to us now." 61. Bolhoba awoke and bowed to the Three Gods, and replied, "We are wishing at this time for a son in our home life." 62. Two of the gods, Brahmadeva and Shiva, said, "Your wish will be gratified." Thereupon the Lord-of-Heaven [Vishnu], asked him what kind of a son He should give him? 63. Bolhoba answered in reply, "Give me a son who will be a world-saviour, and a Vaishnava, one who in *kirtans* [services of song] will sing of Thy goodness. 64. Thou didst see the love of Damashet, and his wife, Gonai, and Thou gavest them Nama as their son. In that same way, O Supreme Being (Vishnu), fulfil my wish." 65. As he thus spoke in loving words, the Husband-of-Rukmini answered, "Your longing will surely be granted, let your heart carry this conviction. 66. Your eyes will see in the form of your son the crown-jewel of all saints." Bolhoba then walked around the God, and prostrated himself on the ground before Him. 67. Such was the vision that his mind saw, and then Bolhoba awoke. He at once awakened his wife Kanakai, and told her what had happened in his dream. 68. After a short time both of them saw with their eyes the birth ceremony of a son; for Kanakai was with child, and a son was born. 69. This was the son promised by Shiva, and they named him Savaji. Listen with loving attention you Vaishnavas, to the extraordinary events that now took place.

A Conference Takes Place in Heaven.

70. On a certain occasion when Shri Hari was in Heaven, a circle of saints sat around Him, a joyous assembly. 71. You may perhaps ask who they were. Listen to their names. In the mere hearing of their names the craze of evil desires at once passes away. 72. There were Sanak, Narad, Tumbar, Pralhad, Dhruva, Akrura, Udhav, Ambarish, that noble Vaishnav, Shuka, that Prince of Yogis, and Parikshit. 73. Bhishma, Rukmangada, Pundalik, that mine of devotion. Nivriti, Dnyanadev, Sopan, Mukta, the mine of Vaishnavism. 74. Nama, Kabir, both noble Vaishnavas, Bhanudas and Changa Vateshvara, Sanvatamali, Narahari, the goldsmith, Visoba Khechar, and Eknath. 75. Sena, the barber, Chokhamela, the loving *bhakta,* Gora, the potter, who by his continual worship made the Lord-of-Heaven subservient to him. 76. Banka, and Bahira Pisa, the loving Janak, and Parasa, the Bhagavat. Tulasidas, Kamal, whom the Lord-of-Heaven delights in. 77. Kanhopathak, Suradas, and the four sons of Nama, Narasi Mehata, the crest jewel of saints, and Vasara, the mine-of-Indifference-to worldly-things. 78. Ramdas, Ramananda, chief of sannyasis, Joga, Rohidas, that noble Vaishnava, the noble Nagnath, the possessor of all siddhis, and Vishvambhar the prince of *bhaktas.* 79. Keshav Chaitanya, Raghav Chaitanya, Amabai, that mine of goodness, Gonai, Rajai, Mirabai, and Kanhopatra. 80. Such was this circle of *bhaktas,* and Krishna sat in their midst. Just as the moon looks in the midst of the planets, so Krishna looked resplendent on that occasion. 81. Just as Shiva among the ascetics, or as great Meru among the mountains, or as the son of Anusuya among the perfected ones, so seemed Vishnu whose pleasure ground is Vaikuntha. 82. It was the mine from which all beauty

in the animate and inanimate world has come. If any poet seeks to compare its beauty with anything else, his voice fails him. 83. Such was Hari, the incomparable, that wish-tree to all wishing *bhaktas,* the soul of all his *bhaktas,* and thus with love He spoke. 84. "Among Vishvambhar's descendants is one Bolhoba, a *bhakta,* loving and pious. I have promised him a son who shall be a world saviour, and a world-*guru.*" 85. Krishna then asked the assembled *bhaktas,* "Whom shall I send?" Those noble Vaishnavas, hearing these words, shouted Victory! Victory! 86. The Life-of-the-world then asked Nama, who was sitting before him, to rise. Nama, that chief jewel of all *bhaktas,* the loving and the perfect saint did so and Hari taking him aside spoke with him.

87. Said Hari to Nama, "Age after age I have to become an *avatar* for the purpose of establishing righteousness, and destroying the wicked. 88. I want you to become *avatars* on the earth, and with love worship me. I want you to proclaim loving worship, which brings salvation to the humble in heart. 89. Now listen, my dear *Bhakta,* my choice place of rest, become an *avatar* and tell men how to worship. 90. *Bhakti* is supreme over the four *muktis,* so I have said in Bhagavadgita and the Bhagavata. Make that plain, and sing my praise. 91. Formerly you made a vow that you would offer to me one million verses. Some remained to be written. That they should be completed, is my command. 92. The *Vedas,* with their deeply abstruse contents, I want you to churn, and bring out their true meaning in detail, and then reverently serve it with love to those who are hungry for receiving it. 93. And erect a water-stand of Hari's name for (thirsty) travellers on the Road-of-*Bhakti.* Make *Bhakti* with love the cold water

to be given to cool all the animate and inanimate world. 94. I give Final-Salvation to go with you, to be your helper. It will be obedient to you, and go whithersoever you send it. 95. The four *Muktis* will be at your service. *Riddhi* and *Siddhi* will naturally go with you. I know you do not love them, but they are useful to mankind. 96. Now go to the land of the mortals, and cause men to hear of my deeds that call forth praise. And may your love (for me) be tenfold for you deserve love and happiness.

97. Such was the blessing lovingly given to Nama by the Husband-of-Lakshmi. "I agree to thy wish" said Nama, that statue of love, and added the following words. 98. Said he, "The Kali Yuga is an age of untruth. You are already an *avatar* in the form of Buddha, (silent and motionless). Now if we find ourselves in any trouble, on whom shall we call for help?" 99. To Nama's question the Lord-of-Heaven replied, "If ever you fall into distress, I, the Infinite one, myself will remove it. 100. I will put aside my Buddha avatarship, and immediately assume a *sagun* form. I will then speak to you in nectar words. So let your mind be at rest." 101. When the Recliner-on-the-Serpent [Vishnu] had uttered these words, Nama with love prostrated himself at His feet. With His four arms Hari [Vishnu] lifted Nama up, and embracing him drew him to His heart. 102. Equal with God and in His heart was Tuka [Tukaram], His *bhakta*. The Close friend of *bhaktas,* Shri Hari, put Tuka into the heart of Nama. 103. This was as if the Supreme-Lord-of-the-universe had poured into the heart-jar of Nama the nectar of love. Or, as if, the Life-of-the-World had put into Nama's heart the cluster of His glorious six forms of goodness. 104. He put into

Nama the power of an avatar, the power of developing and the power of destroying. Or, as if the glorious-Lord was offering to Nama the *Bhakti* that is above *Moksha* [Final Deliverance]. 105. He who is not lighted up, because He himself is light, had Tuka His *bhakta* in the secrecy of His heart. And in this heart of Vishnu, and becoming one with it, it partook of the similarity to His divine nature. 106. So with the pretext of an embrace, God put Tuka in Nama's heart. And said He, "Be of help to one another, and enjoy the happiness that is accompanied with love". 107. After these words by Krishna, Nama joined his hands, palm to palm, and asked, "Where shall I become an *avatar*? Give me the name of the holy family. 108. A family in which *bhakti* is given to Vishnu, and where the long list of Thy names are uninterruptedly repeated. Where also there is Thy dark-coloured image. Give me birth into such a place." 109. To this request of Nama's The Dweller-in-Heaven replied, "I will tell you the place where I became bound by a promise through the expression of heart's devotion. 110. This my servant, Vishvambhar, who is now dwelling here in Heaven, he is the one who bound me to a promise through his heart's devotion, O Nama. 111 You will perhaps ask how it happened. I will tell you. Listen. Vishvambhar was accustomed to sing my praise in the loud expressions of his love. He adopted the custom of regular pilgrimages to Pandhari. 112. Naturally I, the Eagle-Bannered-One, was pleased, and as naturally came to his town, and there he bound me with a promise. 113. Among his descendants is the *bhakta* Bolhoba. He made me the object of his worship. I expressed to him my pleasure, and asked him to tell me at once what boon he desired. 114. He replied to me, 'Give me a son who will be a *bhakta* of Vishnu, who will be a saviour-of-the-world in reality, who will live for the good of the world, a universal *guru.*' 115. When he had said this, O chief of the *bhaktas* (Nama), I was pleased with him. And now to fulfil my promise to him I wish you, Nama, to become an *avatar* in his family."

Nama Becomes an Avatar in the form of Tukaram.

116. "I agree" said this noble Vaishnava, and with sincerity of feeling he made Vishnu a reverential bow. He then descended to this world of mortals, and as he did so the whole sky was filled with an intense light. 117. People saw that light with astonishment. They exclaimed to one another, "There are falling stars without number; but to-day it seems as if the queen of night has descended to the earth, for, this light we see is most extraordinary. 118. Perhaps it is the fourth *Bhakti* that is above Final-Deliverance, and is the great star Arcturus."

Kanakai's womb might be considered as the ocean. 119. In that ocean was a pearl oyster shell. Nama's love formed the water in that shell, and in that water Tuka was born as the pearl, the loving *bhakta* of Hari. 120. With effort she performed the nine forms of *bhakti;* and they became her completed nine months. Such was Kanakai's special fortune that this Vishnu *bhakta* should come to her womb. 121. Her special wish at this time was a disgust for worldly affairs. "I wish," she used to say, "to go away by myself and give myself to the worship of Shri Hari."

Tukaram is Born.

122. When Kanakai's days were fulfilled, and as she sat alone in her house, an extraordinary light shone around

her, like the brilliancy of the rising sun. 123. And when Kanakai looked into the face of her son, it looked as if it were a face made of light. Or it might be spoken of as the new shoot of the joy of peace. Or if not that, one might speak of it as indifference-to-worldly-things in a bodily form. 124. Or as if a mine of *bhakti* had been discovered. Or that his name was Satchitananda. Or that he was the storehouse of love, which had now been truly opened. 125. Kanakai's heart was full of astonishment. For four *ghatikas* she sat absorbed in gazing. She said not a word. All thirst (for worldly things), and all pride of heart left her. 126. She was drowned at that moment in the deep pool of joy. She had not the least bodily consciousness. This was a remarkable fact. 127. When the child, this Vishnu *bhakta,* appeared, immediately there took place the loss of her strength, and her spirit was united with the Spirit of God; and her heart became full of joy. 128. Just then the image of Pandurang manifested itself in the heart of the child, and said to it privately, "I wish you to live in conformity with the usual conditions of human life. 129. At first I wish you to show in the sight of men the manner in which the affairs of life should be conducted. But later you will see in yourself Right-thinking, and Indifference-to-worldly-things, with loving devotion in your heart." 130. No sooner had Krishna spoken these words to him, than there appeared the Maya-net, Kanakai opened her eyes and beheld before her, her son. 131. As her mind recollected the past events they all at this time seemed to her like a dream. Just then her neighbours came in, and exclaimed to one another, "Kanakai has given birth (to a son)". 132. They went and told Bolhoba of the event. "You have a son born." He replied, "Pandharinath has fulfilled my wish."

THE INFANT TUKA TAKEN TO THE TEMPLE.

133. After twelve days had passed Kanakai received the rite of purification. She then went at once to the temple, and bowed before the Husband-of-Rukmini. 134. She took her infant in her arms and placed it at the feet of Pandurang. "He is your slave, O Recliner-on-the-Serpent" said she, and with that she marked him with the ashes from the incense plate. 135. Hearing these words, the Lord-of-Heaven said to Rukmini, "Take up the child in your arms and place it in her (Kanakai's) lap." 136. Rukmini lifted the child up and held it in Her own arms, and then placed it in Kanakai's lap. 137. Kanakai said to Rukmini, "O Mother, give the baby a name to-day". "I will," she said, and then Mother Rukmini started to go away.

TUKA'S INFANCY.

138. The Husband-of-Rukmini was pleased with the worship of Bolhoba, though accompanied with desires. So that, naturally, children and wealth were added to him. 139. Wherever Rukmini comes, there all the *Siddhis* [Forces that accomplish, personified] are favorable. The happy mother called her female neighbours (whose husbands were living) together, and then they placed the infant in its cradle. 140. Rukmini took the form of a beautiful woman, and adorned their foreheads with turmeric yellow and red powders. She sang softly to the babe, "Jo, jo, jo," and rocked the cradle. 141. "That which is Indestructible and Indivisible, and without the possession of name or form, that which cannot be described by words, yet is all joy, in that joy, sleep my little babe. 142. Where *Aham* (I am

Brahma) and *Soham* (I am He) and *duality* and *non-duality* disappear; and where the four forms of speech, including *Para* become wearied, there sleep my little babe. 143. Where there is no such recollection as that of a thing to be known, a knower, and the act of knowing; where there is no such thing as a thing to be contemplated, a contemplator, and the act of contemplating; where there is not the triplet, cause, action and effect, there sleep my little babe. 144. Where saints preach the doctrinal knowledge, which teaches action without selfish desire, there place your love, the home of joy, and sleep my little babe. 145. Because no one could know anything of the Unmanifested, Pandurang took a *sagun* form for the sake of his *bhaktas*. At his visible feet sleep with love." 146. With such words the Mother-of-the-Universe sang a cradle song. Around her were gathered all the women, whose husbands were living, and they swung the cradle, singing softly "Jo, Jo, Jo." 147. They gained Kanakai's approval, and named the babe Tuka. By whose name there is salvation for the ignorant. 148. Rukmini distributed *pan supari* to all the assembled people, and gifts to the women with husbands. She lastly distributed *ghugarya* (boiled pulse) to the women, and then came back to her temple.

The Boy Tuka.

149. Time passed in which the loving *bhakta,* Tuka, played and crept about. Gradually day by day he began to walk.

150. In the meantime Kanakai again became an expectant mother, and the son promised by Brahmadeva was born. He was given the name of Kanhaya. 151. Thus

there were three sons, Savaji, Tuka, and Kanhaya. Bolhoba seeing this miracle, worshipped the Lord-of-Pandhari. 152. Said he, "The three gods gave me a vision in my dream. It was not at all an untrue one. They have all come true as promised." 153. All fortunes, such as wealth, grain and children were given him (Bolhoba) by Krishna. It was the good fruit of his austerities in a former birth, and he was able to experience delight arising from his fortune. 154. If one should attempt to describe his good fortune, there would be no end to it. The three gods had given him three sons to save the world. 155. It was the manifestation among men of the three forms, composed of the *satva, rajas,* and *tamas gunas.* It was to turn men to knowledge, Indifference-to-worldly-things and *bhakti,* that they were born.

156. Gradually the three sons reached manhood. The mother and father felt great satisfaction in looking at them. 157. Seeing the wealth of property and sons, many rich persons offered their daughters in marriage to his sons. The Brahman astrologers read the horoscope, and the wedding day was fixed. 158. A great deal of money was spent, and the marriage ceremony passed very happily. Kanakai saw it with a very happy heart. 159. A woman truly has no greater joy in her heart than to be an honoured wife, with sons, daughters-in-law and wealth.

160. Every thing was favourable to them. Their business prospered. God, Merciful-to-the-lowly, did not allow them to lack in the least thing. 161. While carrying on his business honestly, Bolhoba at the same time acquired the Supreme-spiritual-riches. He only, in whom the thought, "I am the doer," does not arise should be called one indifferent-to-worldly-things.

Two Opinions Regarding Fate.

162. Saints, and those not in that class, both are engaged in carrying on worldly affairs. But their experiences differ. Listen with your ears to the following statement.

163. The ignorant say Fate is lame. It is by effort that one's business prospers. In our worldly affairs we are always for efficiency, and, therefore, we have no further anxiety. 164. Deeds in a former birth, without effort on a man's part, cause him to be bound through the idea of "I am the doer." In this way men fail to acquire Final-Deliverance from births and deaths, and have to wander back and forth in the eighty-four rebirths.

165. The wise are also engaged in worldly affairs. But they say, "He that does all things is Shri Hari. It is He who pulls the cord of ancient times, and creates the experiences superimposed on Fate. 166. One must receive what is in one's Fate. That which is to happen cannot truly be avoided." It is in accordance with this doctrine that the wise act, and they are called Jivanmuktas [Freed, though still living].

167. Such was Bolhoba's state of mind. The idea that I am the doer, never entered his mind. Therefore, it was that in his daily business affairs he united himself with the Husband-of-Rukmini, thus gaining the supreme-spiritual-riches. 168. Just as the leaf of the lotus, though it is in the water, does not become wet with water, or as when the sun is reflected in a jar of water, one should not make the meaningless remark that the sun is wet. 169. Or as when a sensualist happens to see his face in a looking glass, he is not pleased with the reflection. 170. So the Vaishnava *bhaktas,* while engaged in worldly affairs, yet live

outside of illusory conceptions of life. While carrying on their worldly life, they always have God [The Husband-of-Rukmini] in their minds.

BOLHOBA'S ELDEST SON SAVAJI BECOMES A SANNYASI.

171. Time passed and Bolhoba arrived at old age. He called his son Savaji to his side, 172. and said, "I am now in my old age. You are my eldest son. Now put your mind into our worldly affairs and take the care of what you owe to others, and what others owe you. 173. Look at the Day-book and the Ledger, and bring to mind what cash is in hand." He listened, however, to his father's request, and then bowed at his feet. 174. Said he, "Father dear, I do not want to be entangled in any way in worldly affairs. I want to go on a pilgrimage to sacred places. I feel an indifference-to-all-worldly things. 175. I have felt the responsibility on my shoulders for the care of you, my mother and father. That is why I have remained here at home, entangled in our household affairs. For to leave you uncared for, and go far away is contrary to scripture, and from the point of view of public opinion, very wrong." 176. Recognizing his son's indifference-to-worldly-things, Bolhoba accepted it quietly. He remarked, however, "Things that are destined to happen are certainly curious. One does not know what Fate has in store." 177. Then he suddenly remembered what had happened, and said, "It was Shiva who gave me the boon of this son. He has the same characteristics as Cemetery-inhabiting-Shiva. 178. When the divinities of the *satva, raja* and *tama gunas* are pleased with one who is a seeker after them, they give such fruits as are like themselves. This is a fact of human experience. 179. If one prays to the sun, he gives his piercing rays. Or, if one makes the round moon the

object of his prayers, it gives to its worshippers a state of coolness. 180. In accordance with that principle, Shiva gave me this favoured son. Naturally he does not want the work connected with worldly affairs. My mind understands it now. 181. So with this understanding in his mind, Bolhoba quietly accepted it.

TUKA CARRIES ON THE FAMILY BUSINESS.

Bolhoba then called Tuka, and in a kind way put him in charge of his business interests. 182. He instructed Tuka in the method of buying and selling, and in the principle of conducting business. He charged him to keep his eye on his profit and loss accounts, and do those things that would finally issue in a profit.

183. "You seem to possess good talent for every kind of business." After hearing what his father had to say, Tuka replied, "I agree." 184. Relatives and dear friends began to remark upon Bolhoba's clever son. "Bolhoba has been able to arrange his business affairs very satisfactorily, while carried on in his presence. 185. That a son should act according to the wishes of his father, and that a wife should be endowed with good qualities and faithful to her husband, is the result of austerities in a former birth; one can easily see this. 186. His eldest son is Savaji. He seems to be a great saint, but Tuka appears to be a clever business man, and he is still quite young." 187. It was in this way that relatives and friends talked, sometimes praising Tuka in Bolhoba's presence, and sometimes behind his back. Hearing them talk thus, Bolhoba felt keen satisfaction. 188. Just as a king rejoices in his heart, hearing of the prowess of his Minister, or as when a mother and father rejoice, hearing of the goodness of their daughter, 189. or as a *sadguru* is

happy in his heart when he sees a disciple with an excellent mind. So when Bolhoba saw Tuka's business ability, he had joy in his heart.

Tuka's Second Marriage.

190. Tuka was already married, but his wife was suffering from the malady of asthma. The mother and father gave the matter thought and decided on a second marriage. 191. In the city of Poona there was one Apaji Gulavya, a very wealthy banker. His daughter was of marriageable age. Proposals were made and accepted, and the second marriage took place. 192. When the mother and father saw that Tuka was able to manage his elder and younger wife, and at the same time carry on his business, they were happy. 193. And thus there were mother, father, brothers, good friends, abundant property and money. Because of Tuka, the family was looked upon with honour and respect. They lacked in nothing whatsoever.

Mahipati's Benediction on the Bhaktalilamrita.

194. This book, the Bhaktalilamrita, may be considered as the ancient city of Pandhari. Good-heart may be considered as the saint Pundalik of noble character, who dwelt there. 195. Peace of mind, Indifference-to-worldly-things may be considered as the Bhima and Chandrabhaga rivers, that flow and unite there. Saints, listeners, and loving servants of God, live in this sacred city. 196. The unfailing love is, as it were, the brick, which Pundalik gave to God to stand upon. And the Lord-of-Heaven stands on it with His hands on His sides. 197. He stands in contemplation with His sight fixed on the tip of His nose, and gives His embraces to the pious. And I, dull

of mind, and ignorant, have come to see and worship him. 198. With his abundant verses, his tender *tulsi,* and his love as water, Mahipati ever stands close beside Him, contemplating His lotus feet.

199. Svasti. This book, the Bhaktalilamrita, by merely listening to it, supplies all one's heart's desires. May the pious loving *bhaktas* listen. This is the twenty-sixth interesting chapter.

CHAPTER 27.

Invocation.

Obeisance to Shri Ganesh. Obeisance to Shri Pandurang.

1. Victory! Victory! to Sacchidananda, Supreme-Brahma in visible form! The fame of Thy goodness is immeasurable. In attempting to describe Thy glory, the *Vedas* failed through weariness, and the *Shastras* had to stop their endeavours. 2. In relating Thy glorious deeds, O God-Supreme, the Serpent Shesha [on whom Vishnu reclines] grew weary. Brahmadev looked at Thy deeds with astonishment. Before them what am I? 3. A little child lisps when it talks, but the mother is very happy to hear it. And in her love she replies to the child in the same lisping manner. 4. Just so, when a *bhakta* praises Thee, O Husband-of-Rukmini, though in crude language, his words are pleasing to Thee, because of the strength of his loving devotion. 5. Although the Vedas are so wise, they had to become dumb when attempting to describe Thee, and yet the pious milkmaid (Thy mother) fastened Thee with a rope. Thou

didst obey her perfectly from fear, O Thou, who wast the Saviour-of-the-Universe, the Guru-of-the-world. 6. The great *rishis* perform great sacrifices in order to gain a visible manifestation of Thyself, and yet Thou, with a marvellous courtesy, didst eat the *bor* fruit, which the Bhil woman had already tasted. 7. Thou art the father of Brahmadeva, and yet Thou dost call Thyself the child of Yashoda, ever lying on her lap and demanding impossible things. 8. Duryodhan was a universal king, and yet Thou wouldst not accept from him honour and reverence, but Thou didst go around hunting for the house of the *bhakta* Vidur, the son of a slave. 9. Enjoying the exquisite taste for loving devotion, Thou didst eat what the cowherds left over on their plates. Thou didst push aside the plates with dainty food, and asked for the stems of the greens. 10. In that same spirit the Cloud-of-Mercy must accept my uncouth language, causing me to recollect the stories of the saints, and to relate their noble deeds.

Tuka's Prosperity turns to Adversity.

11. At the close of the last chapter we saw how Tuka turned the wheels of his business. When his father saw how the mercantile business was prospering he was very happy. 12. In the home there were the mother, the father, the brothers, good neighbours, and abundance of money and grain. There was bodily health, and the respect of the people. The family lacked nothing. 13. Thus it continued for a time, and Tuka's mind was absorbed in his business affairs. But suddenly adversity came upon him. How it came, listen, you pious folk.

14. After joy comes pain. This is a prophetic saying proved from the very beginnings of Time. People see

it taking place before their eyes, "After .happiness comes sorrow." 15. Just as when the sun sets, immediately there is darkness. Or after an exceedingly abundant harvest of grain, there comes a great famine. 16. Or where there is intense friendship there comes suspicion between the friends. Or where one is most highly honoured, there insults begin to appear. 17. Or where there is the enjoyment of physical health, there some disease begins to develop. When the ocean was churned there first came nectar, but afterwards poison appeared. 18. So it happened to Tuka, who felt happiness in the joy of his business affairs. But after that joy came the three-fold afflictions. How it happened, listen.

19. When the end of their lives came the mother and father went to Heaven. Tuka was wholly unable to restrain his grief. 20. In the sorrow of his brothers and sisters, his heart felt added grief. It made him exclaim, "The weight of our domestic and business affairs are on my head. How can I endure it?" 21. Though thus sorrowing, he inspired his own heart with courage, saying, "What was to happen has now happened. I could not have prevented it."

22. While thus seeking to inspire his own heart with courage, the wife of his elder brother passed to the Beyond. That also pained him deeply. 23. Savaji had already been a person indifferent to worldly things, and regarded domestic and business affairs as a nuisance. In addition he had the snare of a wife. But that snare now naturally ceased to hold him. 24. So now with a supreme sense of repentance the brother left for a pilgrimage to sacred places. In his mouth was the continual repeating of God's names, that lifegiving nectar. 25. On this pil-

grimage he saw the seven chief cities, the twelve Jyotir-lingas, the Pushkar pool, and other sacred watering places. In this way he rid himself of the difficulties of a worldly life. 26. He naturally performed the austerities of body, speech and mind, thus conquering the six enemies of the soul and attaining to the joy of mental peace. 27. After visiting all the various sacred places, he came finally to Anandavan [Benares]. Here he lived in association with saints, and sought from them the knowledge of the spiritual life. 28. When he had attained the perfect spiritual state he reached the peace of unity with the divine essence.

Now coming back to our story, listen to it, with love, you good folk. 29. In the town of Dehu the Vaishnava *bhakta,* Tuka, was continually in grief. "My mother and father are gone", he said, "and such is the condition of my brother. 30. If his wife were still alive, he would at least come back sometime. To begin with he was one, indifferent to worldly affairs, and (his wife's death) gave him the good opportunity (he wanted)." 31. So Tuka exclaimed, "O Husband-of-Rukmini, O Lord of Pandhari, while my mother and father were with me I did not have the least worry. And now what shall I do?" 32. The father had accumulated much wealth, but now that wealth had become dissipated. Just as the clouds that come in the Cold Season vanish in the sky. 33. Or as the tender grass shoots exist to-day, but in the Hot Season they wither away, or as when one prepares a seat in the shade of a cloud, in an instant the shade is gone. 34. Or as when one looks at a rainbow, in a moment it has disappeared; or look at the nature of a wave. Think you that it is permanent? 35 So Tuka's money and grain all disappeared there and then. In consequence becoming intensely worried, his frequent exclamation was, "What am I to do!"

Tuka Opens a Shop in the Bazaar.

36. People who owed him money did not let him say a word about it. His business did not at all succeed. What was he to do! 37. He had to bear the whole expense of his large family. So he rushed to the market place, and made great effort to obtain a loan of money. 38. But even with loans he was unable to make ends meet. Then he opened a shop in the Square and sat there. As he sat he was continually repeating aloud the names of Hari [God]. And his business principle was to do nothing that was false. 39. As he said, "To give any one small measure, that is contrary to truth and a great sin. One should give to a customer a little more than the usual rate." 40. He (Tuka) had full compassion towards all creatures, and never spoke an untruth. At the same time he was constantly repeating the names of Hari, and did not forget to do so for even a moment.

God was Testing Tuka.

41. In viewing Tuka's misfortunes it is evident that God was testing him. He gained no profit in his new business. Then he attempted other ways. 42. He adopted many lines of trade, but in none did Hari help him. As he saw his capital dwindling his heart was heavy with anxiety. 43. He worked hard day and night. He carried bags of grain on bullock backs. He paid no attention to cold or heat, to sleep or laziness. 44. He then borrowed heavily and attempted big business. But he was unable to make the least profit. He was now overcome with concern. 45. He borrowed still more, and attempted other

methods, but he saw no advantage in them. "O Vithoba," he cried, "What shall I do?" 46. Although his heart was full of anxiety yet day and night he continued to repeat God's names. Finally he borrowed more money, and sold what valuables he had. 47. But the money lenders gathered at his house, weighing things and looking into his accounts. He saw his means dwindling. What was to be done! 48. There were there some evil minded persons and relatives. They spread the report that Tuka was a bankrupt. That brought his creditors, who now remained sitting at his door (demanding payment). That brought tears to his eyes. 49. "O God-Supreme," he cried, "O Husband-of-Rukmini, what evil events Thou hast brought upon me! What is the use of all these worldly things!" Thus Tuka was in dire distress of mind. 50. There were some close friends and relatives, however, who came to his rescue at this crisis. Some shouldered his responsibilities in order to share his troubles.

False Friends Tempt Tuka to Distrust God.

51. Some used their own good credit, and had a loan given him (Tuka). But ridiculing him they gave him the following advice. 52. "Since you have been seeking the supreme-spiritual-riches, you have been constantly repeating God's names. This is the reason why you have miserably failed in your business. You should no longer keep thinking of Vitthal. 53. No one has really profited by his devotion to Vishnu. Our fathers left that principle with us, and you see its truth in your own experience. 54. You do not understand the most important business principles, and at the same time you are all the time repeating God's names. You will find this a true prophecy. You are in fact wishing for poverty. 55. We wish to teach you

this for your good, even though you may perhaps be angry with us. If you will not listen to us, and will continue your worship of God, your debts will increase." 56. After giving Tuka this advice, those grocers returned to their homes.

Wife and Neighbours Oppose Tuka's Piety.

At home Tuka's wife made a great ado. Said she, "What is going to happen to my domestic affairs! 57. Since the master of this home began his contemplation of Vithoba, we have lost our social position among men, and we have not enough to eat." 58. In Tuka's home, his wife indulged in all kinds of nagging, and outside the home the evil-minded laughed at him. But Tuka would not drop his heart's resolution. 59. With feelings of heartfelt love Tuka's tongue delighted in repeating God's names.

Tuka alone in a Thunder Storm.

The queen in Tuka's home was in great trouble, because he was gone away on his business venture. 60. He took four bullocks with him. Three of them were stricken with some disease and died. Thus the Husband-of-Rukmini tested Tuka to see whether he would cease to worship Him. 61. But Tuka worshipped with all the more enthusiasm, and in his love for God he shouted his words. His companions said to one another, "He has truly become a nuisance to us. 62. He knows nothing about proper time, and is all the while babbling. We cannot get a wink of sleep. He gives us the headache." 63. So all these, his companions, gave Tuka the slip, and went on before him. Then when this *bhakta* of Vishnu looked about him, he saw he was in a jungle. 64. There was now no one with him, and one watch of the night had passed. Just then a bag of grain fell from the back of the bullock. 65. Immediately he was in great distress. "Who is there to help me lift this bag?" he cried. Just then a cloud in the sky thundered, and the rain storm turned in its course. 66. A most violent wind began to blow. The dust compelled him to close his eyes. Lightning bolts flashed and thundered in the sky. Immediately drops of rain began to fall. 67. The jungle was now truly frightful, and a great number of wild animals appeared in sight. It now rained in exceptional torrents, and Tuka was in distress. 68. Then Tuka said to himself, "This rascally worldly life is persecuting me. I have thereby fallen into great distress. And to whom shall I tell of it? 69. My mother and father have left me and gone. My brother has become a mendicant. I am to-day a bankrupt. That makes me ashamed of my worldly life. 70. Even the evil minded did once honour me, but now they laugh and persecute me. My wealth has become dissipated. We have not enough to eat at home. 71. My companions have given me the slip, and who will now help me lift the bag of grain?" He cried. "O God-Supreme, O Krishna, I have no one but Thee. 72. Be to me, O Lord-of-Pandhari, mother, father, brother, and uncle. I am about to lose my life, O Infinite-One, come quickly (to my help). 73. Aside from Thee I have no close friend and true neighbour. I am just like an ignorant infant. Who except its mother will take care of it? 74. The power of my will is at an end, therefore, it is that my thoughts are centered on Thee. If Thou dost not come to my help, O Cloud-of-Mercy, the evil minded will everywhere laugh at me." 75. Thus, this loving *bhakta* prayed, and tears streamed from his eyes. "O Mother Vithoba! Helper-of-the-Helpless, care for me, Thy humble (*bhakta*)."

God in Human Form Comes to Tuka's Help.

76. Hearing this love accompanied appeal for help, Krishna assumed the form of a traveller, and arriving just at that moment, began to question Tuka. 77. "Who are you, sitting here obstructing the path, at so late an hour of the night?" To this question of Krishna's, Tuka replied. 78. "My business is that of a grain merchant. This bag of grain has fallen down, and there is no one to help me lift it. All my companions have left me." 79. Having listened to this reply, what did Krishna do, but put his hand to the bag, and at once placed it on the bullock's back. 80. Of course this noble Vaishnava was made very happy by this help, but on account of the darkness he could not see the path. The traveller said to him, "Follow me." 81. Thus Pandurang [God], in human form, briskly showed the way to this *bhakta* of His. But Vishnu's Maya had caused confused ideas in Tuka's brain, so that he did not recognize Him. 82. Krishna went on before showing the path, and the God-loving *bhakta* followed behind Him. When they arrived near the Indrayani river, they found it in full overflowing flood. 83. Tuka began to be anxious, and exclaimed, "How are we to remove this bag of grain from the bullock's back, and carry it across the river?" The Giver-of-Eternal-Life replied, "I will find a place (where we can cross) and will return." 84. But now what did the Life-of-the-World do by his miraculous power? He placed His disk under the water. And said to Tuka, "It will not be necessary to remove these bags from the bullock's back." 85. With these words the Husband-of-Rukmini walked steadily ahead, and the noble Vaishnava crossed the river (on the disk) with the bag of grain undisturbed on the bullock's back. 86. Tuka was astonished, and said to himself,

"God has sent this traveller to-day (to help me), otherwise it would not have been well with me. How am I to repay his kindness?" 87. While Tuka's mind was thus puzzled, he beheld a most wonderful sight. A lightning bolt flashed in the sky, and in the light of that flash he saw 88. his fellow traveller, who was walking before him in His four-armed form. Tuka was filled with infinite joy, as he saw this form. 89. At His waist was a shining yellow garment. On His throat flashed the beautiful Kaustubha jewel, around His neck was the *Vaijayanti* garland. His glorious face was full of charm. 90. His bodily complexion was dark, but shining, and besides this, sandal-wood paste had been rubbed over Him. There were jewels set around the glorious *Shrivatsa* mark, and in His crown precious stones sparkled. 91. Brilliant earrings flashed light. In His mouth His teeth sparkled like diamonds. On His feet the *todar* and *vanki* bells tinkled, and Tuka was amazed at the sight. 92. It was by the lightning's flash that Tuka saw this Ocean-of-beauty-and-joy. It is true that the flash revealed God to Tuka, but no simile will apply here. 93. How can one use the light of a lamp to see the sun? In order to get the taste of nectar, would one add sugar to it? 94. In order to form an idea of the serpent Shesha [Vishnu's couch], would one place before himself a common reptile? Or, would one seek the company of ghosts, in order to call on the Lord-of-Kailas? 95. How can a seeker after knowledge gain it by studying the illusory ideas of the ignorant? It is not by association with the six enemies of the soul that one obtains peace and joy. 96. So it truly was not the lightning at all that revealed the form of Pandurang, but it was because of the loving devotion of Tuka, that Shri Krishna revealed Himself. 97. But coming in this peculiar way,

Tuka recognized His true form, and met Him with love. To this end the brilliant light of the lightning falling on Him as he walked ahead, gave Tuka a vision of what He actually was. 98. But again as Tuka watched Him, He was still his fellow traveller walking ahead of him. Finally the two reached Tuka's home, and the bag of grain was removed from the bullock s back and put in its proper place. 99. While the Vaishnava Tuka was occupied in attending to the needs of his bullock, the Lord-of-Heaven the Friend of *bhaktas* made use of the opportunity and slipped away.

Tuka's Piety Blamed for Business Failure.

100. As soon as the day dawned the town's people heard the news that Tuka had returned from Vanaje, and that his bullocks had died on the way. 101. And now the money lenders, the evil minded and the villains of the town gathered at his house, like Death. Just as when there is a wound (in an animal) the crows assemble at once to peck at it. 102. There is never ceasing enmity between the pursuit for the Supreme-spiritual-riches and the pursuit for worldly riches. In Tuka's case it was that of one swan, and many falcons. 103. Or, he was like a lonely banana tree in a jungle of *bor* trees. Thus Tuka had to suffer persecution in the words addressed to him. 104. "There were four bullocks and three of them died. Now at last you have gained the actual experience of the result of worshipping Shri Hari. 105. Tell us, to whom good has come by holding in his heart the Husband-of-Rukmini. King Harishchandra, courageous in good things, had to suffer great distress. 106. King Nala and Damayanti, held the Husband-of-Rukmini in their hearts, but in their domestic affairs they fell into great trouble. How many

examples must we need give you of this?" 107. One said to Tuka, "You are holding Vishnu in your heart, but you do not feel the least shame from your public disgrace. All you had is now dissipated." 108. Said another, "We give him advice, but he will not listen to it. It is because of this that he has to suffer so much pain. He has borrowed money, and the lenders have lost all. And yet he has no shame, nor any sorrow over it." 109. With these words the evil minded returned to their homes. But great anxiety took hold of this noble Vaishnava. "What am I to do about my business affairs?" said Tuka. 110. "My heart is on the supreme-spiritual-riches, and my body is entangled in worldly things. My life is divided between the two. O Mother Vitthal! When wilt Thou free me? How is it that Thou dost not feel pity for me?"

Tuka's New Business Venture.

111. The Rainy Season had come and gone, and now a severe famine confronted the land. Children and even adults were everywhere in greatest distress from lack of food. 112. On whom could he cast the burden of his business affairs? He could see no help anywhere outside of himself. With this thought this noble Vaishnava conceived a special plan. 113. He had a small part of his principal still in hand, and with it he bought a quantity of *mirchis* [very hot chillies]. He bought enough to fill three gunny bags and (with his pack bullock carrying them) went down into the Konkan [District bordering the sea]. 114. As he journeyed along the way, the air resounded with the name of Vitthal. He held in his imagination God's *sagun* form, and his heart was all the time filled with love. 115. His business venture was really that he might have a distaste for worldly affairs. His choice of this business

was with the idea that in some way his mind might feel a disgust for it. 116. So his thoughts were occupied with the name and form of God. He lost entirely the consciousness of his own body. (Arriving in the Konkan), this Vaishnava *bhakta* stopped outside of a town near the sea shore. 117. There was there a great temple to Shiva, and before the temple a banyan tree. He removed the gunny bags (from the bullock), and tied it (with its rope). 118. He ripped the bags open, and at that very spot prepared to sell (his chillies). But all the while the image of Pandurang filled his heart, and he forgot all about his bodily needs. 119. Men and women gathered around him and said to Tuka, "You have brought these *mirchis* here for sale, tell us at what rate you sell them." 120. The Vaishnava *bhakta* listened to them and then replied, "Do you not know the usual rate? Take at once what you need. Don't hesitate." 121. Just then some one brought a quart of rice. He at once measured it and accepted it. And according to its value this noble Vaishnava measured out his *mirchis* (chillies). 122. "Can you not add a little to it?" said the customer. In reply the Vaishnava said, "Take it with your own hands. Don't hesitate." 123. The customer began to take from the bag, but rather timidly, thinking that Tuka might grab her hand away, but he was not looking there, because though in the body he was not of the body. 124. Just then two women came with six pies [a pie equals a twelfth of an anna]. Tuka measured out his *mirchis*. "Add a little more," they said. 125. He replied, "Take with your own hands as much as you need, and go." One of them put her hands into the bag very timidly, the other remarking to her. 126. that Tuka was a very honourable merchant. He gives true measure. He lets them take out the extra *mirchis* with both hands, and made no effort to prevent them by seizing their hands. 127. Still remarking as above, they pulled the *mirchis* out of the bag with both hands. But Tuka did not prevent them, and the people standing around saw it all. 128. In the mean while some one went into the town, and reported that a merchant by name of Tuka, a grain dealer, had seated himself outside the town. That he was a highly honourable man, and one of noble character. And that he was constantly engaged in the worship of Hari. 129. On top of what he measures out he gives above that twice as much. He does not at all seize the hand that takes it away. Come and see his acts for yourselves. 130. The report spread about the town and people came to look at him. Then they said to one another, "He is a mere simpleton *bhakta.* Let us make use of the opportunity." 131. So they said to Tuka, "If we have to go back to our homes for money, all the mirchis will have been sold (before our return), and our households need a great quantity of them. 132. If you will give us the chillies on short credit, we shall repay very soon." "Take away with you what you may need," said the Vaishnava *bhakta.* 133. Then the noble Vaishnava measured out what they asked for, and then with their own hands they took out for themselves four times as much. Said they, "That all should have more than what is due, is certainly very extraordinary." 134. Seeing his simplicity, every one began to ask him for some. He ripped open another bag, and said, "Help yourselves. 135. You are all asking at once, how can I supply you single handed? I trust you. Take out what you want with your own hands and go." 136. No sooner had the noble Vaishnava said this, than from every side, and all at once, they thrust in their hands. And just as dogs fiercely fight with one another when they see a pile of leaf plates with uneaten food on them, so these people began to fight with one another. 137. Making their worldly affairs a matter of selfish gain, they growled at one another. They paid no thought to what the future would have for them. 138. Some of them were strong, and they took away a whole maund. Some pulled out with their hands a half a maund. Others five *sher,* 139. Some a half a *sher,* a half of a quarter of a *sher,* or two *shers.* To some there came a lapful. Some took a small panful and went home. 140. Thus the two bags of *mirchis* were plundered and their contents taken away. Just then a low villain suddenly approached Tuka and said, 141. "At my home a large quantity of *mirchis* is required. Just now I want a bag full of *mirchis.* If you think I am not telling you the truth, ask the people about me." 142. Listening to him the Vaishnava *bhakta* replied "I trust you implicitly." As soon as he heard this answer, that vile wretch took up a bag. 143. The loving *bhakta* said to him, "Bring the bag back soon." The other replied, "I have no bag to store the *mirchis* at my home. 144. So when you come here again, then I will empty the bag and give it back." Talking thus, the rascal went off to his house. 145. A Vaishnava *bhakta* never understands the insincerity of the human heart. Listen to certain facts that illustrate this. 146. If it is going to rain to-day the ant knows it, and removing its eggs from one place takes them to another. 147. But the same ant gets washed away, when a man throws water on the ground. The ant understands the laws of the universe, but it knows not the mind of a man. 148. So a loving *bhakta* understands the thoughts of God, but fails to understand the hard heart of the wicked. 149. In order that he might not have to pay anything, the rascal took the bag along with the *mirchis*, but Tuka trusted him. He could not understand such a mine of guile. 150. But Tuka was in a very happy frame of mind. "I have made a quick sale to-day," said he, and then went to take his bath, all the time thinking of the Husband-of-Rukmini. 151. A *sher* of rice and the six *pies*, equal to two *pice*, was all he got for his first cash sales. As Tuka looked at these he felt quite happy. 152. I have what I need, now I must prepare my meal. He took his brass vessels, and put the rice to boiling. 153. That God filled all mankind, was Tuka's fixed idea. So bringing into his mind the Giver-of-Eternal-Life, he wagged his head as he repeated God's names.

God Becomes a Debt Collector for Tuka.

154. Recognizing Tuka's condition, the Husband-of-Rukmini said to Himself, "Such is his indifference to worldly affairs, he does not understand the intrigues of the worldly wise. 155. These thieves have made away with the three bags of *mirchis*. The money-lenders at home will press him on his return, and what answer can he give them?" 156. Thus thinking, the Advocate-of-His-*Bhaktas* immediately took human form. He went to one of the houses in the town and said very politely, 157. "Sirs, please pay at once for what you took on credit. We are already late in starting for our home." "Who are you?" they replied. "And what is it that we took on credit, that you are asking for?" 158. Krishna listened, and then replied, "Tuka Shet is a grain-dealer from Dehu, I, Vithoba, am his servant. I have come to ask you for the money due on what you took on credit." 159. To this those mercenary men answered, "He gave this to us for nothing. If he had measured them out to us, then your asking would be quite

proper." 160. The Lord-of-Heaven replied, "Because his hand gives a correct measure, therefore he has received the name of Tuka Shet from the chief men of Dehu." 161. "Well then," said the towns-people, "tell us how much *mirchi* we brought home." When they weighed it, they found it exactly as what the Husband-of-Rukmini told them. 162. And this seemed to them so miraculous that they brought their money at once and gave it to him. Thus for the sake of His *bhakta* Krishna went from house to house. 163. Some, however, showed a vulgar impudence, and on those He, (the Husband-of-Rukmini), showered a flow of vile curses. But though some of them replied to Him harshly, the Soul-of-the-Universe bore it without making answer. 164. Whatever amount He told them they owed, when they weighed the *mirchis,* the weight was as He told them. At this they exclaimed, "Tuka Shet is rightly named," and all marvelled. 165. Hari was under the spell of Tuka's sincere devotion, so He took no thought of what he might suffer, and became for the time being one of low degree, and went from house to house. 166. The Husband-of-Rukmini said with His own mouth, "The people of the town are very impudent. If one asks of them what they owe, they are ready to come to blows, but for this reason, they will get the worst of it." 167. So it was that some who recognized the marvel (of Vithoba's knowledge) brought their money and gave it to Him. Some, fearing a quarrel, came bringing the money to the square. 168. In this way the Lotus-eyed-One collected from every one what they owed, with the exception of that one man who had taken away a gunny bag full of *mirchis.* 169. The Life-of-the-World said to Himself, "How shall I be able to get any money from him? He seems a greater scoundrel than any of them. I wonder what plan I should adopt? 170. Just as there are some kernels in grains that will neither get soaked with water, nor be cooked, so is the heart of a scoundrel. His hard heart never melts." 171. Realizing the difficulty Shri Hari stood before the man's door. And there in an angry tone He spoke roughly to the man. 172. "Tuka Shet," He said, "is a grain dealer of Dehu, I am Vithoba, his servant. You took away a sack full of *mirchis*. Give now at once what you owe on it. 173. To the sight you look like an honourable man, but you brought a gunny sackful of *mirchis* here to your house, and have kept it. My master is waiting. Give what you owe at once." 174. As the Dark-complexioned-One thus spoke, the scoundrel replied, "Come along with me to your master," and with this he began to drag Him along by force. 175. "Tuka Shet is my friend," he continued, "he did me this kindness. Did he measure it out and give it to me? And because of that have you come?" 176. To this statement of the villain the Dweller-in-Heaven answered, "I will not go to him. He would say I was a worthless servant." 177. "Well then," said the other, "I will not give you the money. Let us see how you will take it from me?" Seeing the man's hard heart, what did the Lord-of-Heaven do 178. but take a loose rope and made of it a noose around his neck? "I will take my own life, and will sink this whole town in dismal condition." He said. 179. Seeing His fixed determination, the men and women of his *wada*, gathered around, and in various ways these towns-people tried to shame the scoundrel. 180. "Is there any one," they said, "who would give away for nothing a sackful of *mirchis*? Why are you quarrelling to no purpose? Give him his money at once." 181. The scoundrel replied, "Well take away the sack that is filled with the *mirchis*." The Giver-of-Eternal-Life replied, "To begin with why did you bring it here?" 182. And with that Krishna tied the rope around his neck with his own hands, and his eyes began to roll wildly, while the people looked on. 183. He whose form Shiva in seclusion contemplates in the recesses of His heart, even He, for the sake of Tuka's loving devotion, fastened the noose around His own neck. 184. *Yogis* with their eight-sided severe austerities seek Him, but He is never seen by them, yet He wears the noose of loving devotion round His neck. I consider this very wonderful, indeed!

185. For the purpose of attaining whom, the great *rishis* perform austerities, He, the Soul-of-the-Universe, fastened the noose (around His neck) for the sake of helping His *bhakta*. 186. He who is the father of Brahmadev; He whose feet are adored by Indira; He who is the subject of Narad's song and of others, He became fastened (around the neck) by (the rope of) loving devotion. 187. To continue the story, however, listen to it, you pious folk, with reverence. The towns-people became frightened, and began to beat the scoundrel. 188. They exclaimed, "If this man takes his own life, our whole town will perish." So with kicks and fist-blows they attacked him. 189. Truly God fills all men, and so in these many ways the scoundrel was brought to shame. The towns-people compelled him to measure the *mirchis* and pay their value. 190. When this act was performed, the Life-of-the-world unfastened the noose, and collected all the money together. But He performed another miracle. 191. He assumed the form of a mayor's assistant; and said to Tuka "Take, sir, your money." "What money?" said Tuka. 192. "It is the money for the *mirchis* you gave on credit," said Krishna. "I collected all this money, and have at once come with it here." 193. The loving *bhakta* said,

"Why! I gave it to them to be divided among themselves." The officer replied, "Why did you do that? Do we want to have your goods for nothing? 194. We are well known and honourable citizens, and in what does God let us lack?" With this remark he unloosed the cloth, and placed all the money before Tuka. 195. When they had seated themselves the loving *bhakta* said to him, "Please take those six *pies* there, and go over there, and bring me some *ghi*." 196. "I will do so," he said, and the officer started to go. He brought back a whole brass vessel full of *ghi,* which astonished Tuka. 197. "This looks like a large quantity of *ghi*." The Lord-of-Pandhari replied, "*Ghi* is very cheap here. There is no lack of it in this town." 198. Tuka then said to the officer, "My cooking has turned out well. If you will dine with me, I shall be very happy." 199. Seeing his *bhakta's* sincerity, God-Supreme said, "Thank you, I will." Just then Shiva, taking the form of an uninvited guest, 200. and sitting in front of the temple, said to Tuka, "I am a guest sitting here, and hungry. Give me a place to sit and dine." Tuka heard this request with pleasure. 201. So the officer, the uninvited guest, and the dear God-loving *bhakta* dined together, and afterwards to cleanse their mouths, Tuka gave them *tulsi* leaves. 202. It was because Vishnu and Shiva recognized the sincere loving devotion of Tuka, that the two dined with him. As the uninvited guest left, He glorified Tuka with words of blessing. 203. The officer having made the God-loving *bhakta* as one protected, vanished out of sight.

Tuka is Accused of Hypocrisy.

Just then the people of the town assembled there and began to accuse Tuka. 204. "You are Tuka Shet, a *bhakta* of Vishnu, and you are continually repeating Hari's name. But you came very near bringing destruction on our town to-day. What are we to say to this?" 205. Then they began saying to one another, "He began by a show of piety, then saying that he was distributing the *mirchis,* the towns-people took them away. 206. He is just like the crane, that pretends to be contemplating, and then when a fish comes near it, swallows it down. It seems to us that this Tuka Shet is a *sadhu* of that kind. All of you should know of this." 207. Such was the accusation which adults, and even children of the town, passed to one another. Tuka listened with amazement, and asked one of them (to explain). 208. He explained in full: "A man, by name of Vithoba, your servant, went from house to house, and there quarrelling, collected your dues. 209. The man who took a sackful of *mirchis* would give nothing. Then your servant, there and then, put a noose around his own neck (to commit suicide). 210. Hearing a great hullaballoo, all the towns-people gathered there and kicked the scoundrel, and with their fists struck him in the face. 211. Having pommelled him well, we made him pay the whole account. If we had not done so, your servant would have taken his own life, and our town would have gone to destruction." 212. At this recital of what had happened the Vaishnava *bhakta* was filled with amazement. He said to himself, "If I should say their story was not true, yet I have received for all I gave on credit. 213. If I say it is a true story, (how can I), for I have not employed any servant. Well, it must have happened through the *maya* of Hari, whose Vaishnava deeds are beyond understanding."

Mahipati's Benediction on Chapter 27.

214. This Bhaktalilamrita is the great Manas lake. The fortunate loving and wise listeners are the noble *rishis* on

the shore of the lake. 215. How should one pay them reverence so that *sadhus* and saints will be pleased? That is what the poet has to think of in his mind. 216. With his simple verses, as beautiful flowers, and made into a variety of garlands, Mahipati, as a cultivator of flowers, stands in the midst of an assembly of Vaishnavas. 217. Svasti! This book, the Bhaktalilamrita, by merely listening to it, obtains for one his heart's desires. May it be listened to by loving, pious *bhaktas.* This is the Twenty-seventh interesting chapter.

CHAPTER 28.

Invocation by Mahipati.

Obeisance to Shri Ganesh!

1. I have no power of cleverness. I am not a wise and an able poet I merely call myself the darling of the saints, and spend my time in the contemplation of God. 2. My handwriting is not perfect. I cannot speak in the fifty-six different languages. I cannot talk in Sanskrit. My speech is a disconnected babble. 3. I do not live in a sacred city. My home is in a mean village. I am not backed by some perfect scribe. 4. I am not in good health. Very frequently I am attacked by some disease. In every way I go limping along. O Mother Vitthal, Thou knowest all this. 5. But trusting in Thee, I have begun this chapter. Preserve the honour of Thy humble servant, and permit me to finish it, O Shri Hari. 6. When a violent wind blows, the straw scarecrow begins to sway. How can it have an independent motion? 7. Or as the showman

pulls the strings, and makes his dolls dance in various ways, so sitting in my heart, Thy temple, Thou, O Shri Hari, will, (I know), give me a recollection (of what I should say). 8. If I did not have at least some of Thy gracious help, the saints would not honour my words surely. Just as, if the musk lacked its fragrant odour, who would ask for it in the bazaar? 9. The peacock's tail-feathers have eyes on every side, so without Thy gracious help all my words seem fruitless. 10. Therefore, through the blessing of Thy gracious help, cause me to relate in its details the life-history of the *Bhaktas,* whereby the hearts of the listeners may exude love, as they sit listening.

INNOCENT TUKA DECEIVED BY A KNAVE.

11. In the last chapter the pleasing story was told of how the Husband-of-Rukmini, becoming a servant, went from house to house and collected what was due to Tuka. 12. And how when Tuka had heard of that fact from the townspeople, this God-loving *bhakta* was amazed, remarking, "I do not know with certainty what the Lord-of-Pandhari may do."

13. Saddling his bullock, the noble Vaishnava started for his home (at Dehu). As he walked the path, his heart full of love for God, he shouted aloud God's names. 14. His mind was concentrated on the name and form of God, and, therefore, he was, as it were, outside of his body. Suddenly he was met by a swindler, who entered into conversation with him. 15. He had taken brass bracelets, and plated them with gold. He now showed them to Tuka. "I will let you have them," he said, "if you care to take them." 16. The God-loving *bhakta* listened to his offer, but replied, "I have not sufficient money with me, although I

collected all that was due me." And with that Tuka took out what he had and showed it to him. 17. The swindler then said, "Give me what you have, and the balance I will take gradually. I know who you are." 18. Tuka listened to this offer, and counting out his money gave it to him. The swindler took a different path, and Tuka, continuing his journey, arrived at his home. 19. He was feeling very happy, and said to himself, "Now I must give some money to the money lenders. Grain has become dear, but in place of having nothing to spend, I have gained some." 20. Even in Tuka's dreams he never suspected that anyone could have deceit in his heart. The doctrine was fixed in his mind that God fills the heart of mankind. 21. Just as Dharmaraj, the son of Kunti, searched over the three worlds (Heaven, Earth and Hell) and yet could not find a single corrupt being, so was it with Tuka. 22. Happy in his heart, Tuka had arrived at his home, and as soon as the people heard of it they hastened to his home. 23. Tuka tied up his bullocks, and sat down in front of them. The money lenders now asked him to show them what he had brought back. 24. Said he, "I gave a man the money I had, and bought from him this gold to bring home. Take some of it towards my debt, and let me have some for my home expenses." 25. With this explanation, the pious *bhakta* took off the bracelets and showed them to them. Experts looked at them, and then they burst out in loud laughter. 26. Then they cut a little into them to prove it, and sure enough the brass appeared. The money lenders beat their foreheads, and Tuka's wife cried, "Alas! alas! 27. You had better die! You sinner! You are all the time repeating the names of the Lord-of-Pandhari, and yet it is He who has done away with your worldly feelings. Do not now, therefore, worship that Merciless-One. 28. Just as, thinking some one to be a *pandit,* you take by the hand one really a fool, and bring the idiot home. Or, as if one gave a touchstone, and in return received a pebble. You haven't any common-sense. 29. Trusting that swindler you have brought destruction to our home. I truly cannot see how you are going to carry on our household affairs." 30. After talking with Tuka, the evil-minded people returned to their homes, and in his own home his wife was full of concern. "What am I to do now for our household needs?" she exclaimed.

TUKA'S WIFE BORROWS MONEY FOR TUKA.

31. Tuka had two wives. The name of the elder wife was Rakhuma Bai. The younger wife was called Avali, though her other name was Jijai. 32. Avali, the younger wife, was a very thoughtful woman. She thought to herself in the anxiety of her mind, "How are our household needs to be met? 33. My husband has gone crazy. He is at his worship day and night. He carries on his trade, but meets with no success. He is in straitened circumstances. 34. Still I think I should give a promissory note in my own name, and give that amount to him as his capital. If he makes any profit I shall not fail to apply it to our household needs." 35. With this thought in mind she went to the house of a moneylender, and said, "If you have confidence in my honesty, put the money in my skirt." 36. Avali's brother was a rich man, so the money-lender did not dare to refuse her request. The merchant, therefore, said to her, "Take as much as you need, Jijai." 37. She took two hundred rupees, and gave him her promissory note. Jijai returned to her home, and said to her husband, 38. "I have on my own account borrowed heavily of the money-lender. I have done so in order

that you may go with a company of traders on a distant expedition. 39. The merchants have laden (their bullocks) with salt, and are going to Baleghat. Go with them and bring back some money." 40. She gave the two hundred rupees to Tuka, and this *bhakta* of Vishnu started at once with the merchants. 41. Avali told Tuka, as he started, to be very careful of the capital given him. "If you do not take care of it," she said, "the curse will fall on my head. So don't let that happen by any means. 42. Since you have given yourself to this constant repeating of Hari's names, no one has confidence in your business management. So I borrowed this money, and I have had to give a promissory note in my own name. 43. If you give away any of this capital to anybody who asks you for it, you know well my character." After this warning, his wife returned to her home.

Tuka's Successful Business Venture.

44. To continue our story, Tuka also loaded his bullocks with (bags of) salt and accompanied the caravan of traders. 45. In the region of Baleghat they sold the salt, and filled their sacks with raw sugar [*gul*]. All the traders then wended their way back to the city [Poona], the loving *bhakta* being among them.

46. And he may be likened to a pearl fallen in the dust, which no one notices; or, like gold in a heap of brass, which no one except an expert recognizes; 47. or, like the touchstone [*paris*] among pebbles. Who would know its miraculous power? Or, like a diamond among quartz crystals. Such was our noble Vaishnava in that company. 48. Or he was as if the Vedas were bound with a book on Erotology. Or like a great pandit who

loses every form of greatness in an assembly of Muhammadans. 49. Or as if a wealthy banker should find himself in a great gathering of thieves. Or as if a beautiful and devoted wife should find herself in a company of prostitutes; 50. or a great distinguished Yogi among a set of lunatics; or as if one found nectar in an intoxicating drink. If a man of loving disposition should be seen in a company of scoffers, how would anyone know to pay him respect? 51. So amongst this company of untruthful traders, was Tuka, a statue of piety, knowledge, and indifference-to-worldly-things. Time and again they scoffed at him, they who had no scruples of conscience. 52. They remarked amongst themselves: "This Tuka who has come with us, doesn't know how to conduct business by false representation. How then is he going to make any money? 53. He puts aside all concern for his worldly business, and sits mentally repeating the names of the Lord-of-Heaven. He is worshipping all the time. He makes our heads ache." 54. Thus these evil-minded traders discussed Tuka among themselves, but Tuka though in the body was not of the body. He experienced not the least (worldly) joy or sorrow.

55. But enough of their conversation. The caravan arrived at the city [Poona] and there sold all their raw sugar, and received cash for the same. 56. Along with them this *bhakta* of Vishnu also sold his sugar. He received cash, and with it in hand, started to return (to his home).

Tuka Gives away all his Money to a needy Brahman.

57. The traders in their journey home rested in a bazaar. Let the intelligent listener pay attention with reverence to what happened there.

58. A Brahman, with a wooden plough hanging from his neck, and with the hair of his beard grown very long, came along begging. "Help me, I beg you" he cried. 59. The merchants answered him, "A great many people come to beg. We haven't any thing to give. Get out from here at once!" 60. The poor man pleaded in this way. "Some gave me two-anna or four-anna bits." Tuka watched this scene and then said to the man, 61. "Tell your story from beginning to end." The Brahman listened to his request and said, "I had the hereditary rights connected with the office of Patil [village mayor]. Relatives deprived me of my rights. 62. They easily bribed the judge, and I was being sent to prison. The town committee of five heard of it, and saved me from this shame. 63. But the king is a very thoughtless man, and I am a weak, helpless Brahman. He demands three hundred rupees as the price of my freedom. I have given him fifty rupees. 64. In order to raise the balance I and my family are begging it. The king has detailed a soldier to go about with me, and he permits me no happy moments."

65. When Tuka heard the Brahman's story, he felt pity for him, and then assured him that he need not let his mind be troubled. 66. He then gave the worthy Brahman two hundred and fifty rupees in silver coin, and gladdened his heart. When the merchants saw this most unusual transaction, they all burst out laughing. 67. Said they, "He is throwing a whole cloth on the thorny bushes. We had better not associate with him further. When Jijai is told of it at his home she will loudly weep. 68. His wife and children haven't enough to eat, and he scatters his money any and every where." With this fling at Tuka the merchants left him and went on their way.

69. The Vaishnava *bhakta* remained there to complete the service he was rendering to the Brahman. The money was sent by the hand of the soldier to the judge's court. 70. The servant of Vishnu then called a barber and had the Brahman's hair cut. He called the Brahman's wife and set her to cooking a meal. 71. He provided the materials and feasted ten Brahmans. Tuka thus rejoiced the hearts of the couple, and they blessed him.

72. "May God-Supreme, Husband-of-Rukmini, ever care for you. No *bhakta* of Vishnu, as generous as you, is to be seen on this earth. 73. If for twelve years we should have begged with the plough around our necks, we should not have been able to collect as much (as you gave us). May God bless you," said the Brahman. 74. Tuka's heart was full of joy. Said he, "I have spent my money in a good cause." But he had a terrible fear of what at home he must expect from (his wife) Avali. "What shall I tell her?" he said.

GOD PAYS TUKA'S DEBTS.

75. Krishna knowing what was in Tuka's mind, said to Himself, "He has spent all, capital and profit. 76. If the merchants go and tell Avali, she will be in a rage. Then she will give Tuka a beating, and the money-lenders will demand what is due them." 77. So what did the Lord-of-Pandhari do to save Tuka from this disaster, but take the form of Tuka, and pay the money-lenders their money. 78. He paid them back the capital and the interest on it, and took back the promissory notes. "And now please go," he said, "and give Avali these five gold pieces, [*hon*]." 79. The merchants said, "Go yourself and give it to her." "No," said God, "she will be angry with me,

I am afraid to go. 80. She will say you have been gone many days, and you have not made any profit. Take the promissory note and these gold *hons* now and give them to her." 81. The moment he said this, this Giver-of-Eternal-Life left them. And the merchant took the promissory note and the gold *hons* and went to Avali's house. 82. He told her what had happened. She enquired where Tuka was. He replied "He is probably sitting somewhere repeating to himself the names of God." 83. Such was the miracle God performed, but no one recognized the clever act. Men's minds were bewitched by the seductions of Maya, so that no one recognized God.

Tuka Returns Home.

84. After a number of days the Vaishnava Tuka returned to his home. His wives told him of what had happened in his absence, but he was unable to learn what the true facts were. 85. On the one hand the merchants (with whom he had gone) spread the story that Tuka had taken all his capital and profit and made a gift of that sum, and freed a prisoner. 86. Others said God paid off the debt. Still others declared that such a statement was false.

Jijai practised a little deception, and thus preserved the credit of the family. 87. She said to herself, "That Black-complexioned-fellow [Krishna] is a cunning one. One can never understand His curious deeds. He has made my husband crazy. Public esteem is no more." 88. The tale told by the merchants of Tuka's foolishness, however, became public property, and knowing what had happened, people refused thereafter to let him have any more capital.

TUKA FALLS INTO PITIFUL POVERTY.

89. Now soon after this a severe famine took place. The price of grain was now two *payali* measures (to the rupee). Rain absolutely ceased. Cattle died from lack of fodder. 90. Tuka then experienced great distress in his domestic life. If you will listen to his experiences in a kindly spirit, your own severe troubles will disappear.

91. With the dissipation of Tuka's wealth he seemed to the public as one deserted by Fortune. They who once paid him reverence now insulted him. 92. When hard times came, he lost credit among the people. No one would let him come to his house. That gave Tuka's heart great pain. 93. There was now no food at all in his home. The children had to fast. No one would lend him anything, experiencing as they did the terrible famine. 94. Seeing his children's distress, he went here and there to beg for food. Now you listeners, with growing doubts, are perhaps asking the narrator of this story, 95. that "after Indifference-to-worldly-things had entered Tuka's heart, why did he go begging from house to house?" To this question, which you wise ones have proposed, give the reply a listening ear. 96. If one swallows a fly, one vomits, but the bile keeps coming up. One then puts the fingers down the mouth and brings up all the bile. And this means health for the body. 97. Just so the Seeker after spiritual-things makes his mind disgusted with worldly things, and plans for those causes that will make people insult him. 98. "Once or twice before this the Lord-of-Pandhari had saved me in time of distress. If word of this should become known to the people," said Tuka, "they will call me a saint." 99. In order that this might not happen,

I must be despised by men. In order to create disgust with every thing, I must wander from house to house begging."

100. The Vaishnava *bhakta* said to his relatives and friends, "My children and the other members of my family are dying of hunger. You must quickly find some remedy." 101. The evil-minded at the same time said, "It is a dreadful famine. It is the same in every house. How much more can we tell you?" 102. When he asked a loan of the money-lenders, they shouted, "Get out of here! First bring back what you borrowed, and then take away what we give you." 103. One of them, when he saw Tuka, scowled at him, and said, "You have shut out worldly prosperity with a thorn fence, and why should you now persecute us? 104. Get out of here, you miserable wretch. You have made us sick and tired of you." And taking him by the hand, they whirled him around.

105. Tuka pitifully turned to his friends and relatives for help. Tuka therefore said to them, "Lend me some money. I will soon pay it back. 106. If you will keep us alive while the famine lasts, we shall regard you as mother and father." To all he described his pitiable condition, but none of them took pity on him.

107. The unkind words which Tuka had to listen to, made him feel ashamed. So retiring by himself, he tried to think what to do. 108. And just as he brought Pandurang into his thought, he suddenly remembered that he still possessed a few things. He had at his home some gunny bags, some trays and a bullock saddle. These he quickly sold to the merchants. 109. With this he purchased eight *sher* of grain, though with great difficulty. He made of it a thin gruel, and thus kept his family alive.

110. But when this grain was exhausted, even his dearest friends neglected him. Then his condition became so severe that he determined not to go to any one. 111. If he went to a rich man's house, he would drive him away. His public credit was ruined, and his worldly affairs turned to dust. 112. People treated him with insults. His relatives grew weary of him. The famine was at its height. A *sher* of grain for a rupee. 113. But even that much no one could obtain, and living beings passed on to Death as their home. Tuka's condition was of the worst; and he said to himself, "What am I to do?" 114. "In this Kali Yuga life entirely depends on food," so say all men everywhere. Once in two or three days they were able to get some gruel, and they also ate greens and leaves.

Tuka's Elder Wife Starves to Death.

115. Tuka's elder wife (Rakhumai) died, calling out, "Give me food, food." This filled his heart with shame. Said he, "All my worldly affairs have gone to nothing." 116. His relatives and the townspeople now said to Tuka "Now at least wake up, and do what we tell you. 117. The reason why your worldly affairs have gone to utter destruction is, because your mouth is all the time fondly repeating the names of God. 118. It is because you will not listen to us that your disaster is so great. And you will see the same thing in the future." Such were their wicked words. 119. It was like the plunging of a sharp knife into a boil over a bone. But Tuka was an ocean of perfect peace. And his reply was as follows:

120. "What is to happen can never be avoided. Why do you waste your breath in vain? Very well! Those who do not worship the Lord-of-Pandhari, do they escape

death? 121. In this great famine enormous numbers of living beings have died from lack of food. Were they all repeating God's names? What are the real causes of these deaths?" 122. Such was the answer given by this noble Vaishnava in reply to them.

Tuka's Eldest Son Dies.

Give ear now to what further took place. 123. Tuka's eldest son, by name of Santoba, whom he deeply loved, passed on to his death-home. 124. When he, on whose account he bore a very heavy load of domestic sorrows happily, had passed away, Tuka's heart was full of grief. 125. His wife and son were in the peace (of death). This Vaishnava *bhakta* was in sorrow. Said he to himself, "Damn this worldly life! I ought to abandon it. 126. Beings who live in the midst of worldly affairs experience anxieties. And this is the great root cause of remorse."

Listen you saints, and good people, to some illustrations of this fact. 127. When Shiva swallowed the poison his whole body felt the heat. As soon as he began to be anxious about it, He worshipped Shri Ram. 128. Any one who feels the burn of the Three-fold fevers, feels also a sense of remorse. The Pandavas experienced a variety of calamities, and that is why Shri Hari dwelt in their hearts. 129. When Hiranyakashipu, in various ways persecuted his son Pralhad, then when calling out under remorse, Shri Hari manifested himself in the pillar. 130. These illustrations are sufficient. Beings suffer the three forms of hell. Then when they repent they attain to Final Deliverance. 131. So it happened to Tuka. In his worldly affairs he experienced calamities. I will mention them in their chronological order. May you hearers listen with reverence.

A List of Tuka's Reverses.

132. When he was thirteen years of age his father put on his shoulders the burden of his business. He seemed efficient in business, and his father took comfort in him. 133. In his seventeenth year his mother and father died. The wife of his elder brother also died suddenly. 134. In his eighteenth year (his elder brother) Savaji went away to become a pilgrim to sacred places. Separation from him made Tuka sad. 135. In his twentieth year seeing his sons, his wife and himself entangled in worldly affairs, he developed a desire for it. But from then on let us see what God-Supreme did to make his heart disgusted with it.

136. In his twenty-first year Tuka began to experience his time of adversity. As soon as he became bankrupt his relatives began to laugh at him. 137. His (elder) wife, an ignorant and common woman, died, pleading, "Food, Food." Sons are a great snare, and their death is a great calamity in worldly affairs. Amongst the people the news of (his wife's death) caused unpleasant remarks. 138. Thus the first half of Tuka's life ended, in which he experienced a variety of sorrows. He had great hopes about domestic happiness, but that illusion had now disappeared. 139. When the night of ignorance passes away, and the sun of knowledge suddenly manifests itself, it gives the heart of the Seeker a joy that cannot confine itself in space. 140. When the ocean was being churned the gods felt fatigued, but when the god Indra saw the nectar with his eyes, he rejoiced. 141. Or, as when the house wife churns the cream, for the moment she feels it hard work, but when she sees the butter with her eyes, she is happy. 142. Or like the efforts of the ploughman,

which seem to him very hard, but when later the crop appears densely thick, the farmer is happy in heart. 143. Or as when the sugar cane juice is being strained, it requires hard work, but finally when the sugar assumes its solid form, the eater recognizes its sweet taste. 144. So at first the Seeker experiences pain, but at the end he has joy that is beyond compare. Those who have awakened right thinking in themselves, know this fact well. 145. Well, enough now of such talk; giving illustrations, however, is a poet's privilege. Now give your attention to the story that follows, and listen you *bhaktas* of His, and you pious folk.

Tuka Decides for a Wholly Spiritual Life.

146. As soon as Tuka's elder wife and son died, he repented of his worldly life, and going off by himself alone he gave himself to melancholy thinking. 147. He said to himself, "Until to-day the more I endeavoured to form my house, the more sorrows of various shapes I had to encounter which indeed are too many to recall. 148. If the outside of a piece of charcoal is rubbed off, it looks all the blacker within, so by experience I have proved that there is in the worldly life a mountain of sorrow. 149. If one can sleep in peace on a bug-infested bed, then only one can in the visions of a dream see happiness in the worldly life [*samsar*]. 150. The sweetness of the poisonous *bachnag* is felt in the beginning only, but in the end death cannot be avoided. Know this to be absolutely true. 151. If Shukadev had the firm conviction that union with God was possible while in this earthly life, then why was it that he becoming God-mad sought isolation among mountain crags? 152. My own life, how short it is, and even that has been spent in the illusions of

a worldly life. Now in what remains of my life I should devote myself to the worship of God [Husband-of-Rukmini]"

Tuka Retires Alone to a Mountain.

153. With this fixed determination in his heart, Tuka retired to the mountain of Bhambanath. His going was like that of a faithful wife on the pyre of her husband [*sati*]. She abandons everything. 154. Just as she no longer brings to mind her mother, father, son or property, but leaps into the fire in order to go and meet the lord of her life. 155. Just so this Vaishnava Tuka went up the mountain, and there bringing into his mind the Lord-of-Heaven, appealed again and again for mercy.

156. He closed both eyes, and brought before his mind the image of Pandurang. Then he prayed, "O God-Supreme, O Husband-of-Rukmini, give ear to my plea. 157. I do not know how to meditate on Thee. I know nothing whatever about it. Show me how I, who plead with Thee, am to see Thee. 158. Tell me how to praise Thee, and how to really serve Thee, and what feelings I should have in order to meet Thee, O Husband-of-Rukmini. 159. How am I to sing of Thee in hymns (of praise)? How am I to bring before my mind Thy true form? In what manner shall I live amongst men? Do Thou tell me. 160. Thou art inscrutable, inconceivable, then how am I, a poor sinner, to bring Thee into a conceivable form? Even Yamadharma, Varun and Kuber could not know the depths of Thy being. 161. The moon, the sun, and the multitude of stars really revolve about Thee. Indra and the other gods do not know the depths of Thy being. What am I compared with them? I am but

a mosquito. 162. Brahmadev is Thine own child. He hunted for Thy lotus navel, but he was unable to know Thy limits. Then he at once began praising Thee. 163. Anxious to have a sight of Thee, Shiva and Parvati kept recalling Thy name. Thou Lord-of-Heaven wast very difficult for them to see Thee, then how will my desire have any avail?"

God Reveals Himself in His Symbolic Form.

164. With these thoughts in his mind, Tuka brought before his imagination the image of Pandurang, and Krishna, seeing his loving devotion, did (a remarkable thing). 165. For seven days Tuka had been concentrating his mind with closed eyes. He ate no fruit, nor drank water. He was ever repeating the names of God. 166. With his body, his speech and his concentrated mind he was pleading with feeling of love for God's mercy. Just at that moment the Husband-of-Rukmini manifested himself in a strange form. Listen you pious, and good people.

167. Krishna took the form of a black enormous serpent that circled round Tuka, with his tremendous power, just as Great-Death encircles. 168. He lifted up his enormous hood, and began to hiss. Tuka was in no way afraid. He kept his eyes firmly closed. 169. Suddenly there was a voice from Heaven, that spoke to Tuka with a mystic symbolic meaning, that the Husband-of-Rukmini was there in the form of a great serpent. 170. The voice said, "Open now your eyes, you loving *bhakta* and look. Hold no fear whatever in your heart." Such were the words Tuka heard. 171. And after hearing them this God-loving *bhakta* said to himself, "If God has come taking the form of a serpent, I will certainly not look at

Him. 172. The Vedas and Scriptures say that God pervades all beings. But all men see the Universe. How can it be said they are saved? 173. Water is but one substance, but the *Chatak* bird will not drink the water that is on the earth. So I am a worshipper of Pandurang, and I will not look at other forms. 174. If the Giver-of-Eternal-Life will assume the form for contemplation as described in the *Vedas* and *Purans,* and as the saints have stored up that image in the depths of their hearts, then only will I look."

God now Reveals Himself as Described in the Purans.

175. The Lord-of-Heaven, recognizing the feelings of Tuka's heart, revealed Himself openly, for God is one who is bound by a devotion of love. 176. God seeing the love of His *bhakta* manifested Himself as four armed, dark complexioned, and holding the conchshell, the disk, the club, and the lotus. 177. Tuka now opened his eyes, and there before him stood the Husband-of-Rukmini. In his ears there sparkled the brilliant earrings, shaped like crocodiles, and beautiful. 178. Then in a moment God-Supreme, the Lord-of-Pandhari, lifted Tuka up and held him at his side, in the way a mother in her love comforts her little babe. 179. Said He to Tuka, "You are my darling child. Now open your eyes. I will never leave or forsake you." Thus spoke Krishna.

180. Tuka at first lost all consciousness of body, and then arrived at the state of undivided contemplation. The Husband-of-Rukmini woke him up, and said, "Look steadily at me." 181. Tuka opened his eyes, and beheld the *sagun* form of the Recliner-upon-the-serpent (Vishnu). In this spectacle he saw something of even greater worth

than he had seen before. 182. He had been thinking of the Unscrutable-One with deep interest, but now in the form before him he saw what was of very special value. Tuka sat looking at Him intently and wonderingly.

KANHA SEARCHES FOR HIS BROTHER TUKA.

183. You have listened to the tale that I have already told, how Tuka became indifferent to worldly things, and withdrew into the wilderness. No one knew where he had gone.

184. Tuka's younger brother, Kanha by name, was hunting for him day and night in the caves of the mountains. 185. He had made his determination that he would eat no food until Tuka met his sight. His determination was absolute. 186. Bharat was in extreme anxiety through separation from Shri Ram, and it seems to me Kanha's determination was of the same kind.

187. For seven days Kanha searched awful jungles, and great mountains, and finally and suddenly came upon Mount Bhambanath. 188. There he saw God and His *bhakta* together, and the sight gave him a sense of peace. Though he was in the body, he became as one without a body, and changed into the divine nature. 189. Without having made an effort he now saw the Husband-of-Rukmini in His shining yellow robe, and His crocodile-shaped ear-rings. 190. In his crown jewels sent out rays of light, that dimmed the brightness of the sun. Around his neck shone the garlands Kaustubha and Vaijayanti, and he was holding Tuka on his hip. 191. God and His *bhakta* had become one. As Kanha saw this his eyes filled with tears. He then prostrated himself flat on the ground like a log, while a stream

of tears flowed from his eyes. 192. The Merciful-One then said to Tuka, "Ask me for such blessings as you may desire." Hearing these words the wise *bhakta* replied, "May I never forget Thee. 193. A mother never forgets her infant child. A doe never forgets her young. In the same way, O Krishna, care for me, Thy humble servant." 194. To this the Life-of-the-World replied, "I had to take this form for your sake. What other cause could there be for becoming *avatars* age after age? 195. For Pundalik's sake I remained standing on the bank of the Bhima, where I receive pious *bhaktas*, my two arms akimbo. 196. Your ancestor, Vishvambhar, worshipped me with the utmost devotion. I gave him the blessing (he asked for) and remained at Dehu." 197. As Krishna thus spoke Tuka fell at His feet, and Kanha exclaimed, "Blessed is this strange and wondrous sight." 198. And then he began to repeat verses of praise as a wave offering to the Husband-of-Rukmini.

Conclusion of Chapter 28.

And now you saints, listen with reverence to the next interesting chapter. 199. Any one who listens to the story of the saints, the Lotus-eyed-One will meet with him. His heart will become righteous and holy. And the whole Three worlds will seem as though they were himself. 200. Those who sing of or listen with feelings of love to this story of Tuka's worldly affairs, the Husband-of-Rukmini will take pleasure in them and will not let them experience disasters in their worldly affairs.

201. You saints are listening to my uncouth language, which somehow or other I speak. Just as when a little child lisps its words, its mother lisps to it in return.

202. Just so I am an ignorant man, I know neither little nor much, but you by your show of kindness must honour my verses. 203. You are accustomed to give waves of inspiration to those who are intelligent, and you are now increasing the dimensions of this book by the pretext of doing honour to Mahipati.

204. Svasti! This book, the Bhaktalilamrita, by merely listening to it, obtains for one his heart's desires. Listen then you loving Vaishnava *bhaktas* to this twenty-eighth interesting chapter.

CHAPTER 29.

INVOCATION.

Obeisance to Shri Ganesh!

1. Victory! Victory! to Satchidananda, Statue-of Compassion! The whole Universe is inadequate to contain Thy praise. Though Thou art such, yet Thou dost pay attention to the earnest desires of those who love Thee, O Husband-of-Rukmini! O Vitthal! 2. To those who have acquired a knowledge of Brahma, and who practise the severest forms of austerities, Thou hast made known the difficult system of *Yoga*. But to Thy ordinary, innocent minded *bhaktas* Thou dost make known the principles of the Bhagavata [devotion to God]. 3. Brahmadeva was dumbfounded when he heard the extraordinary question put by Sanak and others. Then he with feelings of love began to give Thee praise. 4. Having heard the praises of Brahmadeva, Thou didst come there in the form of a swan, and in

Thy mercy Thou didst make known the Chatushloki Bhagavata. 5. As Brahmadeva listened to Thy nectar words, he became full of joy, and then he made known to Narad the ten Commandments of the Bhagavata. 6. Narad with his mind full of joy, was continually dancing, while singing of Thy praise. Dvaipayana met Narad and reverently said to him, 7. "Hear me, Svami, I wrote the eighteen Purans. I have also composed other *shastras* and histories of deep significance, and detailed stories (of the gods). 8. Yet although I seek to have an unfickle mind, my mind finds no satisfaction. Tell me some remedy for this." And with this Vyasa fell at his feet. 9. Hearing the question of his good disciple, the son-of-Brahmadev rejoiced, and composing the Hundred-verse Bhagavata, made it known to Vyasa. 10. The *sadguru* then said to the son of Parashar, "Explain this Bhagavata fully and recite it. By doing so your heart will find rest, and you will obtain what is good for your soul." 11. So then Dvaipayana, full of love, fully explained the Bhagavata, and composed a work of eighteen thousand verses, which merely convey the meaning of the Upanishads. 12. Then Shuka, the great Yogi, studied it, and preached it to King Parikshiti with love. And many other seekers (after God) have been saved, and their number no one can count. 13. Thus Thou, Lord-of-Heaven, art the very loving and close friend of those who love Thee. And Thou hast created this religion of the knowledge of God as a ferry-boat, in which Thou dost take men across this sea of the earthly life. 14. In this *Kali yuga* all have not understood fully the meaning of this Bhagavata [Knowledge of a personal God], therefore, Thou hast become an *avatar* in the form of saints, in order to preach these truths to the common mind. 15. It is, therefore, Thou, O-Lotus-eyed-One, who art narrating the many stories of the saints. I, Mahipati, am merely Thy instrument. I have no independent mind of my own. 16. When a taught parrot speaks, what is there novel about it? So aside from Thee, O Infinite-One, there is no one who enlightens those of a dull mind.

TUKA THROWS PROMISSORY NOTES INTO THE RIVER.

17. The story at the end of the last chapter was that while Tuka was on Mount Bhambanath, his brother, Kanha, came there, and saw the Husband-of-Rukmini. 18. And when God saw these His *bhaktas,* He vanished from their sight. The spot where the feet of God touched is still there. 19. Kanha then erected a pile of stones, and on it placed bas relief footprints there. And bowing prostrate before Tuka, the brother experienced the joy of love.

20. The two brothers then hastened towards Dehu. When they reached the deep pool in the Indrayani river, Tuka seated himself. 21. For seven days both of them had fasted. But now at the rising of the sun they bathed in the river and there broke their fast. 22. The Vaishnava *bhakta* then had Kanha bring from his house all promissory notes. These notes were those that had been given to his father by different people. And now Tuka said to Kanha, 23. "The knowledge gained from books is valueless to one who lacks experience. So is it with wealth that has passed into the hands of another. It makes one's mind always uneasy. 24. I shall always be thinking of these promises rather hopelessly. Will these debtors give me what is my own, or will they not? So I am going to throw these promissory notes into this pool of the Indrayani." 25. But to this announcement of the God-loving *bhakta* Kanha replied, "You have become one indifferent

to worldly things, but the whole support of the family is on my shoulders. 26. In fact, I should not advise you who are my elder brother, but what are our children going to do in the future?" Understanding what was in Kanha's mind, Tuka carried out the following plan. 27. He divided the papers in half, and his half he threw into the water. The other half he gave to Kanha and said to him. 28. "From to-day all I want is a blanket to keep off the cold. I will gain my food by begging, and in this way my livelihood will be secured. 29. To you will fall the carrying on of business affairs in the rounds of the worldly life. The two ideas of life cannot be united in one person. Hear why this is so. 30. That begging and business should never be mixed together, so it has been declared by the mouths of the *rishis*." 31. Kanha listened to his brother, and carried on by himself the family business affairs.

Tuka's Ascetic Life Begins.

Now listen to the strict renunciation which Tuka adopted. 32. He threw aside all ideas of being ashamed, and gave his mind to the task of contemplation. Through the power of his indifference to worldly things he compelled his organs of sense to observe certain laws. 33. He became a very moderate eater, and thereby his organs of sense weakened. He no longer felt sleepy or lazy. With the thought of repentance in his heart, he spent his time in worship. 34. He would bathe in the early morning, and then go to the temple of Pandurang. After performing his worship, and making his offerings, he was accustomed then to go into the wilderness. 35. Mount Bhandar was six miles to the west of Dehu. Tuka had the habit of going there and sitting alone by himself.

Explanation of Tuka's Ascetic Life.

36. Perhaps you listeners, having some doubts in your minds, will ask the speaker, "Tuka had already met the Husband-of-Rukmini, in his *sagun* form, and in direct vision. 37. If once God has been met, why is it necessary to uselessly conform one's organs of sense to a rule of law?" To this question by you, good people, I reply, and ask you to listen. 38. When the sun rises all living beings behold it. But it is not under the power of any one. It does not stand still a single moment. 39. So by good fortune Tuka met the Husband-of-Indira, but Tuka had in his heart that God should always be near him. 40. When *bhaktas* have attained the presence of God, they continue to render Him loving worship. When the Ganges has met the ocean, it still continues to flow rapidly in its downward course. 41. Air extends through the whole universe, and pervades every space. Yet it does not anywhere lose its active nature. It remains motionless not a single moment. 42. Just so, men, devoted to God, are united with His essence in such a way as to make no difference between them. But that unity is again divided into two parts so that the one continually worships the other. 43. Vishnu lies on the body of the serpent, for that reason both are wholly united. 44. After performing the wave offering over a god who, it is assumed, is going to his bed, the worshipper retires to his home. But the serpent has not the least possibility of a separation, still it continues to worship Shri Hari. 45. So it was with Tuka the noble Vaishnava. His love was great and unsullied. So going to the mountains, he was there accustomed to worship God. 46. He put aside all idea of self. It was the same to him whether among men or where there were no men. His

"I" had now no name even, not even in his dreams. 47. If the idea of "I" has been removed from its very roots, then naturally the fears of this worldly life will have dissolved away. If the body has ceased to exist, could any one have an illness? 48. So it was with Tuka. He discarded his "I" which is the root of worldly living. He regularly went to some place alone, and there sat repeating the names of the Husband-of-Rukmini. 49. Tuka was fully convinced, that aside from the repeating of God's names, there were no other means (of meeting with God). And so he was constantly worshipping God. 50. He would close both eyes, and bring the image of Pandurang before his mind, saying "O Krishna, aside from Thy name I have no other place of rest. 51. Repeating Thy name is alone my severe austerities. Thy Name is alone my repetition of *mantras*. Thy Name alone is my many sacraments. By Thy Name I shall become sinless. 52. Repeating Thy Name is alone our family method of worship. Repeating Thy Name is alone the grand rule of our family line. Now, O Shripati, it is my resolve to have no other support aside from Thy Name. 53. Aside from Thy Name I know not how to speak of anything as being wealth, or property or any thing else. So, now, O Vithabai, ferry me across this worldly life, to the other side.

54. By Thy Name Shiva became tranquil. By it Valmiki wrote the story of Shri Ram. Through Thy Name alone the *bhakta* Pralhad became distinguished in all the Three-worlds. 55. Such is the great glory of Thy Name, known to the saints, the noble Vaishnavas. The child Dhruva, truly by Thy Name, took his seat in that immovable place [the North Pole]. 56. The child Upamanyu was saved by Thy Name, and so was Bibhishan,

Thy loving *bhakta,* to whom Shri Ram gave the whole of the unending kingdom of Ceylon."

Public Opinion of Tuka's New Life.

57. Tuka always went apart alone, and in seclusion appealed to God's pity. When evening came he returned to the town, and danced in the temple. 58. People, seeing him, said, "Tuka has gone crazy. Day and night he is repeating in song the Names of God. He has abandoned all desire for a worldly life." 59. Others said, "He met with loss in his mercantile business, and so he says that trading is a false way. And hence the stream of words from his mouth, and his senseless babbling in the public square." 60. But another remarked, "Tuka threw away into the Indrayani all his promissory notes. He has definitely abandoned the worldly life, and as something better, has grasped the supreme-spiritual-riches." 61. A third observed, "If you give special thought to it, of what value is it to abandon one's worldly life? Has any one thereby lost his stomach? The body cannot continue to live without food. 62. Tuka abandons his children, and goes off to sit alone in the mountain. And yet he has to beg from house to house, as soon as he gets hungry." 63. To this one replied, "Why do you, not minding your own business, speak evil of him for nothing? Many have suffered disasters in their worldly affairs. Do they all worship God [Govinda]?"

64. Thus men of different natures spoke of Tuka in different ways. But Tuka, with a happy heart, had no thought for his bodily needs. 65. When the elephant passes along the royal road, dogs bark furiously at him, but the elephant has no fear of them, and continues his steady gait.

66. When the *rishi* Agasti heard the roar of the ocean he was not afraid, so although people spoke evilly of Tuka, he felt in his heart no unkind feeling. 67. When the wave of public insult dashed upon him, he let peace fill his mind with each gulp. He destroyed the path of desire and anger. His actions were remarkable and beyond compare. 68. He had crushed out of existence desire, longings, temptations, illusory cravings, lust and anger. And in the future the Vaishnava Tuka will become Brahma Itself. This is indeed true. 69. With feelings of love in his heart he continually worshipped the image of Pandurang. During the daytime he was by himself in the wilderness, where he worshipped God with love.

Tuka Guards a Farmer's Grainfield.

70. Along the banks of the Indrayani there were *Karanjaya* Water-deities, and there the Vaishnava *bhakta* Tuka sat, worshipping God. 71. Nearby him a farmer had sown a field of grain. It had now ripened, and the ears were densely filled with the kernels of grain. 72. After looking all over his field the farmer hastened and stood before Tuka, and said, 73. "Tuka Shet, Hear what I have to say, Watch my field. I will give you a half a *maund* of grain, whereby you can support your family. 74. If you sit at home and do nothing, how will your worldly affairs be carried on? So continue to sit here in this field, and here worship Hari." 75. The noble Vaishnava listened and replied, "I will." Then getting up at once he went along with the farmer. 76. Such was Tuka's nature that he would listen to whatever was asked of him, and being inclined to be helpful to others he resisted no appeal for help. 77. Tuka was just like an infant

child, into whose hands whatever you gave, whether good or bad, it immediately puts it in its mouth, without any hesitation of mind. 78. Or just like water, if you put sugar in it, it becomes sweet. Or if you mix salt with it, it at once becomes salty. 79. This was Tuka's character. There was no such thing as urging him, because he would do whatever or whenever any one asked him. 80. The farmer thus took Tuka along with him, and gave him a bird-sling, saying, "Go and sit now on the raised platform. 81. I have put the field in your keeping. Watch it day and night. The agreement remains until the reaping. 82. I have agreed to give you half a *maund* of grain. And I shall give it from the winnowed heap." With these words the farmer went away, 83. leaving for that part of the country where grain was cheap, in order to bring some home. He had seated Tuka in his field, and had told the people in his house of having done so.

84. Now Tuka, the Vaishnava *bhakta,* climbed at once up on to the raised platform, looking like a scarecrow but without life. Just then he saw a flock of birds settling on the field. 85. Said he to himself, "These are God's living creatures, and they are all hungry. If I call myself a Vaishnava *bhakta,* I must not drive them away. 86. Some time ago there was a great famine, and now it is the world's good fortune to have a good crop. If I drive them away I shall make myself reponsible for a sinful act." 87. So saying, the God-loving *bhakta,* sat quite still on the raised platform like a scarecrow which appears like a man, but is without the least life in him. 88. When the sun was up two *prahars,* he said to the birds in a sweet tone, "If you have eaten enough, it would be well for you to go where there is water." 89. So speaking to the birds, he

remained sitting perfectly still and continuing his worship His intoning of Hari's names made a far reaching sound, which the townspeople heard from a distance.

90. Tuka's queen was waiting for him at home, and remarked, "He has not come home yet. Where could he have gone, to sit (and worship). In what jungle shall we hunt for him? 91. Casting aside shame and pride, he wanders aimlessly among men or in the jungle. He has poured water on all worldly things [abandoned them]. What am I to do, my friends?" 92. She then said to her daughter, "Go out and find where that crazy fellow, your father, is sitting. I am hungry, but I cannot eat without him." 93. The elder daughter, Kashibai, started on the run, (and finding her father) she said to him, "Come home to dinner." 94. Tuka replied to her, "I am sitting here to protect the field. The farmer has promised me grain. Go home and tell (your mother)." 95. The daughter hastened home and told her mother what had occurred. So Avali sent food to him there, and she then sat down to her own meal. 96. While Tuka was eating his bread he thought to himself, "I might as well remain here day and night. Why go back and forth to my house needlessly?" 97. So taking his early morning bath, he would then worship the image of Pandurang in his temple, then hasten back to the field, and continue his worship alone by himself. 98. Once when it was evening he said to the birds, "Off with you all. It is beginning to get very unusually dark. You will not be able to see your way." 99. With these words the Vaishnava *bhakta* at once drove them away, but said to them, "As soon as it is morning, come back quickly to this place." 100. As Tuka watched the habits of the birds, he wondered at them. He thought, "The birds eat

a few kernels here, and take nothing home. 101. O God-Supreme, when wilt Thou make my soul like these birds! Who aside from Thee, O Krishna, can supply our needs? 102. May my existence cease. May I lose my name and form. May I see all mankind as myself. May I have no consciousness whatever of my body. 103. May my good relatives and friends no longer look to my comfort. Let them do what will prevent their knowing whether my body is alive or dead. 104. As the fallen leaves fly before the violent wind, so may my movements be. My mouth shall praise Thy goodness. Give me this good gift. 105. Birds, beasts, the noble trees, beings, from Brahmadeva down to the ant, are all pervaded by the one Intelligence. Make me to regard all as one. 106. O Shripati, make me such that gold, earth and stone will look alike to my sight. May wrong desire never arise in my heart. 107. If an unkind word falls on my ear, or if any one praises me, may both seem alike. Make my character such."

The Farmer returns and Blames Tuka.

108. Such was the way that Tuka was constantly thinking with the deep longings of his heart. Pandharinath filled his heart, which was ever filled with joy. 109. He collected there dry dungcakes and kindled a fire. And if he felt at all sleepy, he would immediately awaken himself. 110. All the birds of the town now began to come there every day. And as they ate the kernels of grain this Vaishnava *bhakta* felt a sense of satisfaction. 111. Just as a benevolent giver feasts Brahman guests at his home (and feels satisfaction), so in the same way Tuka felt a satisfaction, as he supplied the cravings of the hungry birds.

112. A month had passed in this way, when suddenly the farmer returned from his errand, and said to himself, "I must now go and see how the grain field has ripened." 113. Thus thinking to himself he hastened to his field, when behold! all the black ears were empty, not a single kernel was to be seen. 114. He felt an overwhelming anger. He gnawed his lips, and bit his tongue. Said he, "Tuka has accomplished his grudge against me; and now to whom shall I appeal for justice?" 115. Thus thinking, he wandered to the four corners of his field examining as he went. Afraid of him, all the birds flew away. 116. Just as when Brahmans are eating, if an outcaste should come amongst them, they would rise at once and leave the place where they were dining.

117. After the farmer had wandered in every direction and examined the field, he saw that the birds had devoured the field. Not a single kernel was to be seen. 118. All this while the kindly Tuka was sitting on the raised platform, worshipping God. The farmer hastened towards him, uttering many imprecations. 119. In great anger the farmer said to Tuka, "See, how you have destroyed my very home. I engaged you as a servant on a six *payali* measure as a wage for the month. 120. I trusted you, and made my journey to bring back grain. You have fed my field to the birds, and you have carried out your hostility." 121. Following his imprecations with a fierce look, he seized Tuka by the wrist and dragged him along. "Now," said he, "you have met with a person who is determined. There is no getting away from me now." 122. A bad man and a saint, a poisonous bulb and nectar, brought together by Fate, such was the coming together of these two. 123. Or the ocean and the *rishi* Agasti; or the demon Rahu

and the moon. These may be brought together by Fate. Such was the coming together of Tuka and the farmer. 124. Or like a meeting for a moment of a swan and a falcon, or of a Vedic Brahman and a murderer, or of an adulteress and a faithful wife. 125. Or an accidental coming together of a wicked, crooked reviler, and a kindly Vaishnava *bhakta,* one pure, the other vile.

The Farmer Drags Tuka to Court.

126. The farmer dragged Tuka along in that manner, and brought him to where the *Patil* and the town scribe were sitting. 127. Smiting his mouth and beating his breast, he made a hue and cry. All said, "The kunbi is mad, and has brought destruction on himself." He does not know what good fortune had brought him. 128. But seeing him in this state of mind the towns-people asked him what was the matter. The farmer then told them the story from the beginning to the end, and added, "Now what shall I do?" 129. They then asked Tuka, and the kindly *bhakta,* whose words could never be touched by the least bit of the filth of untruth, told them the exact truth. 130. Said he, "The farmer gave me the promise of half a maund of grain for watching over his field. I agreed to this. 131. He said to me this much, 'Sit on the raised platform and look out for the birds.' If I had driven the birds away they would have very soon died. 132. The birds flocked together, and ate a few kernels every day, but they took nothing away with them to their homes. Then why should I prevent them? 133. He said to me, 'Look out for the birds,' and, therefore, I cared for them". Hearing these words of Tuka's all broke out into a hearty laugh.

134. The farmer, seeing what was taking place, was very angry and said, "I am going to pick up my basket and go. You can look after the field." 135. The townspeople then remarked, "It will be necessary to the Kunbi to pay the Government taxes. If the farmer runs off, it will not be well. 136. So they casually asked the farmer how much grain he usually harvested. "Tell us the truth, knowing the value of truth." 137. The farmer answered "I usually get two *khandis* from the field. I am telling you the truth. There are plenty of witnesses to this fact." 138. The townspeople said to Tuka "By your own mouth you have acknowledged that the birds devoured the field. You do not seem to have any property at home as security, still you had better write out a promissory note, and give it to the farmer. 139. If you will not listen to us, the farmer will run away, then who will pay his tax, and Government will fine us. 140. So we tell you to write a promissory note, and give it to him. And then you can take to your own house the empty ears of grain." 141. "I agree," said the Vaishnava *bhakta,* and wrote the note signed by witnesses. It was given into the hands of the farmer, and he was satisfied. 142. This fool was overjoyed by this paper wealth; but by it he prevented his own welfare. He knew not of the power of Vishnu.

The Miracle of a Wonderful Crop.

143. The quarrel was thus ended through the efforts of the town Committee of five. And said they, "Let us go at once and see the field that the birds have eaten." 144. So they started accompanied by the town officers to see the field. Suddenly the Lord-of-Pandhari performed a miracle. Listen to what it was, you pious *bhaktas* of His. 145. The ears of the grain were now densely crowded by more than

ten times the usual number. Other things also happened. All this the townspeople saw. 146. They looked for the places that the birds had pecked, but not in a single place could they discover one. As they saw this they were all filled with amazement, and exclaimed, "This is a strange and unfathomable miracle." 147. The farmer who had brought the quarrel before them now said to them that he wished to return the promissory note to Tuka and regain possession of his field. 148. The towns-people replied to him, "Why should the Panchayat (the town Committee of five) reverse its decision? We must not act in a way as to incur the blame of any one. 149. The empty ears have now full ears, but this is the act of Vithoba. God is caring for Tuka. We have the evidence of this. 150. The agreement which he wrote and gave to you cannot be annulled. He will give you what is your due of grain from the heap of thrashed out grain. And what remains he will take away." 151. Then turning to Tuka they said to him, "Sit now in your field and watch it." The Vaishnava listened but replied, "That cannot be. 152. If while taking nothing away from the field I met with such dreadful curses, if I now accept the whole field, I don't know what future penalties I may have to suffer." 153. Thus replying, the Vaishnava *bhakta,* with feelings of love, continued his acts of worship. So the towns-people hired a man, and seated him there to watch the field. 154. Then they engaged labourers and bound the straw into sheaves. When it was thrashed and the heap of grain was measured, lo and behold! it came to seventeen *khandis,* to the astonishment of all. 155. They exclaimed, "No one in this town ever had a crop of this size. God's acts are of the impossible. He displays them in many a miraculous form." 156. Some one remarked, "During the famine there was very great suffering at Tuka's home. In order that he might be quickly delivered from his fasting, Shri Hari has thus come to his aid." 157. Another replied, "Your observation is not true. It is the farmer's great good fortune, for otherwise the bankrupt Tuka Shet would never have paid him as long as he lived." 158. But a third remarked, "Tuka allowed the birds to devour the kernels of grain, it was an exceedingly noble act. The effect of it we clearly see, in this bountiful crop."

Tuka Refuses Grain for himself.

159. Thus people of different characters expressed their various opinions. But all agreed that the amazing maya of Vishnu was beyond their comprehension.

160. They then gave two *khandis* of grain to the former owner of the field, and took back the promissory note that Tuka had written and given him. 161. And now the townspeople said to Tuka, "Take away this grain, and store it in your house. Your heart is indifferent to worldly things, therefore, Shri Vitthal came to your aid." 162. Although the towns-people said this to him, the God-loving *bhakta* would not listen to them. No wrong desire could enter his heart, for he was all the time indifferent to worldly things.

163. The chief characteristic of Indifference-to-worldly-things is desirelessness. Therefore, desirelessness alone should be termed knowledge. Only a wholly desireless Seeker (after God) is impressed by the worship of the *Sagun* God. 164. Where there is desirelessness there is peace of heart. Indifference-to-worldly-things enters only into the heart of

one who has no desires. Indifference to worldly things belongs only to one who is desireless, and in whose heart there is continual joy. 165. One indifferent to worldly things has true and right thinking. And people respect only those who are desireless. And all the Powers stand ready to serve one who is without desire. 166. Why talk of other characteristics, for the *bhakti* that must be finally chosen is the *bhakti* devoid of worldly desires. God meets only with such. Other ways are those of hypocrisy.

167. All the characteristics of such a state had entered into Tuka's heart, and therefore, the Husband-of-Rukmini displayed His many wonderful miracles for his sake.

168. Turning now back to what was happening, Tuka would not take the grain that was given him. The people of the town were therefore perplexed as to what to do, and could think of no right solution. 169. There was, however, there a very pious town officer by name of Mahadajipant. He took the grain, and stored it in his house, 170. saying, "This has ripened through the will of God. It must be used only for benevolent purposes."

Mahipati's Humble estimate of Himself.

In the development of the next chapter good people, when they listen to it, will be pleased.

171. But listen! This book, the Bhaktalilamrita, should be considered as if it were supreme nectar. Only the fortunate Vaishnavas drink it in their love for it. 172. Those who having really conquered the six enemies of the soul, and live amongst men without enmity, they only will enjoy it. Others have no right to it. 173. Those

who have a longing to attain God, find the worship (listening to words about God) sweet. They alone, therefore, will like this story (of Tuka). Others will not find it sweet. 174. Therefore, I, presuming on my friendship with you, saints, with boldness utter my uncouth and humble words, impertinent through ignorance. 175. If a rich man wears on his finger a brass ring, people will look at it, and assume that it is a golden one. 176. In the same way, if you, saints, listen to me, ordinary people will say that Mahipati's talents are very great and known.

177. Svasti! This book, the Shri Bhaktalilamrita, supplies all one's desires by the hearing merely. Listen, therefore, you God-loving, pious *bhaktas*. This is the 29th interesting chapter.

CHAPTER 30.

The Fruit of Listening to the Lives of the Saints.

Obeisance to Shri Ganesh.

1. To-day good fortune from an endless number of births has arisen for you listeners, and, therefore, the words needed for the description of the lives of the saints come to be spoken. 2. It is due to the good fortune of the king's subjects that clouds shower abundant rain on the earth. It was by the good fortune of the gods, that jewels came out of the sea. 3. Because of the great good luck of the swan, the ocean produces pearls. Or that it is in order to ornament the persons of beautiful men, that brilliant gold is found. 4. Or that it is to make the earth brilliant that the sun appears in the vault of the sky. Or that in order

to make the night appear glorious, the moon rises. 5. Or that in order that the *sagun* idol may be worshipped, God created the flowers. Just so, these stories of the saints have been created that they might be ornaments to the ears of you listeners. 6. For after listening there comes thinking, later meditation is developed; and then the Seeker after God has a direct revelation of Him. Seek the evidence of this in experience.

Tuka's Wife Grumbles.

7. In the last chapter there was the story of the birds devouring the grain field, and of the miracle the Lord-of-Pandhari performed in the extraordinary yield of grain. 8. Also how Tuka refused the grain for himself, and continued all the while in worship. He turned away from all the anxieties of a worldly life, to the unceasing worship of Hari.

9. At his home, however, his wife raised a hue and cry. Said she, "The grain came to him, but he would not take it. He has thrown our domestic affairs into the water, just as he threw the promissory notes into the river. 10. People say the crop ripened, but at home here the children are dying of hunger. 'God gave, but Fate took away.' It is this that has happened to us."

Tuka Repairs a Ruined Temple.

11. As I have said, the wife was making a hue and cry at home, but Tuka was full of joy in his heart. And now a thought struck him. 12. "The ancient temple of Pandurang is in ruins. If I pull it down and rebuild it, it will do for a watch-night service, where we can sing of

Hari's deeds. 13. After listening comes thinking, and after thinking comes contemplation, and then, following a direct manifestation of God, the Seeker attains experimental knowledge." 14. With such thoughts in his mind he began to pull down the temple, his own hands wielding the pickaxe. With water he made the needed mud. 15. The Lord of Pandhari knowing that there was little hope for the restoration of the temple, with Tuka working entirely alone, came to his help in the following manner. 16. He appeared to Mahadajipant in a dream, saying to him, "The grain you have stored in your house should be with absolute honesty applied to the work on the temple." 17. Accepting the command with bowed head, he discussed the question with the towns-people. "I have had a dream of this kind," he said, "let us go and see how things are." 18. Wondering in their minds what all this meant, they went to see the temple, and lo! there was Tuka with the pickaxe in his hands digging out the wall. 19. Remarking to themselves that the vision had come true, they decided to help him. They hired five labourers, and had some skilled workmen brought. 20. They purchased rafters, bricks, and used them in rebuilding the temple of Vishnu. The temple was very soon made ready, and all the grain was spent. 21. The concluding ceremonies, however, still remained to be performed, but there was no grain left for feeding the Brahmans. And Tuka was deeply concerned as to what was to be done. 22. The Husband-of-Rukmini, recognizing Tuka's perplexity, did a very remarkable thing. He showed himself in a vision of the night to Mahadajipant, who was alone by himself, 23. and said, "All you towns-people and Committee of Five are great sinners. How is it that you made your decision without thinking of the justice involved? 24. You caused Tuka to give to the farmer the full amount of the grain due him, but why did you keep back from Tuka the half *maund* due him for watching the field? 25. Now wake up to your duty, and calling the farmer to the public building, take from him the grain due Tuka with interest. Only by doing so will you all be blessed." 26. Mahadajipant wondered greatly at this vision, and when it was morning, he went to the public building and told of the dream. 27. The towns-people also were greatly astounded, and said, "A failure has occurred, it is true. We are rightly charged with having angered the Husband-of-Rukmini." 28. They, therefore, called the farmer, and all the towns-people said to him, "You took all the grain that was due you. Why did you keep back the half-maund (due Tuka)?" 29. The farmer replied to them, "I also had the same vision. If I do not give Tuka the half *maund*, Pandurang will certainly be angry with me." 30. He, therefore, hastened to his home, and brought back the grain due, and gave it to Tuka, with interest. Seeing this most wonderful miracle, other very helpful things were done (for the final ceremony). 31. Some provided wheat-flour, others rice. Some *ghi*, some raw sugar, greens and *dal* (a kind of pea). Thus all the necessary materials were provided. 32. An auspicious day was chosen, and the idol (of Krishna) was installed on its throne. Krishna was bathed with the five nectars, accompanied with the recitation of *mantras*. 33. The Vedic Brahmans with their own hands anointed the god, dressed him in gay clothing, and performed all the other requirements. 34. The forehead mark, garlands of flowers, clusters of tulsi leaves added their beauty to him. Incense, lights and other offerings were offered, and the worshippers prostrated themselves before Him. 35. Tuka, full of true love, danced in the pavilion. The love displayed on this occasion was extraordinary. Words cannot describe it. 36. These various ceremonies having been accomplished, they circumambulated the idol, and the Brahmans then sat down to their feast. The *pan supari,* and some gifts were given them (at the close). 37. These dedicatory ceremonies over the temple gave Tuka great joy. He regularly worshipped this *sagun* idol, and the love in his heart was ever new.

Writings of the Poet-Saints Attract Tuka.

38. Tuka now began to wish to perform *kirtans,* and he committed to memory the verses of the ancient saints. 39. At first he had never studied them, but now a love for them arose in his heart. Namdev, the author of the billion verses, had composed his poetry in Marathi. 40. Tuka committed his *abhangs* to memory, and repeated them as he danced. On days devoted to Hari he would fast, and have a watch-night service in the company of other saints. 41. On the twelfth day of the fortnight he would break his fast, and according to his ability feed the Brahmans. He would march in a procession with musical instruments and banners, and thus he became characterized as a Vaishnava. 42. He studied the books of many other saints, among them those of the *bhakta* Kabir, a distinguished Muhammadan. Tuka read with love his nectar words. 43. Dnyaneshvar had composed a very important book on philosophy. Tuka, the noble Vaishnava, was able to procure a correct copy of it. 44. Eknath, the *avatar* of Vishnu, had written a commentary of the Bhagavata. By special effort he was able to obtain a well-written copy of it. 45. In order to study these books what solitary place did he choose? He chose the beautiful Bhandar mountain, and there he went and sat. 46. This chief

jewel of a *bhakta* there read the book from beginning to end, giving by means of previous study close attention to the meaning and connections, helped by the Giver-of-Eternal-Life. 47. Tuka did not have to make great effort to commit the book to memory. As he was continually studying them the words seemed to lodge in his mouth. 48. Eknath's inspiring composition, the Bhavartha Ramayana, Tuka, with feelings of love, committed the whole to memory. 49. The Shri Bhagavata, with its interesting stories, related by the great man [Vyas], Tuka took pains to become familiar with, containing as it does the special deeds of Shri Hari. 50. Then also the Yogavasishtha, and Amritanubhava composed by Shri Dnyaneshvar, he studied and searched into their meaning. 51. Many people listen to the Purans, but do not study them, hence they forgot their contents and their minds wander in the frightful worldly life. 52. If the heart is not pure, though one sits alone worshipping God, the mind begins to recollect its desires, and they make his mind wander far afield from his book. 53. But it was not so with Tuka. He first made his heart pure, and then going to some secluded spot, he would search for the true meaning of the book.

TUKA'S WIFE SCOLDS GOD.

54. Although Tuka was accustomed to go to the Bhandar mountain to sit (and study) there was no water there. But listen to the cause that led to its existing there.

55. People everywhere said that Tuka's wife was hard-hearted, but her heart was devoted to the interests of her husband. She would not serve herself with food without having first served him. 56. So she regularly took

bread and water, and climbing the mountain, gave them to him. This regular going and returning made twelve miles, and they made her very weary. 57. Her very life was with her husband, but she carried on a continual quarrel with God. She refused to go to the temple to see God. She used to say, "I do not want to see that Black fellow. 58. It was our ancestor, Vishvambhar, who brought that enemy here. That great demon is persecuting our whole family line. 59. The wife and many children make a large family, and they cannot get food or clothing. He has thrown on to me all our domestic concerns, and he goes and sits there on the mountain. 60. When the night has advanced four *ghatikas* he comes stealing into the temple. There he dances before that Black fellow, having gathered together other vagabonds. 61. At early dawn after his bath he worships that damn thing [mela]. In some or other of his former births he became a debtor of God's and is now paying back what he borrowed. 62. If he only remained near the town, I could then give him bread with or without sauce. How many times am I to go back and forth! I certainly don't know."

Krishna Takes Pity on Tuka's Wife.

63. Tuka's wife in her home was thus in perplexity. TThe Lord-of-Pandhari, Helper-of-the-Helpless, Vithoba, then had pity on her. 64. He said to Himself, "Tuka goes and sits on the mountain, and she annoys me in many ways. I will show her a way by which this going back and forth may cease." 65. Thus thinking to Himself, he did a wonderful thing that day. Avali was carrying a cake of bread and a gourd full of water. 66. The heat was terribly fierce, and it was now noon. Krishna now did a strange thing; listen to it with reverence, you pious folk.

67. Avali was walking along the path, with her eyes on the mountain, wondering what distance remained for her to go, and suffering from the severe heat. 68. She had no sandals on her feet, and the stones in the path hurt her. She began to feel faint. Just then another catastrophe overwhelmed her. 69. There was a large Karavandi thorn lying in the middle of the path. In stepping on it, it pierced her foot. 70. This also made her feel faint, and in a swoon she fell to the ground. The gourd full of water tipped over, and the water was spilt. 71. When she finally opened her eyes, and looked at her foot, she saw that blood was flowing from it. "What shall I do?" she cried and then began to scream. 72. "There was some enmity between us in my former birth," she thought, "and he is still carrying it on. My enemy is still persecuting me, and my domestic life is all spoiled. 73. Only because he fastened a marriage string around my neck, he is to be called my husband. He goes off by himself and sits in a mountain. Oh dear! Oh dear!" 74. Then in the midst of her sobbing she tried to remove the thorn, but she found it impossible to do so, and said to herself, "What am I to do! 75. My Fate acts curiously. And what Fate has written on my forehead can never be escaped, even to the end of Time. That is why I am suffering all these misfortunes. 76. My father spent a lot of money in giving me a grand wedding, and my knot was tied to a crazy fellow. But in the end Fate declared itself. 77. Somehow or other my brother managed to take me on the supreme pilgrimage (to Benares). That worthy deed, however, stands for nothing to-day. I have lost sense of shame in my domestic affairs. 78. He spent an enormous sum of money in paying my weight in gold, but now I have not food enough

to satisfy my hunger. And my worthy deed (in going to Benares) has gone for nothing."

79. Thus Tuka's queen, Avali, mourned over her fate, but she could not utter the cry, "O God," for, said she, "My enemy will come running to me. 80. My adversary, the Husband-of-Rukmini, must not know of my misadventure. If he should suddenly come, he would laugh at me. 81. And say, 'Because you curse me day and night, therefore, this thorn has pierced your foot.' It would delight him (to see it), so may he not happen to come at this time. 82. When times of distress press upon one the pangs should be born by oneself only. But they should not be revealed to an enemy. This should be a principle in life. 83. Objects of sense seem pleasant to one, but people as they meet in the public square speak evil of him, and say a worthless fellow has been borne by his parents. 84. If your enemy gets hold of your secret, you should not go to him for compassion; even if it brought you to the point of death; you should not go to him as a suppliant."

God Reveals Himself to Unwilling Avali.

85. With this determination (not to call on God for help) Avali continued sobbing. Her efforts to remove the thorn were unavailing, and she kept thinking, "What shall I do?"

86. The Dweller-in-Heaven recognizing (Avali's condition) said to Himself, "Tuka is sitting up in the mountain hungry, and she is in this state," and so saying, Shri Hari manifested Himself to her. 87. Dark-complexioned, beautiful-in-form, lotus-eyed, and clothed in his heavenly yellow garment. In his crown there sparkled many kinds of jewels, that brought paleness to the sun. 88.

Brilliant earrings shone in his ears. Around his neck were the Kaustubh jewel and the Vaijayanti garland. On his feet little bells and *vankis* tinkled. This was the sight Avali suddenly saw. 89. Avali at once exclaimed to herself, "Why has this damn fellow come here! He has made my husband crazy. The misfortunes of my domestic life are through this fellow. 90. Seeing my unfortunate condition, He will laugh at me." So exclaiming, she turned her moon-face at once towards the West. 91. But there also the wonder working Lord-of-the-Universe appeared before her. She tried to escape him by looking in each of the eight directions, but there was no absence of Him there.

EXPLANATION OF GOD'S REVELATION TO ONE HATING HIM.

92. You listeners, with doubts in your minds, put a question to the speaker to explain how it was that Avali, who was not a God-loving *bhakta,* and in her hate was continually cursing God, 93. should have a revelation of God forced upon her. You feel a serious doubt. You ask me to remove it. 94. You good folk, ask me this question, and I, the speaker, answer the question with pleasure.

Through hatred God has met with many. This fact is brought out in the Purans. 95. One may seek Ram through a spirit of devotion, but He may not thereby come into one's contemplation; but through a spirit of hatred, Ravan saw Ram everywhere in Lanka (Ceylon). 96. So also Kans hated Krishna, and declared that He was his enemy, and yet Shri Hari was never far from his sight. 97. And so it was with the wife of Tuka. She said to herself, "I will not look at that black fellow," so He without her effort had to walk around her. 98. Just as in a room lined with mirrors, and with an image of Vishnu installed in it, in whichever direction one looks one sees

Krishna. 99. Even this illustration is not adequate here. For when Avali wearied looking at Him, she closed her eyes and kept quiet, but lo and behold! she saw the Soul-of-the-Universe in her own soul.

100. Said she, "Without my heart's wishing it, why does this enemy of mine appear needlessly to my sight? Why is he persecuting me?" As she thought thus, she gave herself to angry muttering. 101. The Lord-of-Heaven seeing Avali was in such a state of mind said to Himself, "I must plan something by which she will love me." 102. So the Lord-of-Pandhari placed His assuring hand on Avali, and said to her, "My daughter, you should not hold this anger in your heart. 103. You call me an enemy, but what enmity have I shown you? You say to me, 'You have made my husband one who has lost all consciousness of body [Videhi].' This charge of yours lacks sense. 104. When a fruit has become loose on its stem, the moment a wind touches it, it falls; in the same way I have become the instrument of Tuka's condition. 105. Tuka fixes his attention on Name and Form and goes and sits in the jungle. My state is just like yours. I am always following after him. 106. You did not have food to eat, so, I created a dense crop, but Tuka would not take the grain. What injustice of mine is that?" 107. Thus speaking, The King-of-Pandhari took her foot on his lap, and drew out the thorn without the least pain to her. 108. As God looked at Avali with an eye of compassion, she forgot all her former troubles. Even Brahmadev and the other gods cannot fathom the wondrous acts of the wonder working God-Supreme.

109. "I am very late" said Avali to herself. "My crazy fellow is sitting somewhere in the mountain, and I

must hasten to where he is." 110. Thus thinking, Jijai placed her basket on her head, and walked along with Krishna walking behind her. 111. As they began climbing the mountain, Tuka opened his eyes and looked, and was utterly amazed. "This is a most extraordinary sight," he said. 112. "I see darkness and the sun occupying one place. Or it is as strange a thing as would be the union of the ocean with the Rishi Agasti. 113. Or that through friendship a Pandit and a goatherd should become one. Or a mixture of poison and nectar become one. I have the same feeling of surprise. 114. Or to see a falcon and a swan come together through friendship. So to see Avali and Vishnu together is the most extraordinary surprise." 115. Thus thinking to himself, the noble Vaishnava felt great satisfaction. "The two were enemies," he said, "but now that enmity has entirely gone. 116. Our domestic quarrels have been bad. Every moment I feel troubled about them, but now that the King-of-Heaven has met with Avali, my heart is happy."

117. While the God loving *bhakta's* heart thus overflowed with joy, the two, Avali and Krishna, gradually approached. 118. Tuka at once arose and grasped Shri Krishna's feet. Overcome by the eight feelings of the heart, he was choked with emotion. 119. Tuka, Avali and the Life-of-the-World, these three, sat down together in silence.

Tuka, Avali and Krishna Dine Together.

The God-loving *bhakta* then said to his wife, "Serve Vithoba with something to eat." 120. Hearing this suggestion, Avali felt a sense of shame. Said she, "There is only one cake of bread, how will it be sufficient for two?"

121. She was greatly distressed in mind, and said to herself, "Even here this Black fellow has brought his enmity. To my sight he looks strong and fat. What am I to do?" 122. Although she thought thus in her mind, yet she served the one piece of bread on God's plate. She did not save any of it for herself or Tuka, and Krishna was pleased with her act. 123. Hari, seeing her guileless spirit, created many kinds of food, and Avali's basket overflowed with good things, but it was covered with a cloth. 124. Once in former times Shri Krishna was hungry, and Draupadi gave him some greens. Nothing remained of it, and then He created many kinds of food. 125. Thus although Avali did not have the spirit of worship, yet Vishnu was pleased with her, and this even though she had the feeling of enmity against Him. So Vishnu said to Avali, "Serve Tuka now." 126. Hearing this suggestion of the Husband-of-Rukmini, Avali felt a sense of shame (not having any bread to serve). However, she removed the cloth (that covered her basket) and when she looked, lo and behold! it was full of dainty food. 127. Full of supreme amazement Avali said to herself, "The female deity of our family has come to protect me. Bhairav, or Khandoba, or Bhavani has come to help me. 128. I do not know whose act it is that has preserved my reputation. (Whoever he may be) I must approach Him with all my heart and my every life." 129. Perceiving what Avali was thinking, the Husband-of-Rukmini said to her, "He to whom you should come as a suppliant, you should recognize as me, the Infinite-Being. 130. I created this food while you were looking. Know that it was really my doing." Although the Lord-of-Heaven thus told her, it seemed to her false. 131. She thought to herself, "If He has all this power why did he eat the kernels of grain offered by

Vidur? He spread His hand before Draupadi and greedily ate the stalk of the leaf. 132. He has the habits of a glutton, and yet in the services of song his praise is sung. He ate the *bor* fruit that the Bhil woman had tasted, without any hesitation. 133. If He has all this power, how is it that He was seen coming out of a Mahar's house? He dragged Chokhamela's dead cattle along, and then asked him for something to eat."

God Creates a Spring of Living Water.

134. Such were the various thoughts that Avali brought before her mind. Then with her own hands she took the food and served the two. 135. When the thorn pierced her foot, the gourd of water had spilt. There was no water at all near at hand on the mountain. 136. This greatly distressed Avali, and she said, "What shall I do?" Knowing her thoughts, Krishna said to her, 137. "I see a spring of living water in that ravine over there. You will find a spring of water there. This is my absolute assurance." 138. Avali could not believe his statement as true, but when she used her hands, and lifted up a slab of stone, lo and behold! a pure spring of water coming up from below, to her great astonishment. 139. Said she, "In a waterless forest He has made water to flow. This His act is beyond all belief. He created also the food right here. No one but He could have done this. 140. He must have learned some magical *mantra,* and become skilled in sleight of hand. He has bewitched my husband, and made him a crazy fellow." 141. She brought many such thoughts to her mind. However, she filled the gourd with water, and with her own hand served food on the plates. The Husband-of-Rukmini began to eat. 142. Gods

sitting in their chariots of light [*viman*] hovered over them to see the wonderful sight. They said to themselves, "Blessed is this extraordinary power of a *bhakta*," and with this they showered flowers upon them. 143. The Life-of-the-World then said to Tuka, "Eat this morsel, I give it you as my blessing. Let not your heart be troubled. I will carry your efforts to success." 144. Thus speaking, God, with his own hand, put the morsel into Tukar's mouth. God dined along with Avali. The Soul-of-the-World does not hold the thought of duality. 145. As Tuka tasted the divine food with love, he felt a sense of joy. Krishna gave Tuka water with which to wash his hands, and then said to him, 146. "Listen, O Tuka, to my words. I am God who fills all mankind. You must look at the animate and inanimate in my form, just as in an ornament you see gold. 147. Or when you look at cloth carefully, is it without the fibres that compose it? So the Universe does not exist without Me. Learn this through your experience.

God Ends Avali's Wearisome Journeys.

148. From to-day do not come regularly to this mountain to be alone. It is very wearisome for Avali. Listen to this word of mine." 149. When the Merciful-to-the-Lowly thus spoke Tuka fell prostrate at His feet. Said he, "I am Thy dear one, therefore, Thou dost have compassion on me. 150. I know nothing of repeating of *mantras*, of austerities, nor how to read the *Shastras*. I know not the eight methods of attaining Yoga. I have no knowledge of metaphysics, nor the knowledge of Brahma. I am in every way a sinner. 151. Thou art the Brother-of-the-Lowly, the Protector-of-the-Helpless. This Thy reputation is known world wide, Loving *bhaktas*

sing of it in their *kirtans*, and Thou hast shown it to be true, O Pandurang." 152. Hearing these loving words of Tuka's, the Cloud-of-Mercy, said to him, "Remain (in peace). A mother protects her infant child. This is her natural instinct. 153. So you are wholly mine, the child of my old age". Thus speaking, Krishna embraced Tuka. 154. The happiness of His heart, which remains hidden, untold even to the wise, Krishna gave to Tuka, seeing his loving devotion. 155. In that state God and His *bhakta* became one. So that no one of them desired the other. When the Lord-of-Heaven realized this, 156. He said, "Tuka has reached the state of oneness with me. He has discarded the idea of duality. Just as when water is poured into milk it is then nowhere to be seen. 157. Or just as the soul pervades the body, or as the air fills the sky, or as in the golden bud the honey lies concealed, 158. or as sound gradually disappears in a bell, or as sweetness exists in sugar, so Tuka has become one who recognizes no duality. If there is no duality, then loving conversation is stopped. 159. If no duality exists, then if I think of something wonderful to whom shall I whisper my secrets? Also whom shall I hold neck to neck in an embrace?" Thus thought the World's-Supreme-Lord to Himself. 160. "If Tuka attains unity with Myself, then who will there be to call on me for help? Who would there be to whom I must rush to help? And who will sing my praises?" 161. Realizing this possibility, the Merciful-to-the-lowly said to Tuka, "Whenever you are dancing in your services of song [*kirtans*] there I, Krishna, am present." 162. While the Close-friend-of-*bhaktas* was saying this, Tuka opened his eyes and looked. Using the opportunity afforded by his questions, God gave to Tuka the joy of *bhakti*.

GODS APPLAUD THE CONVERSATION OF GOD AND TUKA.

163. This conversation between God and his *bhakta* was listened to by gods in their chariots of light. They remarked to one another, "This noble Vaishnava, Tuka, will be the salvation of many. 164. We have attained the Heaven of Indra no doubt, but we have been largely deprived (of the joy of love) while this *bhakta,* Tuka, has snatched the joy of love by way of *bhakti;* and made Krishna subservient to him. 165. Blessed! Blessed! is this world of mortals. Its glory looks to us extraordinary. All the means for joy are here, while we (gods) have to go to the Heaven of Indra to experience joy. 166. Blessed is this mount Bhandar, for God's feet have touched it. Blessed is the sacred town of Dehu, where this Vaishnava has descended as an *avatar.* 167. Blessed is all the region around here. Blessed are the stones and the earth, for here the Husband-of-Indira has wandered, whose limitless glory we are unable to describe". 168. Following this praise by Indra, the gods returned to his Heaven. Then Krishna, taking leave of Tuka, vanished out of sight.

MAHIPATI GLORIFIES TUKA.

169. To my imagination Tuka's heart was a perfect lotus, and Shri Hari was a bee that came and lived in it out of love. 170. Or, I imagine this *bhakta's* heart to be an ocean in which the Husband-of-Indira shines as a fish as he swims about. Egoism is, as it were, the demon Shankhasur whom the Lord-of-Indira (Vishnu) killed with his own hands.

171. In his loving *bhakti* Tuka has uttered blessed words. One should recognize them as having come from the *Vedas.* There can be no opposite opinion. 172.

Those who sing his verses in faith and in reverence should be considered as noble *rishis*, and those who accept the authority of his words will increase the number of his noble followers. 173. His is a limitless glory. Comparison is of no use in the case of the incomparable. By the extraordinary love he showed in his *bhakti* he made the best of men subject to him. 174. In the Kali Yuga the Buddha *avatar* took place. This is well known from the *Purans,* but in order to fulfil the longings of Tuka, God became *sagun* [took visible form]. 175. Just as the calf of the Wish-cow, even before it is evening sucks her udder, and just as in her love her milk flows without any reference whatever to the time of day. 176. Or just as one sitting under a wish-tree conceives a desire for something extraordinary, the tree pays no regard to births, this present one or the future one, and fulfils the wish. 177. So it is that the Merciful-to-the-Lowly, although there is no occasion to become an *avatar,* assumes His *sagun,* pure form, and at once meets his *bhaktas*.

178. But enough of these illustrations. The wise listeners will grow weary. (As we have seen) Krishna, after meeting with Tuka, arrived at His heavenly city.

179. And then the Vaishnava Tuka, together with Avali, came back to his village.

Mahipati Regards Himself as God's Instrument.

I wish you to listen to what the friend of the loving *bhaktas* will make me relate in the next interesting chapter. 180. Due to a violent wind, the scarecrow swings to and fro. But people imagine that he is a farmer, sitting there watching his field. 181. Looking at the matter in the same way, all consider it to be the skill of the poet, and call him a wise man. But the wise say that it is not so. It is the Lord-of-Pandhari who causes him to speak. 182. The mendicant's horn plays many a tune, and is heard by all the people, but the blower of the horn is quite different from the horn. It is he whom the people see as the skilful player. 183. So the wonder-working Pandurang is really Himself relating these stories of the saints. He uses Mahipati the ward of the poet-saints, as His instrument.

184. Svasti! This book, the Shri Bhaktalilamrita, fulfils all the desires of the heart by merely listening to it. So may the loving pious *bhaktas* listen to it. This is the thirtieth interesting chapter.

CHAPTER 31.

God's Blessing Necessary.

Obeisance to Shri Ganesh.

1. Aside from Thy name, I truly know no means of salvation, O Krishna. I do not at all know the repeating of *mantras*, austerities, or religious ceremonies in their various forms. 2. If I depend on performing correctly religious ceremonies (I fail; for,) I am suffering from lack of food. If I ought to wander to sacred places, I cannot, because my body is without sufficient strength. 3. If to attain Thee, O Shri Hari, I should make gifts to those who deserve them, I have very little wealth, so how can I attain Thee? 4. If it is by seeing Thee in every thing whatsoever I behold, the animate or the inanimate, I see both good and evil in them. My mind does not possess the conception of equality in all things. 5. If I ought to study the *Vedas,* I cannot, for my mind is no longer youthful.

If I say I will look into philosophical books, I do not have faith in them. 6. But the stories of Thy saints form a large pumpkin raft, which I with love and faith have fastened on my back. So looking towards me with Thy merciful eye, O Supreme-Being, cause me to reach the shore of the other side.

Tuka's Benevolent Character.

7. In the last chapter there was the story of how a great thorn pierced Avali's foot, and how after drawing out the thorn the Husband-of-Rukmini met Tuka. 8. After this, the Vaishnava *bhakta* came to remain in the town, and became engrossed in the service of saints. He paid them great reverence, and with his own hands washed their feet. 9. And when he took into his mouth the water (with which their feet had been washed) he regarded divine joy as inferior to it. That all the sacred waters are to be found at the feet of the saints, was the conviction of Tuka's mind. 10. This noble Vaishnava would decorate them with garlands of *tulsi* leaves and flowers, and worship them. So also Tuka paid reverence with sincerity to the noble Brahmans. 11. The moment Tuka learned of the state of any hungry Vaishnava or Brahman he would make great effort for their relief, and with reverence provide them with a meal. 12. He believed that there was no means of attaining God more effective than a service rendered to saints. And whatever words they uttered, Tuka held in his heart as truth. 13. When the saints performed *kirtans,* Tuka led in the chorus. In this way he had the opportunity easily of listening to them, and then in privacy he would meditate (on what he had heard). 14. Although Tuka had met the Husband-of-Rukmini, still he gave himself to doing good to others.

Where the noble Vaishnavas danced (in their *kirtans*), he with his own hands swept away the little stones. 15. According as he saw the necessity in the *kirtans*, Tuka held the little torch in his hands, and this without any sense of shame, keeping the audience awake by his repetition of God's names. 16. When the saints sat down in the *kirtan*, he watched over their shoes, and when they were ready to leave, he would present to each one his shoes and in sincerity made an obeisance to them. 17. When Tuka led the chorus there was aroused an extraordinary enthusiasm. His own voice trembled with emotion caused by his love, and tears flowed from his eyes. 18. Repeating the names of God in a loud voice, he would speak to the audience moved by his feelings of love. All illusions were gone, Tuka alone remained with Vithoba his close friend, whose names he was repeating. 19. The characteristics of a good *bhakta* are described in the Shri Bhagavata. Every such characteristic belonged to him. He did not lack in a single one. 20. As people looked at him they would exclaim, "He is love-crazy, he babbles without sense, He never rests day or night. 21. He spoke the truth, He did good to others, and sympathy with all creatures dwelt in his heart. If any man or woman asked him to do anything, he would at once put his own hands to the work. 22. If any one had a desire for anything, and if Tuka happened to possess it, he gave it to him; but never physically, by word of mouth, or in thought did he ever deceive any one. 23. There are those who with their mouths preach wisdom to men. "I am altogether Brahma," they claim, but they are ready to sacrifice their lives for the sake of a *kavadi*-shell. Then of course, their preaching goes for nothing. 24. But Tuka's acts were not such. He acted amongst men just as he talked. He regarded the whole universe as himself. He saw no duality even in his dreams. 25. When seeing your own infant child crying, and that of another, to have the same sympathetic feeling towards each, that is the characteristic of a saint. 26. If any one should hear that a thief has robbed him of his money and property, and should feel not in the least troubled by it, that man is a saint. 27. If a king gave one diamonds and precious stones, and a common citizen brought him some greens, to regard both gifts as equal, that is the characteristic of a saint. 28. Or supposing some one praises one in various ways, and another speaks evil of him, and yet neither pleasure nor displeasure are awakened in his mind, he is a saint, and such was Tuka's nature.

Tuka Gives Away his Wife's only Garment.

29. It happened on a certain day that Tuka's wife was taking her bath. She had only one old garment, and she had folded it and placed it on the wall. 30. The noble Vaishnava sat outside worshipping with love and reverence. To him the whole universe was filled by the Husband-of-Rukmini. There was nothing else but Him. 31. Just then a weak Brahman woman came there, and pitifully appealed to Tuka. Said she, "If you will give me a garment it will mean to you the value of numberless good deeds. 32. The Brahmans' domestic affairs are in a very straightened condition. I have no other garment for bathing. If you have some old tattered garments, give them to me." 33. This request of the Brahman woman excited compassion in Tuka's heart. So by a gesture he pointed out his wife's garment, and told her to take it away with her. 34. Avali was bathing in the back yard and had placed

her garment on the wall. The Brahman woman came to it, and pulling the garment off the wall went off with it. 35. The Brahman woman was greatly pleased in her heart and thought, "What a good nature this man has!" She gave Tuka her affectionate blessing and said, "May the Husband-of-Rukmini come to your help". 36. Tuka motioned to her not to talk, and to go away quickly. And after giving her this hint he himself went off at once. 37. He sat down on the bank of the Indrayani and there worshipped full of love. But now what happened in the house is for you, wise people, to listen to. 38. After having bathed, Jijabai [Avali], looked about for her garment. But it was not where she had placed it. Her mind was greatly disturbed. 39. Said she, "The Mighty troublesome Karma has come to the front. My garment was taken while I was not looking." And then she began to think. 40. "My servant Bubai is not at home. She has gone far away to bring dung-cakes. My little infant Ganga is playing outside." She was greatly perplexed. 41. "Mahadev has taken Vithoba with him and gone to bathe (in the river). He is developing the same characteristics as his father. It is a long time since he has gone. 42. A leper may not have a leprous son, but five spots at least may be seen on his body. And, therefore, 'Like mine, like earth,' is a proverb, men repeat. 43. Kashi and Bhagirthi are clever girls both of them, but since they have gone to their mother-in-law's there is no one in the house to look after things. So he takes up anything and gives it away to anybody. 44. My husband was sitting in the house, and that Brahman woman was asking for a garment. And I also heard her voice asking. 45. This mad man has lost his common sense. He is throwing whole cloth on thorny bushes. I had only this one garment in the house. He gave that away and then ran off himself. 46. That damn black-faced husband of mine has gone away silently to escape me, O dear! just as a scorpion, when it has done its evil deed, sits hidden somewhere. 47. Otherwise, he is accustomed to go outside, and shout aloud the name of the Black-face [Vithoba]. He is remaining silent to-day, because he is remembering the evident wrong he has committed. 48. Thief! glutton! indeed! He is persecuting me and carrying out his enmity. He is not my husband, but my enemy, and is carrying out his revenge for our enmity in our former births. 49. What sort of a woman could that Brahman woman be! And he gave my garment to her. He did not say a word to me, and went off into the jungle, to sit there, and escape from my notice. 50. My father, Apaji, bought that garment for me. I have never eaten food earned by my husband. 51. Because he (my husband) fastened some black glass beads around my neck, he is to be called my husband, but he has been a damned and useless husband. I know his doings. He is sitting there a bankrupt. 52. In the famine his elder wife died, crying for food. A sense of shame never occurs to him; and (with impudence) he shows his face to everybody. 53. Rakhuma Bai had many deeds to her credit, and so she went before me. I was to suffer great misfortunes, therefore, I have been kept in this worldly life. 54. If I should now go into the house, there are towns-people standing in front. I cannot think what to do." And she began to cry. 55. Just then some relatives and the fathers of the bride and bridegroom were going along together to a marriage ceremony. They all came to the house to invite Jijai [Avali], and called out, "Jijai, come out here." 56. Having called out to her all the people entered the house. Avali was sitting unclad on the bathing slab, and very much ashamed. 57. Said she to herself, "If he who holds a grudge against me (my husband) were here in the house, I would whack his face. But now what shall I do! I can't think of anything I should do." 58. So as the slanderous crowd began to come near her, the fire of her fear was kindled. The oil of mourning fell on the fire, and it flared up fiercely. 59. The faggots of love were set on fire, and they were all in blaze from the wind of desire. And when the flames touched her sense of shame, her mind was utterly overcome. 60. The fire burned with the three forms of heat, and Avali exclaimed, "What shall I do!" Suddenly Vithabai rushed to her help, and performed a most wondrous thing. 61. From behind she threw over Avali a yellow garment. Thus the compassionate Husband-of-Rukmini preserved the modesty of his handmaid. 62. To my imagination I think of Avali as being on fire with the three fevers, and that the Husband-of-Rukmini as a cloud showered rain upon her. 63. As Avali saw the shining garment, she was overcome with astonishment. Said she, "This seems to be the doing of the Black-one. No one, but He, would do so. 64. He performs many miracles, but I am not at all under obligation to Him. He has made my husband a lunatic, and, therefore, He has to protect me again and again." 65. Avali quickly dressed herself in this garment, and without a moment's delay she came into the house. The garment produced light in the house, and all the slanderous crowd marvelled.

The Slanderous Crowd Slander Tuka.

66. They exclaimed, "We have seen many very costly garments, but never one equal to this. Whose house has Tuka reduced to bankruptcy, and with the proceeds bought his wife this yellow robe? 67. In his home there is a well-furnished kitchen, but outside in public he pretends

poverty with a show of loud lament. And now he is adopting the pious look of a crane, and pretends indifference to worldly things. 68. As we look at the dazzling brilliancy of this garment, our eyes have to close. And the sweet perfume from it more than fills this room." They were overwhelmed with wonder. 69. Some one remarked, "He must have kept this garment hidden in a box up to now. And she has now taken it out to wear. One does not know the limit of Tuka's acting."

70. Thus speaking to one another, they said to Jijai, "We hope it is all well with you. Make haste and come to the wedding." 71. Avali replied, "Our affairs are not known. My husband has discarded all desires for a worldly life, and has become one without bodily consciousness." 72. To this reply of Jijai's those slanderous men anwered, "Tell us at once, whether you will or will not come to the wedding?" 73. Knowing the weakness of her domestic affairs, they said to themselves, "From whence will she obtain the wedding gifts?" The selfish slanderers began now to speak outwardly in words of reverence. 74. Just like the temporary shadow of a cloud. A moment after, and there is none. Or just as when the least sunlight falls on a butterfly, it loses its colours. 75. Or like the contemplative appearance of a crane, that from a distance looks as though it is absorbed in some special thought. Or like an actor on the stage, who acts the part of a beautiful woman, but is not fit to associate with. 76. Or like the flowers of the *pungal* creeper. From a distance they look beautiful, but when held up to the nose, they have a disgusting evil odour, which nauseates one. 77. Or like a gilded coin, that is all brass within. It is like these, that one should judge the outward reverence paid by slanderous men.

78. Recognizing the extremely discourteous manner of the invitation, Avali replied to them, "If I find my family affairs in a favourable state, then I shall surely come a little later." 79. After their empty compliments, these slanderers left. What happened later is what the wise should listen to with reverence.

Tuka Confesses his Sins before God.

80. Because he had stealthily given the garment away to the Brahman woman, and because of Avali's harsh words, Tuka, the noble Vaishnava, went off hastily into the jungle. 81. He naturally sat down, and bringing the image of Pandurang into his contemplation, he prayed, "O God-Supreme, Husband-of-Rukmini, hear my request. 82. All sins being collected together, I am made a statue out of them. O Purifier-of-the-fallen, Merciful-to-the-humble, may this be known to Thee. 83. I am a heap of every kind of sin. But Thy service-thief is at Thy feet. Punish me, O God, in a way that I may lose all worldly honour. 84. I outwardly call myself as one belonging to Thee. I have turned my worldly affairs into dust and earth, but in both I, Tuka, am a shirker. Thou knowest my heart, O Vithoba."

85. With the sense of repentance in his heart, Tuka continued his worship with feelings of love. When four *ghatikas* of the night were passed, he came to the temple. 86. He took two stones to use as cymbals, and in love spent his time in dancing. His house was near by, and Avali understood that he had returned. 87. She had by this time entirely lost her anger, because God had given her that yellow robe to wear. So by the hand of her daughter she at once sent him some bread and greens. 88. He ate

with pleasure, just a small amount, and then stood up to perform a *kirtan* with loving enthusiasm.

TUKA OVERCOMES HIS DESIRE TO SLEEP.

Some pious people used to come there and sing, and listen to the stories of Hari. 89. Tuka carried on his *kirtans* in the temple, until the second watch of the night. Until then there were people in the temple. After that they returned to their homes. 90. But Tuka would not sleep at all, and sat alone in the temple. He would repeat with love the poems of the saints which he had committed to memory. 91. During the day time he spent his time in the jungle. At night he carried on his *kirtans* until the second watch. He would sometimes nod, but he would rub his eyes, and keep them open. 92. A seeker casts aside all self-conceit, and thereby gains a direct vision of the soul, but the physical nature undergoes no change. It operates through its past momentum. 93. Just as, even after the consciousness of the body has gone the organs of sense still continue to function. 94. Or just as a potter whirls his wheel, and then suddenly removes the handle. Because of the acquired momentum it continues to rapidly whirl. 95. Or when a whirlwind has ceased, the trees continue to sway for a short time. Even after the rain-cloud has passed four days, it leaves much moisture behind. 96. After the sun has set it is still light after four *ghatikas*. So would one expect the body to lose its function all at once? 97. Hence frequently Tuka would fall asleep. But in order to overcome that tendency, what did that noble Vaishnava do 98. but tie a cord to his tuft of hair, and with his own hands fasten the cord up (around a peg). Said he to himself, "When my neck feels a jerk my drowsiness will leave me." 99. For four days he did this, and absolutely conquered his tendency to sleep. He also lost slothfulness, packing it off to a distant land. 100. What one should not hear that Tuka's ears did not hear. What should not be seen that Tuka's eyes did not see. His tongue knew what was not to be spoken; and these were the natural characteristics of Tuka. 101. Although his mind was not unswervingly fixed on the everlasting, although his hands did not offer worship to Vishnu, still his feet hastened where he could help others, because that is counted for innumerable good deeds. 102. The man who does good to others, if his previous births have been pure, will in future have health of body, and the enjoyment of many things. 103. Tuka's unselfish nature, anxious to attain the Husband-of-Rukmini, spent his strength in doing good to others. Listen how he did it.

EXAMPLES OF TUKA'S KINDNESS.

104. If Tuka happened to meet a traveller on the road, he would take his load on his own head, and so give the traveller a short rest. 105. If a traveller was caught out in a very heavy rain, and was looking for some place to lodge, he would show them the public rest house or the temple. If those failed, he would at once take them into his own house. 106. If pilgrims, walking along the road, suffered from swollen feet, he would heat some water, and shampoo their bodies. 107. Merciless owners would let their weak cows and oxen loose (to find their own fodder). Tuka would caress them, and give them water and straw. 108. He would keep in some place a mixture of wheat, flour, sugar and *ghi,* and put it in the holes of ants, out of his constant love for God. 109. He was sympathetic towards every creature, even the smallest. He disliked the act of killing. 110. As he walked or moved about, if he

happened to see an insect, he took care, lest it be crushed under his foot. His heart moved with compassion, and (at the sight of suffering) he was like a fish out of water. 111. During the heat of the hot season he would fan those sitting in the *kirtans.* If there was any one suffering from hunger, he would make an effort to provide him with food. 112. In the hot season when there was no water along the road, he made great effort to supply it. He used to fill a large earthen jar with water, and carry it to the road. 113. The right use of speech he considered the highest form of the system of austerities. He never spoke an untruth. He spent his body in doing good to others. There was no slothfulness in him whatever. 114. If a traveller was taken ill on his journey, and there was no friend or relative near him, he would make a place for him in the temple precincts, and prepare medicine and suitable food for him. 115. The *rishi,* Jadabharat, has been described in the Bhagavata. Tuka's character was just like him. If any one asked him to do some hard work, he would at once do it. 116. He put away all selfish thought, and personal desires, and did for others what they asked him to do.

Tuka's Kindness to a Lame Woman.

Once Tuka was sitting worshipping on the bank of the Indrayani. 117. Suddenly a crowd of traders came along on their way to Umbare Navalakh. As a joke they said to Tuka, "Come along with us." 118. "I agree," said this Vaishnava *bhakta,* and at once started to go with them. But he continued his worship with feelings of love, not wishing to be silent even for a moment. 119. Suddenly they met a weak, old Brahman woman, whose body had lost its strength. She was on her way to the bazaar, slowly hobbling along with the use of a cane. 120. When Tuka saw her, his heart was aroused to pity. Said he to her, "Mother! You seem very weary. Come and sit on my back." 121. Hearing these words of Tuka's, the Brahman woman replied, "If you will go and bring back some oil for me, then I will go back to my home." 122. "I agree," said the kindly *bhakta,* and the woman's heart was happy. She placed her money in Tuka's care, and gave him the vessel to take along with him. 123. The old woman returned to her home with a happy heart. And Tuka went to the bazaar for the sake of doing a kind act to another. 124. Even there in the bazaar, with his kindly spirit, he began to do whatever the traders asked him to do, but he kept up his worship with the enthusiasm of love. His heart was filled with the spirit of goodness. 125. Buying the oil, the next day he brought it, and gave it to the Brahman woman. Said she, "I have nothing with which to repay your kindness."

THE WIDOW'S OIL THAT LASTED LONG.

126. After some days had passed the Brahman woman began to tell people that there was a matter that greatly astonished her, and she did not know to whom to tell it. 127. "There was brought to me by Tuka oil sufficient for eight days surely, but it has lasted very many days. I think this very strange." 128. This remark of the Brahman woman spread from ear to ear, namely, "The oil that Tuka brings lasts many days." 129. One said "He, fortunate indeed! In his own home his children have not enough to eat. His wife died from lack of food, but his heart feels no shame." 130. Some wanted to test the miracle, and had Tuka bring them oil. They reported that the oil lasted many days, and they too thought it a wonder-

ful thing. 131. Some greedy people then said to Tuka, "O Tuka Shet, go to the bazaar, buy some oil, and take it to my house. I shall never forget your kindness." 132. "Very well! my *mabap* [mother-father]" said he in reply, and many oil-cans were brought to him. He fastened his bag around his neck, and people threw their money into it. 133. When the news spread in the villages along the path the people brought vessels and money and gave them to Tuka, and he was made happy by it. 134. Some placed bamboo cans in his hands, and some hung them around his neck. But this did not trouble Tuka's heart, for he was one who had lost consciousness of body. 135. So hastening to the bazaar he looked for the oilman's shop. Here he passed over to him all the bamboo cans and all the money. 136. The oil-man said to Tuka, "How much oil shall I put into each can?" Tuka replied "I don't know. Do what you think is proper." 137. While thus engaged in talking with the oil-man, other shopkeepers called out to him. "O Tuka, help us to put up our shop-tents. We are very late." 138. And Tuka in high glee carried their bundles for them on his head. With his hands he brushed off the ground, and helped the shopkeepers to put up their tents. 139. Whatever kind of work anybody asked him to do, this Vaishnava *bhakta* did. He would tie the pack animals, and bring them straw and water. 140. Seeing God in every creature, he served horses also. All liked Tuka. He was not disliked by any one. 141. At night time he went into the temple and performed a *kirtan*. Pious people listened to him with love, and repentance came to their hearts. 142. As soon as it was dawn the traders began calling him. As soon as Tuka heard their call he ran to them. 143. But all the while his loud repeating of God's names was heard all over the town. He said to people, "Do not waste this worldly life of yours without the sincere repeating of God's names." 144. He packed their goods into bundles for them, and helped them all to lift them. Whatever work was asked of him, he did it without feeling any vexation. 145. He then went to the oilman's who told him he had properly filled the bamboo cans. "I agree to it," said the noble Vaishnava, and taking them started on his way. 146. People were waiting for him along the road, and as they recognized their cans they took them from him. But at this juncture The Husband-of-Rukmini performed a wonderful thing, which you hearers must listen to with reverence. 147. An equal amount of oil had been placed in each can, and Tuka had no idea at all how to distribute it, but according as each person had paid money he saw the value of that money in the amount of oil. 148. Just as innumerable living beings die and their bodies turn to dust, still in their next birth in various ways Fate selects each of them. 149. So Tuka was filled with the idea of the sameness of all things on earth. He saw nothing as more or less, but Vishnu made His selections. 150. The saints who have this conception of the sameness of all things, a king or a subject is the same to them. But God-Supreme appoints Fate to make some suffer poverty and others to enjoy power.

151. When the Vaishnava *bhakta* returned to Dehu he went at once into the temple, and prostrated himself with true sincerity. 152. As he saw the dark-complexioned Krishna his heart was filled with supreme joy. Just as when a mother meets again her infant child, she is full of joy. 153. Then the people came and selecting their own oil-cans took them away.

When Avali saw this she used very derogatory words. 154. Said she, "These damned, evil minded people, now that my husband has become crazy, put a fire-brand in that crazy fellow's hands, and make him work for them. 155. They make one man carry a load that belongs to an ox. If my husband should die, they would be pleased."

156. When Avali was quarreling in this way, some one said to her, "If your husband wouldn't listen to people, why would they ask him to do things? 157. One whose character is especially good, he is bound by that very character. Because the wild cow has a very charming white tail, it gets cut off. 158. If a parrot will not listen to what is being taught him, then how would he experience confinement in a cage? A man is injured by his own good nature, recognize this as true. 159. At the command of the monkey-man the monkey makes his salaam to the people. It is because of that that it is strongly tied and made to wander from house to house. 160. So listen, Jija Bai. Your husband has become one who has no consciousness of body. Whatever is asked of him he listens to it. Now what have you got to say against the people? 161. The oil that he brings lasts a long time. Many have experienced this miracle. That is why they give him many oil cans, and frequently call on him to bring their oil. 162. Tuka is a *videhi* [one unconscious of body], and seems crazy. Why do you charge us with using denunciation. If one's own coins are false, why quarrel with others?"

163. Avali listened to these illustrations, and then remained quiet. She thought to herself, "It is my Fate that is false. I am disgraced before the people."

TUKA'S HUMILITY, KINDNESS AND TENDERNESS.

164. Such was Tuka's condition. He considered all womankind as Prakriti and men as the God, Pandurang,

and, therefore, he had compassion on every creature. 165. He would get up very early in the morning, and bring water to a Brahman's house. He would sweep his front yard, and clean and decorate the place. 166. Hunters caught many birds. If Tuka saw them, he would speak to them in a humble way, and somehow or other he would get the birds released. 167. He considered himself the bought slave of saints and *sadhus,* and drank with love the water in which their feet were washed. Divine nectar seemed to him inferior to the food left on their plates. 168. The Shri Bhagavata has described the characteristics of saints. And all those characteristics were found in Tuka. Not one was lacking.

Miraculous Feeding of a Multitude.

169. Avali was in fact ignorance itself, and, therefore, Tuka kept himself far from her. And, therefore, she quarrelled with him day and night and used rough language.

170. One day, Jijabai [Avali] said to Tuka, "To-day is the holy anniversary of your deceased parents, and we have nothing at all in the house with which to prepare the feast." 171. The noble Vaishnava, on hearing this remark, said, "I will at once go into the jungle, and will bring back a large load of greens, which you can cook, and feed them." 172. So saying the kindly Tuka, shouting aloud the names of Vitthal, started to go into the jungle, keeping in mind the Lord-of-Heaven. 173. As he brought the image of Pandurang before his imagination, he closed both eyes, and with a heart full of love, he prayed for God's mercy, as he (walked along) alone. 174. "Victory! Victory! to Thee Husband-of-Rukmini, kind to

His *bhaktas,* Purifier of the Sinful, Merciful-One, Saviour of the lowly, Shri Vitthal. 175. In body, speech, and heart, I have become Thy suppliant. Thou alone art my dearest friend, and my relative, and dost deliver me from many a calamity. 176. In past days I devoted myself completely to the worldly life, but thereby I only increased my sorrows, realized in many forms. 177. But now I put aside all desire for things that are perishable, and come as a suppliant to Thee, O Husband-of-Rukmini. I place all my burdens on Thy head. Whatever Thou dost plan to do, do it."

178. Thus praying, this loving *bhakta,* continued along the path. Suddenly he came upon a wheat field, ripe and with a heavy crop. All the hired labourers were harvesting it. 179. They said to Tuka in fun, "Hurry up and (help us) reap this wheat field." Tuka, who had no thought for his body, heard their call and said, "I agree," 180. and along with the labourers he began to reap in the second swath. But all the while he was reaping, he was shouting aloud the names of God in love. 181. The others were doing their work in a careless way, so the noble Vaishnava went ahead of them. Tuka's pure heart would not allow him to spare his body. 182. In the mean time, however, Tuka entirely failed to remember that he had started for the jungle to bring home greens, and that his Queen was waiting for him at home. 183. His heart was absorbed in God's names and form, and, therefore, he became lost to all thought of body. He was feasting all the time on love, and he looked well fed and stout on this food.

184. Turning now to his home, his wife was using abusive words. Said she, "Damn that thief and glutton. He is up and off. 185. Whose wife does he expect me

to be, and provide the home with clothing and food? Here at home he has invited his deceased parents [represented by Brahmans] at his house; and now he is wandering in the jungle. 186. He developes a great deal of strength to work for other people, but he has no friendly relations with me. What am I to do to carry on my domestic affairs?"

187. While Tuka's wife was thus worrying in her mind at home, the Lord-of-Pandhari began to feel a sense of pity for her, and said to himself, "I must help her. 188. When my *bhaktas* lack anything it reflects on my good reputation. I must act the part of a servant to those who are my servants in sincerity." 189. Thinking thus to Himself, Krishna took the form of Tuka, and approached the house with a load on His head of the necessities for the feast. 190. He who is the object of contemplation for Yogis, object of worship for Shiva, He, when His *bhaktas* lacked, thought not at all of His own dignity. 191. He whose abode is the Ocean-of-Milk, He whose feet are rubbed by Lakshmi, even He, Krishna, personally carried on His head this load of material for the feast. 192. He, whom Brahmadev and the other gods, and the great *rishis* continually contemplate, He the advocate of His *bhaktas,* the Lotus-eyed-One, paid no thought to His dignity. 193. He whom Indira obeys, accompanied with the eight *Siddhis,* even He, in His own person, performed this heavy labour, He, Lord-of-Heaven, the Guru-of-the-World.

194. Krishna put down his load, and said to Avali, "Take from this load whatever you need, and start your cooking. 195. I will go to other houses and collect some vessels." Thus remarking, Krishna at once arose and left.

196. When Jijai [Avali] came outside, and undid the bundle and looked (at its contents), lo! and behold!! there was everything in it that was needed. And she was filled with amazement. 197. There was wheat flour, dal, *ghi*, rice, sugar, greens and raw sugar, cumin seed, ginger and black pepper. All these she saw before her eyes. 198. Jija Bai took these cooking materials and started to cook them. Just then the Recliner-on-the-Serpent [Vishnu] approached, having collected the needed vessels. 199. Krishna then went from house to house and gave the invitation (to the feast). "To-day we are observing the holy anniversary of our deceased parents; come at once to the feast." 200. At this invitation of the Life-of-the-World, people began to wonder. Said they, "To-day at least Tuka has put his mind into worldly affairs." 201. One remarked, "Can he be at all relied upon? There is nothing at his home of goods and chattels, and no materials for a feast. Tuka is a thoughtless fellow, unmindful of bodily concerns, and yet, he has invited the whole town." 202. In this way different people said different things, but they all agreed, "The invitation of this liar cannot be verified, unless we dine at his house."

203. When the hour of noon approached, the cooking was completed. God had gone from house to house, and asked all to come to dine. 204. All went down to the bank of Indrayani river, and after their bath came (to Tuka's house). God seated them, and worshipped them. 205. The compassionate Husband-of-Rukmini brings to full completion the good deeds of those saints, who, forsaking all other affiliations, come to Him as sincere suppliants. 206. Krishna washed their feet, and presented them with bouquets, fragrant oil, and the *tulsi* leaf, while Jijai, happy in her heart, served the meal. 207. Whatever she had

prepared she served on their plates, while Krishna served the *ghi,* and repeated the Sankalpa (religious formula). 208. With this assistance of the Husband-of-Lakshmi, the food had a delicious taste. They ate all their stomachs could contain, so that there was no room left for any water. 209. This wonder-working Saviour-of-the-World again and again pressed upon them to take whatever was pleasing to their taste. 210. After the guests had washed their hands, He gave them the *pan supari* with the thirteen ingredients. The guests were astonished, and said to Avali, 211. "Jija Bai, you need not from to-day be troubled about your domestic affairs. It appears that Tuka has again put his heart into his business." 212. Avali listened to them but said to herself, "I am not so sure of that." All the guests returned to their homes, with minds well-satisfied. 213. And then many beggars and Mahars came for some food. The Husband-of-Rukmini served them food in abundance. 214. Avali thought to herself, "There has been over-abundance of food." The Husband-of-Rukmini collected together all the vessels, and said to Avali, 215. "I am going to take these vessels back to those from whom I borrowed them. After that we shall sit down to eat with care-free minds. Don't be impatient." 216. The Soul-of-the-World washed the vessels in the water of the Indrayani, returned them to whom they belonged, and then became invisible.

217. Turning now to Tuka, the noble Vaishnava, he cut a very large quantity of the wheat. The farmer thanked him and gave him a few sheaves. 218. He put them on his head and started for home.

Tuka is Attacked by Bees.

As he walked along, the straw touched a bees' nest.

The bees swarmed about him, 219. and began to sting him on his body, but Tuka would not brush them off. He said to himself, "This body of mine is a perishable thing, and one should spend it in doing good to others. 220. Or this being the holy anniversary of my ancestors, perhaps they have all come in the form of bees. So that this Vaishnava *bhakta* made a full offering of his body to Brahma. 221. But Shri Hari, seeing Tuka's determination, came in an invisible form, drove all the bees away, and brought relief to his body.

Avali Tells Tuka of God's Miracle.

222. The God-loving *bhakta* having returned to his home, said to his wife, "Roughly grind this grain, and serve our ancestors with food." 223. Avali replied to Tuka, "Are you crazy? You did everything that was required," and with that she showed him the cooked materials. 224. She related to Tuka what had happened from beginning to end. Tuka heard her with amazement. Tears filled his eyes. Said he, "I have made hard work for the Life-of-the-World." 225. His voice choked with emotion as he exclaimed, "O merciful Vithabai! If you do not come at this time, I shall not eat at all." 226. The Wearer-of-the-Yellow-Robe heard Tuka's piteous cry and came. In his ears were the crocodile earrings. His hands were adorned with the conch shell and the disk. 227. When Tuka saw this form he grasped its feet. And Jijai placed a plate before Him and served Him with food. 228. Then Tuka by the use of words worshipped the Husband-of-Rukmini. God and His *bhakta*, with feelings of love ate together. 229. And the Husband-of-Rukmini was satisfied with Tuka's sincer-

ity. God then vanished out of sight, to the amazement of Jijai.

The Bhaktalilamrita Likened to a Lake.

230. This beautiful book, the Bhaktalilamrita, is lake Manas. The various stories are large, blossomed lotuses. 231. The zealous and wise listeners who enjoy the love odour are as bees here who buzz through love.

232. The next chapter is full of extraordinary interest, the relater is the Husband-of-Rukmini. Mahipati is His darling one, whom He has slowly taught to speak.

233. Svasti! This book, the Shri Bhaktalilamrita, fulfils all desires by merely listening to it. May loving saints and *bhaktas* listen to it. This is the thirty-first interesting chapter.

CHAPTER 32.

Mahipati Calls His Language Uncouth.

Obeisance to Shri Ganesh.

1. The ignorant and dear infant first prattles, and then learns to speak. The mother and father enjoy this prattling very much, and ask the infant to repeat the same by imitating it. 2. In a rich man's home there is no lack of the daintiest food, but as a change they gladly partake of various common foods. 3. Just as if one should offer curds as an offering to the Ocean-of-Milk, so my uncouth words must seem to my audience of saints. 4. Or, it is like lighting a wick, and waving it before the sun in worship. Or, as if to cool the moon one should take a fan and fan the moon. 5. Or, as if for a mountain of gold one should make a tinned ornament. So my uncouth language appears before the saints.

TUKA TELLS OF THE SAINTS OF OLD.

6. In the last chapter, and the last story we saw how the Life-of-the-World took the form of Tuka, brought to the house the needed things, and dined all the ancestors. 7. Then how, when the Vaishnava *bhakta* came home, his wife told him all that had happened, which made him exclaim, "For us the Husband-of-Rukmini has had to labour hard." 8. And then how at dawn he went to the Indrayani to bathe, and after worshipping the glorious image, praised God in love; 9. saying, "O Ocean-of-Mercy, O Lord-of-Pandhari, in past times Thou didst save those who came to Thee as suppliants. Thou didst give no thought as to their caste or family line. Thou, Infinite-One, didst care for them in their distresses. 10. When Nama's children were about to die of hunger, and (his wife) Rajai was in great distress, Thou, Krishna, didst become the banker Keshav and bring her a bag of gold coin. 11. Chokhamela was a Mahar by caste, and Thou didst drag home for him dead cattle. And recognizing his great love, Thou didst eat with him. 12. Because of Dnyanadev's love, Thou didst make his wall to move. Thy praiseworthy deeds, O Husband-of-Rukmini, have been described by very many saints. 13. Damajipant was a generous minded *bhakta.* He robbed an immense store (of the king's) grain (to feed the starving). Then Thou didst become Vithu, the Mahar, and paid (to the king) in cash the full value (of the grain). 14. For the sake of Mirabai Thou, Infinite-Being, didst drink the poison. Thus Thou didst protect her modesty, and caused her good name to spread over the world. 15. There was Narsi Mehata, the Vaishnava *bhakta.* God cashed his check. Thou didst become Savalsah, and showed an unheard of marvel. 16. Thus Thy Vaishnava

bhaktas, O Krishna, sing their praises. My dull and weak mind wishes to do the same, in its love."

TUKA'S THREE GREAT PRINCIPLES OF ACTION.

17. As Krishna heard Tuka's praise of Him, He was very pleased, and said to Himself, "Tuka will utter words of inspiration for which I shall pay him his due. I shall glorify him."

18. Tuka had performed three austerities belonging to Body, Speech and Mind. (Belonging to Body) was that noblest of good deeds, namely the doing of good to others. In this Tuka spent his entire strength. 19. Also in the months of Ashadh, and Kartik he went on pilgrimage to Pandhari. And just as a young wife, living at her mother-in-law's, has a heart full of joy when on her way to her own mother's home (so the pilgrimage was to Tuka). 20. Tuka did not ride a horse, he walked barefoot to Pandhari. And as he listened to the enthusiastic rendering of the *kirtans,* he experienced the joy of love. 21. Thus the service of the saints, acts of benevolence, and his many bare-footed pilgrimages to Pandhari, formed the physical penance of this noble Vaishnava.

22. His religious activities [*tap*], as related to Speech, were as follows. In all his talking he never spoke an untruth. He was repeating God's names day and night, without the least cessation.

23. Now as to his mental activities, his heart was fixed on the feet of Pandurang. He was just like the *chatak* bird, that will not drink any water except such as comes directly from a cloud. 24. Or as when an infant child is crying, who but its mother can pacify it? So Tuka's determination was to worship the King-of-Pandhari.

25. Hearing the above, some pious listeners, may feel a doubt in their minds, namely, if Tuka had no other thought aside from Pandurang, then why did he worship men, through his acts of benevolence? Listen to the answer of this question.

26. All the animate and inanimate creation functions through the power of the One, Shri Hari [God]. Now Tuka, in order to respect His wish, was accustomed to bow in reverence before every creature. 27. Just as a dutiful wife, living at her mother-in-law's and loving her husband, mindful of her husband's feelings, tries to please all of her husband's household. 28. The father-in-law, the mother-in-law, her husband's sister, and her husband's brother may speak to her in many rough words, still she works hard for them, knowing that that is the wish of her husband. 29. And yet all the while she has no love for any of them except for the lord-of-her-life. So Tuka's heart was fixed, and in love was lost in Pandurang. 30. There are those Seekers who, instead of worshipping one deity, give themselves to a variety of deities, but they fail to get a direct manifestation of God. One who seeks to be the guest of a great many, ends in starving. 31. But Tuka's heart was not of that kind. In the three departments of Religious activities, Work, Worship and Philosophical knowledge, he was an expert, and he showed it to men by the way he lived. 32. His physical religious activities belong to the Karmakand [System of Works]. By his speech activities, by his worship he sang of God's goodness. Aside from Pandurang he knew nothing. He did not possess perfect self-soul-knowledge. 33. These three religious austerities, as ornaments, were worn by Tuka, and added to his life those good and holy deeds as would test God.

God Inspires Tuka to Become a Poet.

34. Recognizing the above characteristics of Tuka, Shri Krishna thought to himself, "I must give to Tuka poetic inspiration, so that he may sing my praises." 35. So then taking Namdev by the hand, the Lord-of-Pandhari came to Dehu. And while Tuka was asleep at night the Soul-of-the-Universe appeared to him in a vision. 36. The Supreme-Universal-Being patted Tuka on his back with His hand, and said to him, "Tuka, arise quickly, and listen to what I am going to tell you. 37. This Nama is my perfect *bhakta*. Long ago he made a vow that he would compose a billion verses in Marathi. Such was the number in his vow. 38. I gave him poetic inspiration, and he wrote with his own hands his verses. The number of his verses has been counted, and I will tell you the number. 39. Nine hundred and forty-four million, nine hundred thousand brought his verses to an end. The balance in the form of love remained in his heart, and then by his own wish he came to Heaven. 40. Fifty-five million remain to be composed to complete his vow. These, in words that mean blessings, I want you to compose. I will give you the poetic gift with the fervour of love. 41. Truly, through you many will be saved. Now do not waste words in what is of no value, and begin at once to compose your verses." 42. After giving Tuka this vision, God vanished out of sight. And the Vaishnava Tuka, when he awoke, said to himself, "God has shown me a perfectly wonderful thing. 43. In my dream I saw God and his *bhakta* together. My mind recollects all the details of that vision. Krishna has given me the reward [uchit] of His love, and gone away."

Tuka Becomes a Poet.

44. Tuka's easily satisfied mind loved the portions of the saints' words, which he had committed to memory. But now the Life-of-the-World had given him the command to speak those words of blessing. 45. The kind of joy that Tuka's heart felt was such as when at night, when wishing for the light of a lamp, suddenly the sun should rise, 46, or, as when hunting in the jungle for a medicinal vine, one should suddenly see ly the sun should rise, 46. or, as when hunting in a kingdom, when suddenly he was given to sit in his fixed position [of the North Pole], 47. or, like Upamanyu, the Brahman's son, who asked for a cupful of milk, and the Husband-of-Lakshmi being pleased with him, placed him by the Ocean-of-Milk. 48. So Tuka, in that same way rejoiced. Saraswati [Goddess of Speech] sat on his tongue. And with a heart of love, he began to compose verses that showed his love. 49. He had never had any practice in writing the Balbodh script, so he made a book of blank paper, and wrote in it as he felt inclined. 50. The cream of the *Vedas* and *Shastras*, Vyasa has taken it out in the form of the Shri Bhagavata. And in the tenth chapter of the Bhagavata there is described the nectar of Hari's deeds, as the Soul-of-the-Universe played in the homes of the cowherds. 51. Those infant deeds of Krishna, Tuka took as the first subject of his verses. There were nine hundred verses on this theme. Saints and *Sadhus* know of this from personal experience. 52. In his *kirtans*, if he did not have a particular story in his memory, then the noble Vaishnava would compose extempore *abhangs* in quick succession. 53. As his audience listened to his gracious verses, they marvelled. In his *kirtans* the enthu-

siasm was quadrupled, because his words were words of blessing. 54. Just as when after a cloud has poured down its rain, countless tender shoots of grass spring up, or, as when innumerable waves appear on the ocean, which no one can count. 55. So was it in Tuka's *kirtans* when inspired to utter his flow of words. No one now felt any doubts about him. Even the wicked became pious. 56. Tuka was accustomed to hold a *kirtan* regularly until midnight in the temple of Pandurang, and the pious *bhaktas* of the neighbouring villages used to come at that hour to listen. 57. On the eleventh of every fortnight a watchnight service in honour of Hari was held, all the night through. The fame of these *kirtans* began to spread far and wide, and they became exceedingly popular.

Mambaji's Envy Develops into Opposition.

58. It happened at this time that a Brahman by name of Mambaji Bava, had been living for a time at Chinchwad. This great man becoming a *gosavi* [religious mendicant] came to live at Dehu. 59. He built a house for himself, and brought all his family there. He had a small following of disciples, and they cared also for his maintenance. 60. As Tuka's reputation increased, hatred sprang up in the heart of Mambaji. Said he to himself, "How can two swords be contained in one sheath? 61. In our very presence Tuka committed to memory verses from books. Since then his reputation has greatly increased, and even Brahmans bow down to him. 62. Tuka is merely a *Vani* by caste, and I am in this town the highly honoured head of the *sannyasis*. If his fame continues to spread among the people, no one will pay attention to me." 63. Just as when one relates the state of those without desire, those

with desires flare up with anger. Or, just as the (Brahman) astrologers in their hatred despise followers of the astrologer Sahadev, (because he was a Shudra). 64. The planet Ketu says to itself, "The moment I meet the sun I shall throw it into my mouth." Or, as when the planet Rahu sees the full moon it is stirred to anger. 65. Just so Mambaji truly hated Tuka, and said to himself, "I shall some time humiliate Tuka, and thus get my revenge." 66. Although he carried this anger in his heart, yet to preserve his reputation he used to come and sit in the *kirtans*. But Tuka regarded enemy and friend alike. 67. Behind the temple, and to the south Mambaji had planted some trees. His mind was often on them and he erected a fence about them for their protection.

Avali's Buffalo Makes Trouble for Tuka.

68. Apaji Gulavya was the father of Avali, wife of Tuka. Because of his love for his daughter he gave her a she-buffalo. 69. When she was let loose to go to the river to drink, she forced her way into Mambaji's garden. She rubbed against the fence, and got inside, and ate up many of his plants. 70. When he saw this he was greatly excited. He used every kind of abusive language, and then quieted down. 71. After some days had passed, the eleventh day arrived, called the Hari-day. And as the sun set people assembled for worshipping God. 72. In the path around the temple used for circumambulating, Mambaji had put up thorny sticks as a fence. Tuka pulled them up with his hands in order to keep the path open. 73. When that hypocrite saw this, his anger was kindled like fire. To begin with, he hated Tuka, and now this act of Tuka's added fuel to the flame. 74.

Just as when a great serpent is ready to spring, and when on its tail some one steps, it springs forward with violent hissing to take the life of the man. 75. So this Brahman, using all kinds of abusive language, took a stick in his hand, and came upon Tuka. 76. And with anger he began to beat the kindly Tuka. But he with forgiveness, and peace in his heart, answered him not a word. 77. With every angry stroke the stick flew into bits. So Mambaji had to pull up still other sticks to strike with. No pity arose in his heart. 78. Thus in this angry beating he broke ten or twenty sticks. But the noble Vaishnava did not move away from that spot, but continued his loud repeating of God's names with love. 79. In attempting to describe this forgiving spirit of Tuka's no one in the world appears as his equal. In trying to think of some comparison that would illustrate it, none suggests itself, and the poet's imagination is confounded. 80. A merciless man has no tenderness for a creature. How can a meat eater feel a sense of sympathy? So this man appeared a Brahman as to his body, but one should entitle him as an Unmentionable [outcaste]. 81. Just as a farmer thrashes out the grain, so he thrashed the Vaishnava *bhakta.* Only when his hand grew weary did he stop. 82. When that evil man went into his house Tuka went into the temple, and there he told the Husband-of-Rukmini that He had caused him to be soundly beaten by Mambaji, 83. who used abusive words without limit. "And all this is Thy doing. But I do not want association with the wicked. It confuses my heart." 84. And Tuka composed an *abhang* on this theme and recited it. People came there to look at his body pierced with thorns. 85. And the eyes of those, in whose true hearts there was compassion, and who noticed the sad condition of Tuka, were filled with tears and they exclaimed,

"Mambaji has tortured this God-loving *bhakta.*" 86. Avali then took pincers in her hand and pulled out the thorns from her husband, saying, "That Black-One has shown His enmity well, and spoiled all our domestic life." 87. The Lord-of-Pandhari looked with compassion towards Tuka, and the wounds from the thorns were soon healed, and his bodily pain was relieved.

Tuka Returns Good for Evil.

88. On the eleventh day of every fortnight, at the watch-night service in honour of Hari, a very large audience had assembled. When all were seated for the *kirtan,* the noble Vaishnava said, 89. "The great man Mambaji comes to these *kirtans* without fail. What has delayed him to-day?" Tuka then sent some one to invite him. 90. He sent a reply to Tuka that his body was in great pain. As soon as the noble Vaishnava heard this, he at once went to him. 91. Tuka made Mambaji a prostrate bow, and then began to rub his body. Said he, "In beating me with thorny sticks, my Master has become tired. 92. If I had not injured your plants, I should not have merited your displeasure. Forgive me the wrong I did you, and come at once to the *kirtan.*" 93. Thus speaking to Mambaji, Tuka continued for a while sitting by him rubbing his body. Mambaji now felt ashamed of himself, and at once came to the *kirtan.*

Mambaji is Still Envious at Heart.

94. Just as the ocean encloses the internal fire, and water surrounds it on every side, yet it is not put out in the very least, and says to itself, "I will dry up the whole ocean." 95. Just so was Tuka an ocean of patience. Mambaji was to him the internal fire, looking very cool on

the outside, but within raging with hatred. 96. Saints have done wonderful things but the wicked do not have pure hearts. There are many illustrations of this. I ask you, wise ones, to listen to them.

97. In taking the side of the Pandavs, God manifested himself in many wonderful deeds, but the deceitful heart of Duryodhan would not change. 98. A critic sits listening to a *kirtan,* but his mind is wholly taken up in thinking of both its faults and good points. Or if one looks at the pious attitude of the crane, what good deeds does one see there? 99. If a serpent does not eat food, does any one think it is observing the fast day of the eleventh? If the mind is not pure, it is unable to acquire the means of becoming pure. 100. A stone cannot speak to any one. Does that mean that it is to be considered a *Yogi?* A donkey rolls in ashes, but repentance does not come to its heart. 101. A rat sits in its hole, but it is always digging in. So the critic, although he sits listening to a *kirtan,* yet his heart does not melt (with emotion).

The Theme of Tuka's Kirtans.

102. Tuka's impartiality was such that enemy and friend were alike to him. He never had envious feelings in his heart, and performed his *kirtans* with feelings of love. 103. His mind was fixed on the Name and Form of God, and therefore, he became a *Videhi* [one unconscious of his body]. The saints who sat listening to his *kirtans,* also became filled with love.

104. "O Krishna, Vishnu, Hari, Govinda, Achyuta, Madhava, Root-of-Joy, Supreme-Being, Satchidananda, free us from the bonds of this worldly existence. 105. O

Protector-of-the-Helpless, Pandurang, Father-of-Cupid, The Delight-of-Rukmini, so do that the mud of evil deeds may not plaster me, O Shri Krishna. 106. My soul wanders in the whirl of Time, impelled by its *karma.* Quickly free it from this, O Husband-of-Rukmini, Shri Vitthal."

107. Thus pleading for mercy, Tuka danced in his *kirtans* in the enthusiasm of his love. The cymbal and *Vina* sounded their sweet tones, and the air was filled with the sound. 108. There was clapping of hands, and the rapid snapping of fingers. No one felt sleepy or weary. In the *kirtans* all the listeners became unconscious of their bodies, a most remarkable fact. 109. Tuka took up the extremely interesting lives of the saints as his theme; and the pious people listened, and their hearts became attracted by it.

Thieves Steal Avali's Buffalo, but Repent.

110. While Tuka was performing his *kirtan,* his wife was asleep in her house. Two thieves came there, and listen to what they did. 111. They untied the milch buffalo that was tied in the house, and took it away. One of the thieves led her in front, the other drove her from behind. 112. To the west of the town of Dehu there was a hamlet half a mile away, called Bodke's hamlet. When the thieves had gone as far as that hamlet, God heard of it. 113. He said to Himself, "Tuka is absorbed in his *kirtan,* and Avali is asleep in her house. The thieves are taking away her buffalo. I must free her from the thieves and get her back. 114. If I do not go on this occasion, Avali in many ways will make Tuka miserable. So saying, the Advocate-of-His-*bhaktas,* did a strange thing. 115.

Krishna assumed easily the form of a most fierce looking man. He had a club in his hand, and he came upon the thieves to beat them. 116. In attempting to go forward in the path, lo! the fierce looking man was there, with the great club in his hand, and ready to bring it down on their heads. 117. They said to one another, "Who can this man be in our path? We don't know. He looks like a great demon. What are we to do? 118. (In this buffalo) we had put our hands on an unexpected gain, but it is not in our Fate to keep it. The doings of Fate are curious. Who knows what is laid up in our destiny?" 119. Thus saying, they started in haste to take another path, but there also Krishna stood with his club. 120. They were now terribly frightened, and said to themselves, "What shall we do?" They looked in the other eight directions, but lo! they saw Krishna all about them. 121. Said they, "This great monstrous demon comes right in our way. This Brahman-monster, or demon has come to take our lives. 122. It is already dawn. The sun will soon rise, and then anyone may seize us. Now what shall we do?" Their minds were puzzled. 123. Then they thought to themselves, "Tuka calls himself a *bhakta* of Vithoba. We are taking away his buffalo. It is because of that that this demon stands before us. 124. One does not know God's mysterious and extraordinary doings. It is quite true that we have done wrong. We must go back now, and tie the buffalo where she was tied before. Then only we shall escape punishment." 125. After this discussion the thieves turned to go back to the town. The Husband-of-Rukmini followed them, holding the club in His hand. 126. The thieves were still much frightened. "Will he suddenly strike us from behind?" was their thought. Thus threatened by the demon, they re-entered the town. 127. They went into Tuka's *wadi,* and tied the buffalo just where she had been tied before. They started in great haste to leave the town, but there before them stood the Lord-of-the-Universe, 128. with His terrifying fierce form, and the club in his hand. The thieves tried other paths, but there right before them stood the Lord-of-Heaven. 129. They tried to find some narrow passage in the town, through which they might pass, but that demon monster was everywhere. There was no place without him. 130. The thieves now became terribly frightened. Then they said to themselves, "Tuka is performing a *kirtan.* Let us go there, and tell him what has happened." 131. Thus deciding, they came into the *kirtan.* Without hesitation or fear, they spoke courteously to Tuka. 132. They joined the palms of their hands together, and stood before Tuka. They said, "Both of us are thieves. We have done a great wrong. 133. We loosened your buffalo, and were taking her away. But suddenly directly in the way we saw a monstrous demon. 134. He had a club in his hand, and whichever way we turned to go there he stood before us. So we at once brought back your buffalo, and tied her again in your house. 135. We immediately after attempted to run away, but behold! the demon was sitting at the town gate. Whichever way we took, there he was. What remedy is there for this? 136. You are a *bhakta* of Vishnu, with absolutely no hate for any one. Enemy or friend are alike to you. So now Your Greatness must devise some way by which we shall be free from this demon." 137. This plea of the thieves was heard by all the assembled people. And as they listened to this most unusual event they marvelled. 138. Tuka also was surprised and attempted to bring the image of Pandurang before his mind; but lo! and behold! the Husband-of-Rukmini was not in the *kirtan*. And Tuka exclaimed, "The thieves are telling the truth." 139. Tuka then closed his eyes and called on Pandurang to come to his help, "O Lord-of-Pandhari, God Supreme, when didst Thou go from here? 140. While we were carrying on a Hari watch-night service Thou wert wandering hither and thither in the wilds. From the very beginning Thou hast acquired the habit of tending cattle. 141. Where we with true hearts sing Thy praises, there Thy heart had no interest, but taking a hideous form, Thou didst manifest Thyself to these thieves. 142. It is now nearly dawn. At least come in time for the concluding hymns of praise, O Ocean-of-Mercy, Recliner-on-the-Serpent [Vishnu]. This is the right thing for Thee to do. 143. Evidently Thou didst not like our themes though uttered with love, Thou didst hastily get up, and run away. And taking a big stick ran after the thieves. 144. If Thou wert not the close friend of Thy loving *bhakta* there would have been no enthusiasm in the *kirtan*." And now the God-of-Gods, Hari, hearing the call of Tuka, came. 145. As Tuka was dancing in the *kirtan* the Lord-of-Pandhari came from behind with the club in his hand, while all the people around saw him. 146. To the thieves He still looked ferocious and monstrous, but to the other people he appeared in His ordinary form. Tuka then said to the thieves, "Arise, and go your way. 147. If you need the buffalo, untie her and take her away at once." The thieves replied, "Our lives have been saved. That is your gift to us." 148. With these remarks the thieves at once ran away. But because they had experienced this most extraordinary event, they went along shouting aloud the names of God.

Mahipati Suggests the Use of Evil Men.

149. Mambaji saw and heard of the incident, and he was astonished. He said to himself, "Tuka's reputation will increase among men. It is quite evident." 150. With this thought in his mind he continued sitting in his seat muttering to himself. A man with a hateful heart cannot know the glory of a *bhakta* of Vishnu.

151. The story of this impious man is very often re-duplicated through the use of other illustrations. The Goddess of Speech must needlessly be wearied, and listeners will not endure its tiresomeness. 152. By the creation of impious men on the earth, the glory of the *bhaktas* increases. If false coins had never been made, then who would speak of true coins. 153. If the city of Yama [Hell] had never been built, then who would have desired Heaven? If there was no such thing as the eight million four hundred thousand rebirths, who would have cared to acquire Deliverance-from-rebirths? 154. If there were truly no such thing as death for the body, then who would pay attention to nectar [non-death]. So, because of the impious, the *bhaktas* have become widely known. 155. If it were not for the intense darkness of the night, how would the lights in the sky sparkle? It was because of Ravan, that Shri Ram attained his esteemed name. 156. Well, enough of these illustrations. If the thieves had not stolen the buffalo, then, how could the Pervader-of-the-Universe have exhibited the special traits of his saints?

Tuka's Theme, God's Presence with His Saints.

157. The Vaishnava Tuka at this time, sang of God's many deeds, and how Shri Hari answered the call of His *bhaktas.* Listen to how He did so. 158. Because Hiranyakashipu would not listen to words in praise of Vishnu, his

heart was filled with anger (against his son Pralhad). But hearing the call of Pralhad, God manifested Himself in the pillar. 159. In His *bhakta's* suffering His own renown is increased. Because Duryodhan treated Draupadi badly, His fame became more widely spread. 160. Shri Krishna could not endure that His *bhaktas* should suffer loss, and so, He rushed to her aid. He provided her with an unlimited number of garments, and shamed all the evil men. 161. In order to care for His holy saints, and to establish righteousness, without thinking of time or season, Vishnu, dark as a cloud, descended as an *avatar*. 162. It seems to me that Kali Yuga is especially famous for this, that it brings out the extraordinary glory of God. For the sake of His *bhaktas*, the Husband-of-Rukmini has borne many sufferings.

163. Sanvata Mali was a God-loving *bhakta*. Krishna went to him and asked for a place in which to hide. He immediately (took a knife) and ripped his body open. 164. He (so infinite), that the whole universe can be contained in the pores of his skin, even he, was able to be contained in his *bhakta's* heart. And there the Supreme-Being of the Universe lovingly talked with Sanvata on the mysteries (of life). 165. Suddenly Nama appeared weeping, and found that Sanvata had swallowed the Husband-of-Rukmini, but the fringe of His yellow garment was visible, which Nama seized with his hand and drew Krishna out. 166. He thus came out of the body of Sanvata, and so is the own child of Sanvata. Such were the love attracting stories that Tuka related in his singing. 167. The Vaishnava *bhakta* told his hearers that our earthly life was temporary, so that he, who becomes absorbed in the worship of God [Shri Hari], will be one bearing His mark in this Kali Yuga.

168. Thus, preaching in the course of his *kirtan,* the sun began to rise. And then with shouts of Victory! Victory! and clapping of hands, the audience, with loud voice, repeated the names of Vitthal. 169. Then lighting the lights for the wave-offering, they waved them before the Husband-of-Rukmini.

In the next chapter will be found what will arouse interest. Therefore, you hearers, listen with reverence. 170. The real relator of the substance of the nectar of the Bhaktalilamrita is the glorious Husband-of-Rukmini. Mahipati is merely his instrument as you all, wise and knowing, understand.

171. Svasti! This book, the Shri Bhaktalilamrita, supplies all the heart's desires by merely listening to it. Let the God-loving pious *bhaktas* listen. This is the thirty-second interesting chapter.

CHAPTER 33.

Preface to the Thirty-third Chapter.

Obeisance to Shri Ganesh.

1. Victory, Victory! to the Ocean-of-Compassion, The Supreme-Being-of-the-Universe. When Thou lookest on Thy *bhaktas* with the look of mercy, they at once break friendship with their worldly affairs, and Thou dost break the net that binds them to this earthly life. 2. If Thou shouldst give to any *bhakta,* a wife who was all goodness, his love would bind him to her. So Thou dost

give him as his companion a cantankerous wife. 3. If Thou givest to a *bhakta* a noble son, he may thereby get entangled in worldly affairs through his love for him. Therefore, Thou dost bring about a quarrel between father and son. 4. If Thou gavest much money or property to a *bhakta,* he would then engage in the joy of worldly things. Therefore, lest he should be neglectful in his worship, Thou dost give him only a very little of food and clothing. 5. I understand well Thy compassion. Thou removest all false conceptions from those, on whom Thou lookest with mercy. 6. Thou dost place in the wicked a continued misunderstanding, and thus through them Thou dost bring suffering to Thy *bhaktas.* And then, O Husband-of-Rukmini, Thou dost (come to their relief) by Thy many manifestations of help. 7. In the "Thousand Names of Vishnu" Dvaipayana has included Thy name as Causer-of-Fear and Destroyer-of-Fear. I see that this is true. 8. Thus Thou hast all the power, and pullest the string of fate. And so making me Thy instrument, Thou dost speak through me, though with uncouth, foolish words.

The Image of Vithoba Drinks Milk.

9. In the last chapter there was the interesting story of how thieves stole the buffalo, and how Krishna secured her release, and how He displayed to the people what was wonderful. 10. How the time of the Hari-day and its elaborate ceremonies were carried on, and how the watch-night service lasted until the fourth watch in the morning, and finally how the lights were waved before the Husband-of-Rukmini. Now we turn to what the noble Vaishnava did further.

11. Tuka went very early in the morning for his bath in the Indrayani. And then with his usual expressions of love worshipped Pandurang.

12. In the mean time all the people told Avali that her buffalo had been stolen during the night, but that Vithoba had performed a miracle, and had the buffalo returned. 13. Avali was overcome with amazement when she heard of this wonderful incident, and she seated Tuka for his breakfast, feeling full of joy. 14. She had boiled some rice, made some bread, and as a third course she served him with greens. She then brought him a cup of milk. But at this the servant of Vishnu wondered. 15. Tuka said to Avali, "If purifying your heart, you will give me a *tambyaful* (a copper or brass vessel) of milk, I will immediately go, and give it to God to drink." 16. Avali cleaned the brass vessel with her own hand, filled it with milk, and gave it to Tuka. The God-loving *bhakta* went to the temple, and gave it to the idol to drink. 17. It appears to people as a stone image, yet Tuka regularly fed it with milk. He who is not subject to Brahmadev or the other gods, yet becomes subject to one of a pious heart.

18. As many days thus passed, Avali began to have some serious doubts. Said she, "He daily takes a *tambyaful* of milk. I don't understand what it means. 19. With a house full of children all eager to eat, how can I have enough milk to prepare curds? How can I carry on my domestic affairs? I can only make the very least bit of butter." 20. Their youngest daughter, Bhagirthi, went regularly (with her father) to the temple. So Jijai asked her in private, gently caressing her in her love. 21. Said she, "Your father asks me for milk and takes it to the temple. Tell me truly whether the Black-One drinks the milk."

22. Bhagirthi replied, "It is true that the idol does drink the milk. What is left over father drinks, but he gives me just a little." 23. Hearing these words from her child, Avali thought over the matter with amazement. Then on a certain day Avali said to Tuka, "I am going to take the milk to-day to feed the idol." 24. "I am willing," said the God-loving *bhakta,* and Avali went to the temple. This put Pandharinath in perplexity. Said He, "What shall I do? 25. If I should drink the milk, well, but her feelings towards me are not those of love. But if I do not show her some miracle, she will make Tuka suffer at home." 26. Thus thinking, the Husband-of-Rukmini, remained perfectly quiet. He was very much afraid of Avali, because she was always opposed to him. 27. So the Lord-of-Pandhari was perplexed. The question was, to drink the milk, or not to drink it. It was for his *bhakta* that he assumed a *sagun* form, otherwise, as Soul-of-the-Universe, he was without qualities. 28. I very much wonder that the God Shiva could not make Him his own. That (the God Vishnu), the Lord of Gods, inhabitant of the ocean of milk, wanted to taste the milk which Tuka had brought. 29. It seems as strange as to think of darkness confining the sun; or, for the moon-stone to shiver with cold; or, for Death to feel fear hearing that a ghost was coming; 30. or, for a tornado to be confined in a cage; or for the heavens to get caught in an earthen jar, or, for the light of the planets to dim the sun. All this seems impossible. 31. The Eternal, the Unchangeable, the image of the Supreme-Brahma, whom the *yogis* contemplate in their hearts, even He, became perplexed in His mind, because of the power of *bhakti* when accompained with love. 32. As I have said, Avali came to the temple with her *tambya* full of milk. In her heart, however, there was neither love, nor

reverence. So how could her heart be pure? 33. The milk was very hot. That she ought to wait for a moment until it was cool, did not enter Avali's thought, because she considered Him her enemy. 34. She said to herself, "He has made the lord of our home a crazy fellow, given up to His worship." While she was thus thinking harshly of Him, what did Krishna do? 35. As the hot vessel was put to his lips, it burnt the lips of the Supreme-Being-of-the-Universe. It made Him turn His neck and eyes to one side. And Avali was astonished. 36. Said she, "To my eye he appears a black stone, but it has life in it. It is not false then that the lord of our home daily feeds Him with milk." 37. Avali gazed closely at Him with wonder. Her looking at the God had no special purpose, but suddenly she noticed a swelling on His lips. Said she, "This seems remarkably curious to me." 38. After witnessing this miracle, Jijabai, returned home. In the meanwhile, the Recliner-on-the-Serpent [Vishnu] came into Tuka's contemplation, and said to him, 39. "You were lazy, and sent the milk by the hand of Avali. And she put the hot vessel to my lips, without thinking of the consequences. 40. Because you have cast the worldly life aside, she continues her enmity against me. She has given me the name of Enemy. She has no affection for me whatever." 41. Tuka was overcome by what Krishna said to him, and he said to his wife, "How is it that you fed the God with hot milk?" 42. Avali replied, "In your daily songs in the temple, you are always singing of how your Krishna, living among the cowherds, swallowed the fire that broke out in twelve villages. 43. And because my milk was slightly hot, He turned his head to one side, and a swelling appeared on his lips. Go to the temple, and see for yourself. 44. If the stories of those ancient deeds are true, then how comes it that his lips got burned in drinking the milk?" Hearing Avali talk thus, Tuka was overcome with emotion. 45. He ran as fast as he could to the temple and looked at the image; and sure enough! The Lord of Pandhari's neck was turned and a swelling was noticeable on his lips. 46. Tuka's heart was so full of love that his eyes filled with tears, just as a mother's heart is overcome when she sees her infant child scorched by fire. 47. So the God-loving Tuka with throat choked by sobs exclaimed, "O King of Pandhari, Friend of the helpless, Guru of the Universe, Thou hast been scalded." 48. But as Tuka sang God's praises, the swelling went down, but his neck still turned to one side, and all can see it so to-day. 49. For the future the Husband-of-Rukmini planned for witnesses to His miracles. In this way the Merciful-One increased the good renown of his servants.

Tuka Attacked by Mosquitoes.

50. Once upon a time Tuka was walking alone in the Chakan jungle. Suddenly a swarm of innumerable mosquitoes attacked his body. 51. As he looked at them, he paid not the least regard to the pain. Said he, "One's body should be used in doing good to others." And with this he continued sitting quietly. 52. "If I care for my own body, I shall be giving pain to all these little creatures. This temporary body of mine must soon pass away. I fully recognize this as I repent (of my former worldly life)." 53. As the mosquitoes continued to sting him on all sides, he was in great bodily torture. But he paid no attention to the pain, and continued his worship with love. 54. Just then, assuming the form of a wayfarer, the Husband-of-Rukmini arrived on the scene with a date

branch in his hand, because of the attacking mosquitoes. 55. Other wayfarers had come, and had seen Tuka, but because of concern for their own lives, no one cared to drive the mosquitoes from Tuka. 56. No one except a mother feels compassion for her infant child. So the pitying Mother Vitthal came at once to the aid of Tuka. 57. With His own hands Shri Krishna drove away the mosquitoes, and gently rubbed his body, so that it was relieved from pain, and Tuka then continued on his way. 58. As the sun was setting Tuka arrived at his village of Dehu. He immediately went to the temple, and there looked upon the Husband-of-Rukmini. 59. Just as when a staff falls to the ground, and knows not how to rise, so Tuka fell prostrate on the ground as his gesture of love. 60. The moment it was night he began his *kirtan,* in which he sang, "Victory! O Purifier-of-the-Sinner, Shri Hari. Save me in this ocean-of-worldly-life. 61. It matters not, whether I have food, or not. It matters not, if my descendants do not increase. What I want is Thy favour. I have no other thought. 62. It matters not, if my body suffers abuse. Let there be disasters in my worldly life, but I long for Thy favour in my heart. I want nothing else, O Shri Krishna. 63. And just as my voice preaches to myself by my own lips, so will I preach to others, and show them the right path." 64. Thus singing, the Vaishnava *bhakta* continued his worship with feelings of love. In singing the names of Ram and Krishna he made the people listen. 65. The *kirtan* continued until the third watch of the night, and then were lighted the lights for the wave-offering. The Husband-of-Rukmini had the lights waved before Him, and all fell prostrate on the ground in their love. 66. After all the good people, the listeners, had gone to their homes, Tuka assumed his usual posture, and fixing his mind on God's name and form, continued his worship with love..

God Cures Tuka's Son.

67. Some days passed, and then a very interesting incident took place. Tuka had two sons. Their names were as follows. 68. The elder son was named Mahadev, and the younger son was named Vithoba. The elder son had a very painful disease. 69. He was suffering from a stone in the bladder, and often fainted away from pain. Avali used many remedies. 70. Whatever remedy any one suggested, somehow or other she procured it. She got them to prepare food especially adapted to the sick. In her love she wore herself out day and night. 71. She employed many physicians and herbs-sellers, but the boy was not any better. She procured the ashes connected with offerings to the family deities, and applied them. 72. She continually went to the house of exorcisers who remove evil spirits. They told her, "It was a trouble caused by demons. Accept our word as truth." 73. They tied around the boy's neck a cord, made effective by *mantras*. Out of her excessive love for the child, she waved food over him. 74. Thus she used many remedies, but the boy was not in the least better. Avali was greatly troubled, and said to herself, "What shall I do now? 75. The illness is attacking him very severely. He eats nothing at all." And Avali's heart was full of anxiety. "I do not expect any good result," she said. 76. "My husband has become crazy after God, and such is the condition of my child. I have no confidence that he will live." And with this she sighed. 77. In passing water the boy suffered agony all through his body. This so depressed Tuka that he would go off alone to get relief.

78. At the place for getting water, she told the women her difficulties, "My child is lying suffering pain, what effort shall I make? 79. I have been to many gods and shrines. There is no counting the medicines I have used. By day and night I have used the ashes of the offerings. My heart is very disturbed. 80. I have made my boy's mouth a pipe, and poured down it all kinds of medicines. But day by day the pain in his body is increasing. 81. My husband has become crazy after God. He has given up all worldly things, and all desires. My mind is in great perplexity. I cannot think what next to do." 82. The neighbours, hearing her story, came, some of them to her house, to see the boy. When they saw the boy they spoke discouragingly. 83. As they looked at the boy they saw his arms and legs as if they were sticks. Said they to her, "Why do you weary yourself in vain in giving him medicines? 84. Your husband holds the Husband-of-Rukmini in his heart, hence all kinds of difficulties arise in his domestic life. 85. While worshipping Shri Hari, his first wife died. In keeping the Lord-of-Pandhari in his heart, a worse time has come." 86. Hearing these words of her neighbours, Avali's heart flared up in flames of anger. If one were to feed intoxicating liquor to a monkey, and then have him stung by a scorpion, 87. who can tell what sort of antics that monkey would play? But that was what happened to Avali. She gnashed her teeth. 88. To begin with, she was a God-hater, and these neighbours aided her wrath. It was like that evil-minded Shakuni, who whispered evil things to Duryodhan. 89. Hiranyakashipu gave his aid to Hiranyaksha, the two becoming friends, and insulting the Lord-of-Heaven. 90. Or, like the Vishnu-hater Ravan, whom Kumbhakarna aided. His mind turned to evil (as a result he kidnapped Sita). 91. Or, like Tatika,

the she-demon, who harboured in her heart hatred against Shri Ram. She was met in the forest by Shurpanakha, that evil minded one, and she whispered evil things into her ear. 92. Just so Jijabai harboured anger against God, and now all her neighbours began saying to her, that she should not give her devotion any longer to Vithoba. 93. That it was since they had begun to worship Him, that their domestic affairs had met with disaster. And now her boy's illness had become excessive, and he could not possibly lie. 94. After saying these things to Avali, her neighbours returned to their homes. And as Avali looked at her son her mind was troubled.

95. When evening came he was now suffering from a complete stoppage. His abdomen was swollen, and as stiff as a drum. He could no longer move hand or foot. 96. His mother spoke to him, but he gave no answer. His hands and feet were cold. Avali remarked, "This does not look well, what shall I do now? 97. Surely, the boy is dying. He will not escape this time, that is sure. So I will go to the temple at once, and dash my boy on that Black-one's feet. 98. It is He who has spoiled our domestic life, by setting my husband to meditation, and now He has determined on the death of my boy. So, I will dash my boy on His feet. 99. Whatever is to be, cannot possibly be avoided, but I am going to put the responsibility on Him." So saying Avali dragged Mahadev along by her hand. 100. She dragged him rather roughly, and took the path to the temple. In one hand she carried a shoe. "I will take vengeance on the God," she said. 101. So saying, Jijabai arrived at the temple. When the Recliner-on-the-Serpent [Vishnu] perceived this, He was perplexed. 102. The Husband-of-Rukmini thought to Himself, "What plan

shall I adopt? If Avali beats me with a shoe, I shall lose my reputation among men." 103. So thinking to Himself, He looked at Rukmini's face, and asked her for a remedy to avert the evil.

104. When Adimaya, the shadow of the Supreme-Brahma, heard him say this, she said to Him, "O Lord-of-Pandhari, why are you troubled? 105. It is by Thy will alone that this infinite universe is created and destroyed. It would be a vain thing for the sun to be troubled about giving light to the earth. 106. If rain ceases to fall, and water can nowhere be obtained, why should this give concern to the ocean? O helper-of-the-Helpless, Shri Vitthal. 107. When in the hot season the heat is intense, one needs a fan. But why does the moon have to worry about the heat? Think of all this. 108. Those to whom Thou lookest with favor, even if it were a stone, a marble or a pebble, it would become a true *paris* [touch stone]. 109. Thy servant has such power that he can raise the dead to life." Such were Rukmini's words to him, and then she remained silent.

110. In the mean time Avali, roughly dragging her boy along, brought him to the temple. Said she, "I will dash my boy on the God's feet, and then I will slap Him with a shoe." 111. With this determination in her mind, she came in front of the God. She lifted her boy up to dash him on the god's feet, when suddenly Rukmini spoke to her. 112. There was no one else in the temple, and a voice came from behind the image. It said, "I have now made him well. Go back to your home." 113. Avali was astonished. Said she, "Can a stone image speak?" Then she looked at her boy, and behold! he was made well. 114. Avali now took up her boy, and brought him outside

the temple, his physical functions showing that he had fully recovered. 115. The various disorders of his body had now left him, and the first thing he said to his mother was, "Mother, I am hungry." 116. Avali was astonished, and said to herself, "The Husband-of-Rukmini was evidently afraid of me, and that is why He has made the boy well." So thinking, she returned to her home. 117. The boy became very hungry, and Avali gave him food. When Tuka heard of the event, he said, "We have given the Lord-of-Pandhari trouble. 118. The boy was suffering pain. Suddenly he became well. One does not understand the doings of God. He alone understands His ways of wisdom." 119. The Vaishnava *bhakta* then had his meal, and immediately went to the temple. When it was the fourth watch of the night he began the performance of his *kirtan*.

Tuka's Musical Assistants.

120. When the Vaishnava *bhakta* performed his *kirtans*, the following led in the chorus. Listen to their names, for through them love was doubled. 121. There was Gangadhar Maval, a Brahman, who had been living in Kadus. He became Tuka's constant amanuensis, and wrote down his blessed words. 122. The second was Santaji Teli, whose family name was Jaganade. He lived a long time at Chakan, but now was a disciple of Tuka's. 123. These two were sincere disciples of the Vaishnava *bhakta*. They gave up every desire for things of this life, and with their own hands wrote down Tuka's poems. 124. In the daily *kirtans* they followed Tuka, in leading the chorus. By it the enthusiasm became intense, and with love to God they danced. 125. They had cast aside all wrong desires, and held to this good association with Tuka.

They led the chorus, and developed the expressions of love. 126. Just as a charioteer drives the chariot according to the inclination of the traveller, or, as when a dutiful wife falls in with the wishes of her husband for enjoyment. 127. Or, like the king's attendant who gives him his *vida* [*pan supari*], he will wear out his own body in the service of the king, but he will not speak of his obligation, for he has to gain his object. 128. So these two men, the Brahman Gangaji Maval, and the other Santaji Teli, followed Tuka soul and body. 129. They used the cymbal and *vina,* and with them led in the choruses of the *kirtans.* They followed Tuka with the sweet tones of their instruments, developing an outburst of love.

Tuka's Conversation with God.

130. Thus the Vaishnava *bhakta* began his *kirtans* after the night had advanced four ghatikas. In pleading tones, and with a feeling of love, Tuka addressed his songs to the Lord-of-Pandhari. 131. He brought the Husband-of-Rukmini into his imagination, and said to Him, "Wilt Thou, or wilt Thou not, accept me? This is the only thought I have, and which worries me day and night. 132. Art Thou going to give me a sight of Thy feet or not? My heart is worried over this. Art Thou going to speak to me or not? This thought troubles me. 133. Wilt Thou remember me, or wilt Thou not? This is my doubt, O Thou-Eagle-bannered-One. Aside from Thee, dear Krishna, there is no other helper. 134. I lack in good deeds, and, therefore, I feel depressed in spirit, but Thou art the Brother-of-the-helpless, and a cloud-of-mercy. Make this name true in my case. 135. I am not one whose name is great, so that Thou art compelled to respect my request. In every way I am one who fails in ser-

vice. My heart is my own witness to this. 136. I am not of a high caste, a high family, nor pure in deeds. I do not know any secret of yours through which I can effect my purpose. I am wholly ignorant of devotion and love. This Thou knowest, O Perfect-Being. 137. There is no strength in me for religious deeds, nor have I a character given to generosity. I have become merely a burden to the earth. This Thou knowest, O Merciful-One."

138. While Tuka in his love was thus pleading for God's mercy, though still in his body, he became one unconscious of body, and by force of his devotion accompanied with love, the image of Pandurang appeared in his heart. 139. In his love for God he began to dance in the *kirtan,* and moment after moment he would bow prostrate on the ground. (In his ecstasy) Tuka forgot his relation as *bhakta,* and Vithoba forgot his relation as God. 140. Seeing this, Krishna became troubled. He said to Himself, "If Tuka becomes one with me, then who will there be with whom to speak. 141. In time of distress who will call on me, and for whose help shall I rush? In his praising of my name, Tuka has acquired a spiritual body."

142. Thus speaking to Himself, He embraced Tuka to His heart. When Tuka awoke to consciousness of body he again began to plead for mercy in various terms. 143. "O Thou Merciful-to-the-lowly, Lord-of-Pandhari, Thou art my mother and father, my sister, brother, dearest friend, and uncle. Aside from Thee, I have no one. 144. O Vithoba, Thou art my great *sadguru.* Take me Thyself to the other side of the ocean of this life's experiences. I will then sing Thy name without ceasing. Give me this blessing."

145. Such was the theme of his *kirtan*. The lights for the wave offering were then lit, and waved before the Husband-of-Rukmini. In love all bowed to the ground before Him.

God Gives Tuka a Mantra in a Dream.

146. Krishna then said to Himself, "Tuka is Nama's *avatar*. Because of his great love for me in my *sagun* form, I have assumed this visible form. 147. He has no liking for the doctrines teaching non-duality, and, therefore, he does not go to any *sadguru*. This will make a path for others to follow in the future, and will work against the devotion to a *guru*. 148. According to the example set by the great, others, seeing it, follow it. So I will take the form of a Brahman, and give Tuka a *mantra*." 149. But said Rukmini to the Lord-of-Pandhari, "Listen to my request. To whomsoever you give a *mantra*, he becomes truly immortal. 150. I will relate to you some old stories about this, that when all the Yadavs were destroyed by the Brahman's curse, you preserved Uddhav alive. 151. Before your favor the Brahman's curse became powerless. Having explained the Bhagavat to Uddhava, You saved him. 152. During the *avatar* of Ram the *bhakta* Bibhishan, and Hanumant, the son of Anjani, were made immortal as to their bodies, by the laying on of your hands on their heads. 153. Now if you lay your hand on Tuka's head, his body will become immortal." When Krishna heard this remark of Rukmini's, He laughed. 154. Said He, "You have spoken the exact truth. Tuka is my very dearest life. I am going to give him a *mantra* so powerful that Death cannot destroy him." 155. And so saying, the Cloud-of-Mercy waited for a good and auspicious day,

which occurred on Thursday on the tenth of the month, during the bright half of the month Magh [February]. 156. While Tuka was asleep in the night he brought the image of Pandurang before his mind. You saints must listen with reverence to what Tuka saw in his dream.

157. The Vaishnava *bhakta* was on his way to the temple, after having bathed in the Indrayani. In his hands were *tulsi* leaves. Suddenly he saw a Brahman in his path. 158. It was Tuka's practice that whenever he met a Brahman, or a saint he would prostrate himself flat on the ground in his love for them. 159. Whatever one sees in one's waking state, one sees the same thing in a dream. This is the experience of every one. It is an illusion caused by a divine law. 160. Enough of such side references. Tuka, seeing this Brahman in his path, offered him the *tulsi* leaves, and bowed prostrate before him. 161. The Brahman was pleased, and placed his hand on Tuka's head, and gave him the *mantra* of "Ram Krishna" by which he was to save the world.

162. Shri Hari at the same time told Tuka with his own lips the names of the *gurus* in his line. I request you, wise hearers, to listen with your ears with reverence (to these names). 163. "Raghava Chaitanya a Vaishnava *bhakta*. Keshav Chaitanya became his disciple. Baba Chaitanya is my name." So God said to Tuka. 164. "Never leave the worship of Shri Pandurang. Never leave His feet."

Tuka was made happy in heart by this, and pressed an invitation on this *sadguru*. 165. "I ask you, my master, to come at once to my home, and make it holy by (your presence). You can cook with your own hands, and eat until it suffices you." 166. Listening to Tuka's words, the Husband-of-Rukmini said to him, "If you will kindly give me a quarter of a *sher* of *ghi,* I will come to your home." 167. Hearing these words of the noble Brahman, the Vaishnava *bhakta* said, "Certainly", and taking the Brahman by the hand, Tuka brought him to his home. 168. The Vaishnava *bhakta* said to his wife, "God has come to our home. Give him all the materials he may require for cooking, and as much *ghi* as he may ask for." 169. Hearing these words of Tuka's, his wife fell into a great rage. Said she, "Where has this damn Brahman come from? Where have I got the quarter of a *sher* of *ghi* to give him? 170. He brings constantly any sort of Brahmans to our home. He has burnt up our copper vessels, and left me nothing but earthen ware. How am I to carry on my domestic life?" 171. While the quarrel was raging more and more the *sadguru* suddenly left. Such was the dream that the noble Vaishnava had that day.

172. When the Vaishnava Tuka came into his waking state his heart felt remorse. Said he, "The dear *sadguru* met me, and took me over to the other side of the ocean of this life's experiences, 173. and all he asked for was a quarter of a *sher of ghi.* But because the quarrel in our home became so great, God at once left. 174. But he did tell me the names of those in the line of *gurus,* Keshav Chaitanya, Rahgava Chaitanya, and his own name of Babaji Chaitanya, and he gave me the *mantra* 'Ram-Krishna-Hari.' 175. It was on the tenth day, in the bright half of Magh [February]on a Thursday, which he saw was an auspicious day, that He accepted me, and then at once the *guru* left."

176. Tukaram in his love composed three *abhangs* on this theme. If they are continually sung in love by any, they will not be troubled by the cares of the worldly existence.

177. Such was the mercy of the *sadguru,* which was shown to Tuka in a dream. The pious God-loving *bhaktas,* understand this from personal experience as in the Hari-kirtans they listen to such stories.

178. The line of Gurus has continued by the same method [through dreams]. Tuka gave the *mantra* in a dream to whomsoever he especially loved. And that miracle is still going on.

Mahipati is God's Instrument.

179. In the next very interesting chapter the narrator is the Husband-of-Rukmini. So dear *bhaktas,* give close attention, and listen with reverence, 180. Pandharinath is relating this Bhaktalilamrita in order that the praise of his servant (Tuka) may spread over the world. 181. The Husband-of-Rukmini, who is the actor, holds the cord in his hands. He has made me his instrument. He understands this so. 182. Krishna stands on the brick with both arms akimbo. Mahipati is merely one to whom He has given the blessing of singing of His goodness in the *kirtans.*

183. Svasti. This book the Shri Bhaktalilamrita supplies the desires of the heart by merely listening to it. Let the pious God-loving *bhaktas* listen to it. This is the thirty-third interesting chapter.

CHAPTER 34.

Mahipati's Prayer.

Obeisance to Shri Ganesh.

1. I am without a protector and without support in this earthly life. I am lame in every respect. Still I call myself Thine, O Shri Hari. My heart feels the pride of this. 2. Yet I lack in *bhakti,* in knowledge and in strength, and I do not feel indifference to worldly things. Such am I, dull and ignorant. Who is there to help me but Thee? 3. Like the filthy water of a sewer, if it is collected in a tank or well, it will spoil the water of the well, and no holy person will drink it. 4. But if that same filthy water flows into the Ganges, on that day and at that same moment it becomes holy, and it is praised by *munis,* saints and *rishis.* 5. So one, a sinner in every respect, and yet who comes to Thee as a suppliant, though with feelings of any sort of mind, him, the Lord-of-Heaven accepts as His own without looking either to his goodness or blameworthiness. 6. The outcastes are spoken of with contempt in the *Vedas,* but if they worship Thee with true hearts, they become more praiseworthy than the highest caste, through the repetition of Thy name, O Krishna. 7. Such art Thou, the true purifier of the sinner. Thou canst become the universal *guru* of every animate and inanimate creature. Knowing this in my mind, I come as a suppliant to Thee, O Husband-of-Rukmini. 8. And now do as it seems right to Thee. Destroy me or work my good. Thy world-wide reputation as helper is in no wise false. 9. Thou, O Krishna, hast saved an innumerable number of Thy *bhaktas.* The fame of this is well

known in the *Purans*. Among them is I, Mahipati, one dull of understanding, one who needs Thy help.

TUKA IN DEPRESSION DESERTS HIS HOME.

10. In the last chapter the story was of Tuka's receiving the *mantra* in his dream, and that when he awoke, he marvelled over it. 11. It now happened on a certain day that this God-loving *bhakta* went and sat down in the jungle. Said he "I have had to live with this harsh wife. And she has brought discredit on me among all men. 12. She does not like the thought of my acting the part of a householder, or serving unexpected guests or invited guests. And she carries her enmity against the supreme-spiritual-truths. 13. Even in my dreams she never speaks a kind word to me. Well, God has broken the bond. I will not let my mind be entangled in any thing." 14. Thus saying, the Vaishnava *bhakta,* continued his worship in his love (of God). And after the night had advanced four ghatikas, he would come to the temple to perform his *kirtans*. 15. In these enthusiastic *kirtans* he adopted many forms of pleading themes. Many hearers came to listen, those who were God-loving, indifferent to worldly things, and pious. 16. He continued his *kirtans* for four *prahars,* and then went down to the Indrayani to bathe. After worshipping Pandurang, he would go and seat himself in the jungle. 17. If any one brought him any bread, he would eat moderately of it there. But the Vaishnava *bhakta* would not go back to his home, because it meant living with his harsh wife. 18. Two months thus passed without Tuka going back to his home. His wife collected her neighbours, and told them her side of the story. 19. Said she, "That crazy fellow is in town, and yet will not turn to look at me. Go and ask him what plan he has for me? 20. He sits there in the jungle

worshipping, and some one brings him something to eat. And at night he comes to the temple, and beating his cymbals dances there."

21. Now it happened one day that the Vaishnava *bhakta* having bathed in the river, was on his way to the temple, and Avali was bringing back water from the river, and suddenly the two met. 22. She seized Tuka by his clothes, and stopped him in the path. Then biting her lips, she spoke to him with bitter words. 23. She said to Tuka, "You have not come home for two months. Whose wife do you wish me to be in order to carry on my domestic life?" 24. Tuka replied, "Vithoba and Rakhumai are our father and mother. If you will keep their feet in your remembrance, you will have no misfortunes in your domestic life." 25. Avali said to him, "I want you to come home." Tuka replied, "If you are willing to listen to my suggestion, then give me at once your promise." 26. Avali gave him the promise, and took Tuka home.

Tuka's Home-Life is Resumed.

By the door of their house was a *tulsi* altar, and there Tuka sat down. 27. That day was the Hari-day, and some people came to listen to Tuka. But when Avali saw them she scolded and drove them away. 28. Tuka said to her, "Who goes to another's house for nothing? You do not like the honour of a visit to our house. Why do you gnash your teeth at them? 29. Through God the whole universe has become our relative. If you should speak kindly to them, what will you lose by it? 30. People stop their work, and come here to our home. You do not consider this an honour, but, instead, you scold at them and rush upon them." 31.

Hearing these words of the Vaishnava *bhakta,* Avali became quiet, but people ceased to come to their *wadi,* cherishing great fear of her. 32. Tuka sat by the *tulsi* altar and said to his wife, "Now let us concentrate our minds, and sit listening to the praise of God." 33. Avali said to herself, "If I do not listen to him,—but I brought him home, having given him a promise." And so she sat by his side, and listened to him. 34. And the Vaishnava *bhakta,* seeing that they were alone, began to preach to his wife. He said, "Here in the town of Dehu (also human body) we have accepted an assessment. 35. The Government tax is eighty rupees, which we have to give as the assessment. If we do not pay it, then Kaloji (death) the official, will severely threaten us. 36. You will ask me what are these eighty rupees? Your mind will raise the question. They are the eighty elements which make up our bodies. 37. We wear out our sense organs day and night. In that, ten elements are spent. There is no special desire for the five organs, if the heart is continually calm. 38. People say there are five organs of action. They are also spent for God. I forget myself as a doer, so naturally they are already worn out. 39. Ten elements in this way are easily swept away, but there are seventy elements left in the body for which we are not able to make payment. 40. Pandurang is the official in this place, and he says, 'Pay down all the balance.' He asks for our water jars, our other vessels, and our cattle, and all the property in our house. 41. If I had not already established this home, I should not have fallen into His hands. So now by becoming indifferent to worldly things, free me from him, O my wife. 42. Tomorrow is the twelfth day, and a Monday. Take your bath (in the river) and come back quickly. Then invite the Brahmans to come, and have our house looted at their hands.

43. Take no thought at all for food or raiment. If Pandurang, our (heavenly) Father, has His hand on our head, He will never let us lack (any good thing). 44. If you listen to me, your praise will increase in the world greatly, and we can say to ourselves, 'thieves stole our vessels, and our cattle died from lack of food.' 45. Put away all desire, and make your heart like steel. Say to yourself, you have not had any children, and so bring about freedom. 46. Gird up your loins tightly, and discard all desires for things that are perishable, and bringing God, Brahmans and guests to our house, worship them. 47. Becoming the servant of Vaishnavas in sincerity, go with undivided heart as a suppliant to the saints. And repeat the names of Vithoba with feelings of love."

48. There are eleven *abhangs* on this theme in which he preached to his wife in his kindly way. It is called "The Purna Bodha" [Complete Enlightenment]. Any one who hears it read, becomes indifferent to worldly things. 49. If any Seeker (after spiritual riches) commits to memory these incomparable verses of Tuka's, he will most certainly become perfect in *bhakti,* knowledge of Brahma, and indifference to worldly things. 50. I have only quoted in brief the words (of Tuka), and have not given them at length.

Avali Invites Brahmans to Loot Her Home.

Tuka now held a Hari watch-night service and sang, praising many deeds of God, 51. and as the sun arose, lighted the lights for the wave offering. For the time being Tuka's wife had become indifferent to worldly things as she sat beside him. 52. So when it was early morning, she went for her bath, and then invited the Brahmans to her house, and had them plunder the house of everything, the cattle, calves, money, grain, and cooking vessels. 53. Even the ashes that were in the fireplace were taken away by *sannyasis,* saying to themselves, "Let us apply these ashes to our bodies, as we sit indifferent to worldly things." 54. The grain-jars, the stone mortar, the pestle, and the empty earthen jars were all taken away. There were some old clothes, but they were put out to dry in the back yard.

Just then Mother Rukmini took the form of a Mahar woman and said to Tuka, "If you have any clothes, give them to me, Your Greatness." 55. Tuka thought to himself, "This Mahar woman is turning to go away." So he hastened to the back of the *wadi,* where the old garments were lying, and pulled them away. 56. He then gave them to the Mahar woman, making a sign to her to go away quickly, and speak to no one about it. 57. But some of the boys of the village had seen what had happened, and immediately told Avali. 58. They said, "When the Mahar woman asked him for some clothes, he pulled them off from where they were, and gave them to the woman." 59. When Avali heard their tale, her heart turned again to her worldly life. Said she, "I persuaded my husband to come back to the home, and as a consequence this disaster has fallen on me. 60. I ground and pounded the grain here at home, and carried on my domestic life up to to-day. His relations are with those outside the home, and he can live on begging. 61. In this way I was maintaining myself. How was it that I brought this calamity on myself, I do not know. But as I gave him a promise, and brought him home, he has made me give up everything. 62. 'Keep in your remembrance the feet of the Black-One, He will provide food and clothing.' O mother, I trusted this, his illusive promise, and at once had our home looted. 63. During the night I remembered those feet at least twice. At once came the realization, namely, that whatever property I had, that has now gone."

Avali Goes to Crush the God's Feet.

64. Then Avali took a stone on her head, and hastened to the temple. Said she, "I will crush to bits the feet of that Black-One." Such was her fierce determination. 65. With this determination in her heart, she hastened to the temple. In the mean time the image of Pandurang began to tremble violently. "What am I to do"? He said. 66. As Avali came into the temple, Rukmini said to her, "What is this that you are doing?" She replied "I am going to crush His feet. Your husband is a destroyer. 67. Last night my husband preached to me in various words, that if I continued to remember God's feet (I should have all my wants supplied). Instead, behold, poverty has come to me. 68. The Brahmans have taken away my money, grain, cattle, indeed my all. There was left one old, odd garment, but he went and pulled it off (the wall) and gave it away. 69. Now I have no clothing or food, and my husband has become entirely indifferent to his bodily needs. That is why I am angry." Rukmini, hearing her, said, 70. "Do not worry over the thought of your livelihood so far as it affects your body." And then the Primal-Mother [Rukmini] at once gave her a handful of gold coins [hons]. 71. And Rakhumai with her own hand gave Avali a *sari* and a jacket, which she at once put on, and came out of the temple. 72. When Tuka saw what had been given her, he said, "She has been in

too great haste," and he took the gold coins that God had given, and inviting Brahmans, distributed the coins to them. 73. Thus free from all desire, this God-loving *bhakta* continued his loving worship. The fame of Tuka now began to spread far and wide, and people began to come to pay him reverence. 74. And when they saw his wondrous deeds, the people said to one another, "The image of Pandurang actually comes and eats with Tuka."

Ganesh and Krishna dine with Tuka.

75. In the village of Chinchwad this rumour reached Chintaman Dev. When he heard it he was much astonished, and said to himself, "I must invite Tuka here and test this rumour." 76. So Chintaman Dev sent a message to Tuka inviting him to come to Chinchwad, and that after meeting him he could at once return. 77. The Vaishnava *bhakta,* understanding Chintaman Dev's purpose, thought to himself, "Chintaman Dev has a mind to see me. I think I ought to go and visit him." 78. So thinking, he at once started on his way there. While walking along the path, he continued worshipping God in love. 79. When he had gone half the way, he met men bringing a message. "Chintaman Dev wishes to see you, and invites you to come and visit him." 80. "I accept," said the Vaishnava *bhakta,* "I had the very same purpose in mind". He soon arrived at Chinchwad and made obeisance to Ganesh. 81. Just at that time Chintaman Dev was performing his morning ablution and worship, so that he did not know that Tukaram had arrived. 82. He was sitting alone in the Godroom engaged in silent prayer, but he found he could not hold in restraint his fickle mind. Listen to how that was. 83. In his garden he had planted a flower-bed, and the

worshipper remembered it just at that moment. 84. "The plants have been much injured, and much litter is lying on them. I must call the gardener, and give him a good punishment." 85. The moment this thought came into his mind, he at the same time concentrated his mind, and meditating on the form of Ganesh worshipped him in all the ways of worship. 86. After completing his worship in silent mental adoration, Chintaman Dev came outside. When the Vaishnava *bhakta* saw him he bowed prostrate on the ground. 87. Chintaman Dev, however, hesitated as to what to do. He thought, "One should not make a *namaskar* to a Shudra" so he merely welcomed Tuka and said, "This meeting is welcome. When did you come? Tell me." 88. The God-loving *bhakta* replied, "You were at that moment engaged in silent mental adoration, and then your thoughts went to your flower-bed. Just then I came." 89. Hearing this reply, Chintaman Dev was astonished. Thought he, "He is a mind-reader. What public rumour says of him is true. 90. But there is one rumour regarding which I feel a doubt. It is that the image of Vishnu eats with him. Every one says this of him; I must ask him about it after our meal. 91. His fame has become very exalted. Even Brahmans make him a *mamaskar*. If he can show me some miracle, then I will render him honour and reverence. 92. But if it is all mere plain jugglery, there will be no delay in having him punished. However, as soon as the meal is finished, I shall discuss the matter with Tuka." 93. Now if a guest happens to come at the moment when the offering is made to the fire, he is to be considered as the same as Vishnu. The plates were passed to Tuka who was seated in the same line as the Brahmans. 94. But his plates were arranged at an interval of about six feet from the Brahmans. And Tuka had two more plates arranged by the same person (server). 95. Chintaman Dev asked him, "For whom have you arranged the plates? If there are others who should dine with us, invite them." 96. The Vaishnava *bhakta* replied. "One of these plates is for the Husband-of-Rukmini, and the other I have arranged for Ganesh. Will you, my master, please invite him?" 97. While repeating the Gayatri *mantra* the plates were sprinkled, and Ganesh was brought into his mental conception. Closing his eyes, he presented the offering. Then Tuka addressed him as follows. 98. "While bathing in the ocean a *bhakta* was about to drown. He brought Ganesh to his mind, and called on him to run to his help. 99. To draw him out the Son-of-Gauri had stepped into the ocean. I have a knowledge of this event. Now to whom are you making this offering? 100. If you have any doubt about this, wait a moment, and notice the evidence." Hearing Tuka say this, Chintaman Dev was astonished, and remarked, "The state of Tuka's mind is beyond all comparison." 101. Not a half a *ghatika* after this Ganesh appeared, and when he squeezed his yellow robe, behold, sea water dropped from it. 102. Then Tuka said to Chintaman Dev, "Now invite Ganesh to eat. If you actually give him to eat, my mind will be satisfied." 103. Hearing Tuka say this, Chintaman Dev said, "How can an image eat? If one offers it an offering, the fragrance of it goes to him." 104. To this the Vaishnava *bhakta* replied, "You must actually make Ganapati eat here. Only so will your mind be satisfied, otherwise your worship will be in vain. 105. Just as when a field has been properly sown, and the field is dense with ears, but if there is no grain in the ears, then all the labour has been in vain. 106. Or just as when the sky is thick with clouds, but there is not the least drop of rain, so if the deity does not give a direct visible manifestation of Himself, the *mantras* used in worship are useless. 107. Trees and creepers without fruit lack charm; a river without water looks frightful; and a beautiful woman without a child appears devoid of grace. 108. Ornaments for one without a husband, a body without a soul, large eyes, but without sight. All these seem vain. 109. So if God does not give a direct visible manifestation of Himself, worship and adoration go for nothing." Hearing Tuka's remarks, Chintaman Dev, was astonished. 110. Chintaman Dev then said to him, "I have worshipped Ganesh, but to have his image come actually and eat with me, that power I do not possess. 111. You noble Vaishnavas say you have placed the Husband-of-Rukmini under your control, so now bring Ganesh and give him now here to eat. 112. If Ganesh does not come, I will not eat at all." Seeing Chintaman Dev's fixed determination, the servant of Vishnu replied, 113. "By your kindness I will give Ganesh to eat here in your presence." Tuka then composed two *abhangs* of praise, in which love was the theme. 114. "Victory, Victory to Thee, Ganesh, Lord-of-the-fourteen-Sciences, Ocean-of-goodness, Giver-of-all-the-Siddhis, Holder-of-the-Battle-axe, Elephant-faced-One. 115. When Thou dost hang bells on Thy feet and dance, all, including Narad and Tumbar, are awestruck as they look at the strange sight. 116. When Thou lookest on anyone with Thine eye of favour, all hindrances flee in every direction. Thou dost break the snare that binds men to this earthly existence, and protectest Thy *bhaktas* in times of great distress." 117. Such was the praise that Tuka sang, but Ganapati did not come. Tuka continued to plead for his presence. "Let Thy mind be without reserve. 118. Because of Chintaman Dev's devotion, Thou didst cause his barren cows to give milk. I do not ask such a thing now. I only ask that Thou shouldst eat here now the food acquired without effort." 119. Hearing Tuka's pleading voice, the Son-of-Gauri was pleased, and in *sagun* form Ganesh sat down before his plate. 120. Chintaman Dev was fully satisfied at seeing in visible form the deity of his adoration, and in love he prostrated himself. 121. "Now," said he to Tuka, "Invite Vithoba. It will give me joy if He comes, and give Him to eat directly before us." 122. Tuka closed his eyes, and meditated on the image of Pandurang. Seeing this loving *bhakti,* the Husband-of-Rukmini appeared. 123. Dark complexioned, and beautiful in form, with conch-shell, disk, and weapons in his hands, such was Krishna. In his crown jewels sparkled, so bright as to dim the sun. 124. In his ears were the crocodile shaped ear rings, around his waist was his yellow garment. His beautiful face was resplendent. On his feet bells tinkled. 125. Such was the magnificent image that Chintaman Dev saw. He bowed prostrate on the ground, and his heart was unable to contain his joy. 126. One plate was laid for Ganesh, the beautiful four-armed image with one white tusk, and his whole body painted with red lead. 127. Tuka, the Vaishnava *bhakta,* and Chintaman Dev, both had this vision of the actual presence of the deity. But they were not seen by others. 128. When the food was served them on their plates both deities ate it with their fingers. As they consumed the food, the Brahmans looked on with wonder. 129. Here were God and His *bhakta,* and other Brahmans, sitting in their usual order. Whatever any one liked that was served to him, and all were satisefid. 130.

To the images of Pandurang and Ganesh Tuka brought water for them to wash their hands. Then giving them the *vida* [*pan supari*] for the cleansing of their mouths, Tuka fell at their feet in love. 131. Both images then took leave of their *bhaktas* and vanished out of sight.

Chintaman Dev now embraced Tuka lovingly, and bowed prostrate before him. 132. When Tuka saw this, he put out his hand, and taking Chintaman by his hand, raised him up. Said he, "It is your feet that are to be reverenced by me. It is not proper, O Svami, to (worship me). 133. My Svami Pandharinath bears on his breast the mark of the Brahman Bhrigu's kick. All holy waters are in your feet. What am I there, one of a low caste?" 134. Hearing Tuka's remark, Chintaman Dev replied, "One should not call a *bhakta* of Vishnu a low caste man. So it is written in the *Bhagavata*. 135. Like the lofty mountain of gold among other mountains, like Shri Ram among other holders of the bow, or like Shiva, supreme among Yogis, so are you, noble Vaishnava. 136. As the Bhagirthi is supreme among all holy rivers, or as Narad is supreme among all those called the reciters of God's name, or as the son of Anusuya among all Yogis, so are you, Tuka, the chief of those who worship God. 137 You will perform *kirtans* in praise of Shri Hari, and then you will give your body a divine form. This is what comes to my belief as I watch your good deeds." 138. Then Chintaman Dev's lips thus praised Tuka, and said, "It is by your favour, in truth, that I have to-day had a direct vision of Shri Krishna." 139. The God-loving *bhakta* (Tuka) upon this said, "All this is because of the glory of your favour." Tuka then took leave of Chintaman Dev, and returned to the village of Dehu.

TUKA GIVES HIS THREE DAUGHTERS IN MARRIAGE.

140. Tuka's character was now desireless. If anyone wished to give him money, he would not even take it in his hand. Perhaps some of my hearers will have a doubt in their hearts, and will wish to question the narrator. 141. The Vaishnava *bhakta,* as a householder, had some children. How did he get them married? Let us hear about this. 142. To these questions of the listeners the narrator would reply that Tuka had three daughters, and he got them married in the following way. 143. The eldest daughter was Kashibai, the second was Bhagirithi, and the name of the youngest was Gangabai, all born into a good family line. 144. As these daughters arrived at the marriageable age, Avali became much concerned. Said she, "How are we to get our girls married?" and she put the question to Tuka. 145. Hearing these remarks of his wife, he, immediately stepped outside, where boys of his own caste were playing. He brought them to his house. 146. That day happened to be a day auspicious for marriages, and the Vaishnava *bhakta* called in some Brahmans, and applying saffron paste to brides and bridegrooms, he had them married at once. 147. Some milk and rice were prepared in the house, and they were given other delicacies. On the next day the parents of the bridegrooms learned of their boys' marriage. 148. Then the three good relatives, forming a marriage procession, came to Dehu village. The pious people helped, and the marriage festival continued for four days. 149. He who makes Shri Hari [God] his friend, the whole universe will be friendly to him. The Dweller-in-Heaven will not let his servants drown in the Sea of this worldly existence.

A Brahman Goes on a Hunger-Strike.

150. Mose, Gade and Jambulkar were those whom the noble Vaishnava made relatives by marriage. Still he did not allow himself to be in the least entangled in worldly things. He forgot he had a body. 151. In this Kali Yuga Tuka descended as *avatar* to save the universe. Ignorant people did not understand his greatness, and yet he was the friend of the universe, a universal *guru*. 152. He who by singing God's praises was enabled easily to plant his triumphant banner in Heaven whither he went with his body, that Vaishnava *bhakta* maharaj in his mercy gave me also the *mantra* (in a dream).

153. Tuka's characteristic was love. He frequently visited Alandi. Looking with longing eyes towards Pandhari, his throat would choke with emotion. 154. Other events also occurred, to which I ask you, pious men, to listen with reverence.

In the Province of Bid, there was a Brahman, Deshpande by name. He went on a hunger-strike at the temple door of Vithoba in Pandharpur, 155. and assumed most rigorous austerities. He ate no food and continued in a starving condition. He desired for himself skill in understanding the Purans. 156. After he had thus sat for ten days the Lord-of-Pandhari said to him in a dream, "Go at once to Alandi and make your request of Dnyaneshvar. 157. If you will obey his suggestion, the desire of your heart will be fulfilled." After hearing the Husband-of-Rukmini say this, the Brahman awoke. 158. He remembered his dream, and went to Alandi. "I want," he said, "worldly enjoyments and Final Deliverance, and an understanding of the Purans at once." 159. With this desire in mind, he sat down before Dnyaneshvar in a hunger-strike.

He ate no food, and his body was in a wasted condition. 160. After twelve days thus passed, Dnyaneshvar was severely perplexed. Said he, "This Brahman lacks good fortune, and he is uselessly giving pain to his body." 161. Finally he said (to the Brahman), "Go at once to Dehu village. There you will find the Vaishnava *bhakta*, Tukaram, who is actually the *avatar* of Nama. He has descended for the salvation of the world. 162. Whatever favour he may confer on you, if you trust to it, your purpose will be attained." After hearing Dnyaneshvar say this, the Brahman awoke. 163. As the hunger-striking Brahman now thought over the dream, he felt a serious doubt in his heart. He said to himself, "Tuka is a *Vani* of the *Shudra* caste, I hear so indirectly. 164. How can my heart's desires be realized by going to him?" Though he had these serious doubts, still he hastened to Dehu. 165. He came to Tuka, and told him his whole story. The God-loving *bhakta* was astonished, but he understood all that was to take place. 166. Said he, "He by whose blessed means the buffalo repeated the *Vedas,* and when Changadev came to test him, he by whose power the wall moved. 167. Worldly enjoyments and Final-Deliverance stand ever at his door as ready servants. The golden *pimpal* tree grows at his door. What can my *svami* not do?" 168. And so Tuka wondered why Dnyaneshvar, being such as he was, should have sent the fasting Brahman to him? For what could there be lacking in him? 169. "I am not a really true servant of God, but such a reputation has spread among men. Why then, O Dnyaneshvar, the brother-of-the-lowly, have you sent this trouble to my house? 170. Among men I am your darling. Joining letter to letter, you speak in my ear. Or just as a mother churns the milk, and gives the butter to her child. 171. In the same manner you have given me as a favour your words, and because I had them without an effort, I repeat them amongst men. Did Your Greatness lack anything, and, therefore, you sent this hunger striker here?" 172. Tuka wondered at this and then composed eleven *abhangs*. The learned and experienced call these verses, The Most Excellent Wisdom. 173. The hunger striker sat beside Tuka, and the God-loving *bhakta* gave him the verses as he composed them. Tuka gave him as his favour a cocoanut. But the Brahman at once rejected it. 174. Said he, "I desire to understand the Purans, instead, he gives me these Marathi verses, that he has composed. I have come here in vain," and he stand the Purans; instead, he gives me these Marathi verses, on a hunger strike before Dnyanadev's (tomb), saying "Fulfil my desire." To obtain it he performed severe austerities. 176. In the meanwhile Tuka wrote a letter to Dnyaneshvar in thirteen *abhangs*. "You sent the Brahman to me, 177. knowing well that the desired things were not in the Fate of the hunger-striker, yet you so planned it that the disgrace should fall on me. 178. It is like the witness of a liar, which is to be decided by another. In offering my service at your feet I have gratefully acquitted myself, O Dnyanadev. 179. I cannot overstep your wishes. I gave him eleven *abhangs*, and as a favour I gave him a cocoanut, thus glorifying him. 180. But Fortune was against him. He rejected them, and went away." Such was the letter that Tukaram wrote to Dnyanadev. 181. Then Dnyaneshvar at once drove away the hunger-striking Brahman. Such is the effect of his *karma* that a doubt should have arisen in his mind. 182. It is like a man sitting under the Wish-tree and closing his bag. Whatever he had to experience in this world, that he experienced through Fate. 183. A man who was dying suddenly had access to a cup of nectar. But he thought it to be salt water, so he overturned the cup and spilled the nectar. 184. A man saw with his eyes a mine of gold. The luckless one even went near it, but it seemed to him a volcano. Who can withstand fate? 185. Or take some other luckless wretch, who finds a touch-stone, but to whom it seems a mere ordinary stone pebble, and he throws it away in any direction. 186. So Tuka gave to the hunger-striking Brahman most excellent *abhangs,* containing the substance of the *Vedas* and *Shastras,* but on account of his adverse Fate, they seemed to him commonplace composition. 187. So he rejected the cocoanut and went back to Alandi, but Dnyanadev sent him away, as you, my good friends, have already heard.

188. Now turning to the town of Dehu, Tuka the Vaishnava *bhakta,* looking at the (rejected) *abhangs* written on paper, said to himself, "I don't at all understand for whom I have composed these *abhangs.*" 189. But just at that moment a man, Kondoba by name, a great, fat, blockhead of a Brahman, happened to be walking along the path, and noticed Tuka. 190. He was unable to read, and so he had no pride in his heart. He bowed reverently to Tuka at once. 191. The Vaishnava *bhakta* was pleased with his sincerity, and he gave to Kondoba the eleven *abhangs* which he had previously written. 192. And he also gave him the cocoanut, which the hunger-striking Brahman had thrown aside. Kondoba broke the cocoanut open and in it were lustrous pearls.

193. In the city of Ahmedabad, there was a merchant who had vowed to Dnyaneshvar that he would offer on his tomb jewels worth one hundred thousand rupees. 194. In

order to fulfil his vow, the merchant came to worship at the tomb. But Dnyaneshvar told him in a dream to place the jewels before Tuka. 195. The merchant took a cocoanut, cleaned out the kernel, filled it with pearls, and placed it before Tuka. It was on that very day that the hunger-striking Brahman had appeared, and was given the cocoanut. 196. But Fate being against the fasting Brahman, he had scorned it. So Tuka now gave it to Kondoba. Moreover, as he read the abhangs with feelings of love, he began to understand the Sanskrit language. 197. King Shivaji had in his service a learned Brahman who read to him the Purans. The latter had a cook, Kondoba by name, who as a suppliant came to Tuka, 198. and so the saint naturally showed him kindness, and he received worldly enjoyments and Final-Deliverance. He also at that moment acquired a knowledge of the Purans, and became moreover an expert scholar of the Bhagavata. 199. When King Shivaji understood the whole affair, he gave Kondoba garments and ornaments. This made the king think that he should come and pay his respects to Tuka.

Tuka's Increasing Fame.

200. Day by day more and more the fame of Tuka increased. The pious people, as they listened to his *kirtans*, paid him honour and reverence.

201. One day, when the Vaishnava *bhakta* was performing a *kirtan* at Alandi before the great door of the temple, all the people from Lohagav came there, intelligent, indifferent to worldly things, and pious. 202. Bowing at Tuka's feet they besought him to come some time to their town. With this earnest request they reverently fell at his feet. 203. "O Svami," they said, "come as far as our town, and make our abode holy." And seeing their great

sincerity, the noble Vaishnava replied, "I will certainly come." 204. So on the next day they took Tukoba to Lohagav with great eclat. They had dainty food cooked, and satisfied the appetites of the Brahmans. 205. They had erected a pavilion with side curtains, making a very large audience room, and there the noble Vaishnava performed his soul-stirring *kirtans*. 206. The loud sound of cymbals, *vina* and drum made it a veritable din of deafening sounds. In these *kirtans* an affluence of divine enthusiasm moved the audience, such as would be impossible for Brahmadev and other gods to obtain. 207. The pious people listened to the gracious voice of Tuka. Tears of love flowed from their eyes, being overcome with emotion. 208. While drinking in with love these words of Tuka's, no one fell asleep or grew weary. As the sun was rising, they closed by the wave offering to the Lord-of-Pandhari.

209. In the next extraordinary chapter the narrator is the Husband-of-Rukmini. Mahipati is merely the bearer of His badge who extols the deeds of the saints

210. Svasti! This book, the Shri Bhaktalilamrita, fulfils all the heart's desires by merely listening to it. May the God-fearing Vaishnava *bhaktas* listen. This is the thirty-fourth interesting chapter.

CHAPTER 35.

Praise of Vithoba's Image at Pandharapur.

Obeisance to Shri Ganesh.

1. Thy name, O Shri Hari, is Brother-of-the-Helpless. And to my heart this seems true. On the bank of the Bhima river, Thou standest upright on a brick, with Thy

feet parallel. 2. The form of Thy beautiful body gives delight. Thy two hands are placed on Thy hips. At the sight of this unclad image one loses consciousness of body. 3. Thy beautiful idol makes a delightful spectacle. Fragrant powders are sprinkled over Thee. Thy eyes are directed to the tip of Thy nose. The crown on Thy head radiates glory. 4. The pious *bhaktas,* who come to meet Thee, embrace Thee tightly in their love. They place *tulsi* garlands around Thy neck, all of which pleases Thee, O God. 5. Many kinds of sinners, such as thieves, adulterers, haters of Brahmans, killers of cows, are saved by merely looking on Thee. And this was the promise Thou didst give to Pundalik. 6. Seekers (after spiritual things) find it extremely difficult to go to Heaven, so Thou didst found this sacred city of Pandhari among mortals. 7. The various sacred rivers of the Three worlds come to the Chandrabhaga at noon time. The gods, therefore, riding on their chariots of light [*viman*], come here to bathe. 8. There is no further comparison which can be used for the incomparable glory of this sacred city of Pandharpur. So in the composition of this book, give me (the needed) love, O Soul-of-the-Universe, O *Guru*-of-the-Universe. 9. Thou dost happily place in my heart verses already composed. I merely write them down on paper, with nothing to hinder me in doing so. 10. Thou, Lotus-eyed-One, Thou art Thyself relating these stories of Thy saints. It is Thou who hast made me worthy to be Thy instrument, but all the moving strings are in Thy hands.

Tuka's Stay at Lohagav.

11. In the last chapter there was narrated the going of Tukaram to Lohagav, and performing *kirtans,* which stirred the emotions of all the people (of the town). 12.

With much urging on their part they made the Servant of Vishnu remain with them a month. So by day and night the loud music of the *kirtans* continued, yet no one was wearied thereby. 13. As for Tuka, his heart was always without the desire of earthly things. Gold and earth were the same to him. So it was the people, who according to their ability, made offerings to the Brahmans. 14. In order to preserve righteousness in the world, saints have descended as *avatars* in this *kali-yuga*. Neither sinful deeds nor good deeds are a part of their lives. They simply live in the enjoyment of the love of God.

Aged Widow in Lohagav gives a Feast.

15. There was an aged Brahman widow in Lohagav, who reverently invited Tukoba. "Come and dine at my house, and perform a *kirtan* there." 16. The Vaishnava *bhakta,* seeing the sincerity of her love, said, "I accept." She added, "I will make the needed preparations, and I shall expect you definitely on that day." 17. So the widow laboured with her own hands, and made provisions for ten Brahmans. Suddenly, however, a hindrance stood in her way. I ask you, wise people, to listen with reverence to what happened. 18. The widow's hut was just alongside of a wall, belonging to her neighbour's *wada* (house). It had been raining very heavily, and the wall was about to fall. 19. The widow came to Tuka, and wept bitterly. Said she, "The wall will fall to-day. What shall I do? 20. I have made all the preparations in my house for the dinner in your honour." Tuka replied with an assurance that she need not fear. Said he, "Let your mind be at rest. 21. The wall will not fall until we have dined. Vithoba will do away with every difficulty. There is

no doubt of this whatever." 22. The townspeople came to see the wall. The wall was bent over, but had not fallen. Seeing this, a most remarkable sight, all marvelled. 23. When four days were past the Brahman widow cooked food with her own hands, and Tuka was escorted to her house, and duly reverenced. 24. The Vaishnava *bhakta,* along with the Brahmans, dined with grateful heart, and to his full satisfaction. Tuka then said to the Brahman widow, "Now take your own food quickly." 25. As soon as she had finished eating they brought all her things outside. And as soon as all were finally out of the house the wall fell flat. 26. Tuka expressed to the towns-people his wish, and caused another house to be given to the widow. And that night he performed a *kirtan* there in his loving zeal. 27. He, in whose house a saint enters, his troubles flee far away. Shri Hari, with the disk in his hand, protects them in various ways.

28. After the month was passed the Vaishnava *bhakta* left Lohagav. As their fame increases in one place, men, indifferent to worldly things, no longer stay there.

Rameshvar Bhatt Becomes Tuka's Enemy.

29. Tuka's great and good fame increased day by day, just as in the first fortnight of the month the moon increases in her high brilliancy. 30. When men look at the growing brilliancy of the moonlight, they all are made happy thereby, but a thief's heart becomes enraged. He cannot endure it. 31. And so it was that it gave the pious ones a sense of rest to hear of Tuka's good fame, but scoffers, crooks, and the evil minded were enraged thereby. 32. They had pride of knowledge, age, form, caste and family, and had no liking for the teachings of the

saints, just as those who are suffering from fever, have no liking for milk.

33. There was a Brahman in the town of Vagholi, named Rameshvar Bhatt. He had made a study of the four systems of philosophy, and was addressed as Rajamanya [Worthy of a King's honour]. 34. He learned from others of Tuka's exceptionally good fame. Hearing of it hatred arose in his heart. Said he, "Heretics have increased altogether too much. 35. Some proper scheme must be devised so as to send Tuka out of the country. I will do something, however, now that will bring disgrace upon him." 36. With this plan in mind, making use of the influence which he had at court, he charged that, "Tuka was of the *Shudra* caste, and yet was publicly preaching the substance of the *Vedas*. 37. Moreover by performing Hari *kirtans* he has seduced pious people, so that even Brahmans make him a *namaskar*. That seems to me most reprehensible. 38. He puts aside all other rules of duty, and emphasises the all importance of repeating God's names. He has developed the path of *bhakti*, which seems to me heretical." 39. Hearing this accusation by Rameshvar, the chief official of the city (of Poona), became enraged, and sent a command to the patil [mayor] of Dehu to send Tuka out of town. 40. The people of the town showed the letter to Tuka, who immediately composed an *abhang*, that had in it the sentiment of a pleading for mercy. 41. Tuka now said, "What ought I to do? To what other country can I go. If I would live in the town, God does not give me a place of refuge there. 42. The patil and the people of the town are angry with me, and who will respond to my begging for food? There is no joy in remaining with them. I must go and search for Vithoba." 43. Thus saying, the noble Vaishnava began to repeat

aloud the names of Vitthal. He then said to himself, "I will go at once to Vagholi and see Rameshvar Bhatt." 44. Thus thinking, the loving *bhakta* started immediately. Rameshvar was sitting performing his devotions. Tuka prostrated himself before him. 45. And then and there repeating aloud God's names with love, he began a Hari *kirtan.* He put his gracious words in poetic form, and did so without any hesitation. 46. In response Rameshvar said to him, "You are a *Shudra* by caste. The verses which you recite in your *kirtans* bear meanings that are found in the *Vedas.* 47. You have no authority for doing this, and it seems to me contrary to the *shastras.* And if so, then both speaker and hearers will have to endure the tortures of Hell. 48. So from to-day you are not to repeat any of these verses." Hearing Rameshvar's injunction, Tuka was pleased. 49. For the Vaishnava *bhakta* said to himself, "It is the Lord of Pandhari who has commanded me because I have babbled too much, and wasted my voice in vain." 50. Tuka then said to Rameshvar, "You are a Brahman, the image of God. You have commanded me, and from henceforth I will never repeat my verses. 51. In respect to your command I will henceforth not compose verses, but in reference to those already composed what about them?" 52. To this question of the Vaishnava *bhakta,* Rameshvar replied, "Take the verses you have written and with your own hands sink them in the water (of the river)." 53. "I agree" said Tuka, "I bow before your command."

Tuka Throws His Manuscripts into the River.

Tuka returned at once to Dehu, and entered the temple. 54. Seeing the image of Pandurang his eyes filled with tears. He prostrated himself on the ground with thoughts of love. 55. He then stood before the glorious image with his hands placed palm to palm. Said he, "Maker of all things, Husband-of-Rukmini, I am indeed a sinner, and one dull of mind. 56. It was by your command, Vithoba, that I have composed these unconnected, misshapen verses, and now it is Thy wish, O Recliner-on-the-Serpent [Vishnu] that I should sink these verses in the water." 57. Thus saying, the God-loving *bhakta* took all his manuscript books, and going to a deep pool in the Indrayani sank them with his own hands. 58. With cloth he made a bundle of these manuscript books, and placed a stone inside. Then shouting aloud Vitthal's name he slipped the bundle into the water.

59. Those who were pious and lovers of God were entirely overcome in their hearts, but the wicked wagged their necks, and were pleased. 60. Said they, "In composing these verses he brought great glory to himself, but this glory will not last in this world, like the fugitive colour of a butterfly. 61. Rameshvar is a truly learned Brahman. He is like another sun. He has broken down all support to untruths, and our hearts rejoice. 62. Just as Dvaipayana entirely destroyed the Bharat that Jaimini composed, or as Shankaracharya put out of existence the Jain beliefs. 63. Dvaipayana did preserve from the poems of Jaimini one book called the Ashvamedh. And Shankaracharya was pleased to keep the Amarkosh, belonging to the Jain faith. 64. But none of Tuka's were spared. All the manuscript books were sunk in the deep pool." The evil-minded spoke thus, not knowing the power of Vishnu. 65. But Tuka's heart was in peace. For he was without joy or pain. Said he to himself, "God's rule is the authority here. Why should I needlessly complain about it?" 66.

Thus thinking to himself, he continued his worship with love. By this time five days had passed since he had sunk the manuscripts in the water of the river.

The Evil-minded Seek to Irritate Tuka.

67. There were some evil minded Brahmans and some of other castes. Joining together, they came to where Tuka was, and said some very harsh things to him. Listen to them, you pious *bhaktas* of his. 68. They said to Tuka, "When some time ago you threw the promissory notes into the pool in the river, you in that act sank all your worldly affairs, feeling a disgust for them. 69. Then you composed poetry on the theme of the Supreme-spiritual-riches. And now you have thrown all that into the water. Were there any-one else in your place, he would not have spared his life. 70. Now you have sunk both, your worldly riches, and your supreme-spiritual-riches; and still you show your face to people." With these harsh words to Tuka, the evil-minded people returned to their home.

Tuka's Mental Struggle.

71. Those sharp word-arrows struck Tuka, and his heart was divided into two. He thought to himself, "If I should give up my life, it would mean suicide, while in one's present existence. 72. Life does not leave one easi-ly, so what method shall I adopt? I will refuse food and drink, and sit fasting at God's door." 73. There was a stone slab in front of the door of the temple where the *tulsi* altar was, and the Vaishnava, Tuka, went immediately, and sat upon it. 74. His heart experienced repentance. There are nineteen *abhangs* on this event. Said he, "My *bhakti* has reached its limit, and blame attaches itself to

my abode. 75. The Hari *kirtans,* the all-night services on the eleventh of the fortnight have at last borne their fruit. My heart is in a flutter. 76. Alas, I served Thee without special effort. My heart bears witness to that. And now it has come about that I am ashamed to show my face to men. 77. So long as I have not cast my life aside, what shall I say to God? I want now union with Thee, Mother Vithabai, or I shall cause my life to cease. 78. Formerly it came into my mind to go alone, and sit in the jungle. That easily took place with no one to hinder it. 79. When my purpose shall have been fulfilled, I shall then make reply. If I should now compose verses, people would say, 'He has no shame.' 80. This is now the last day on which to make my choice. And the day has come without effort on my part. How can fruition be welcomed without experience? Who cares for mere empty words? 81. I can now no longer maintain my courage. With what is my heart to gain steadiness? If Thou hast not heard my cry, then I have uselessly created empty chaff. 82. Thou, O Vitthal, hast adopted all necessary measures, and now nothing remains for me to wait for. 83. I have come to the end of my way of *bhakti.* I have come straight to Thy feet. There is no special delightful taste to words, since the worldwide hue and cry has taken place. 84. Verses with false sentiment are sung while turning the hand-mill, but one must take them as true. Such, O Lord-of-Pandhari, is the condition of my life. 85. Now this is my final resolve. Why should I winnow chaff for nothing? I will not take my pen in hand carelessly. This is my fixed determination. 86. I speak words pleading for mercy. Thou hast turned Thy back against me. These are all Thy intrigues, and hence this determination of mine. 87. In former times, O mother Pandurang, Thou didst save innumerable *bhaktas*. And now hast Thou grown weary of one person? Why dost Thou not break the bonds of my earthly existence? 88. O Shri Hari, Thou hast obstinately hardened Thy heart against me. (Now I have formed a resolve in my mind no more to open a shop where *bhakti* can be bought.) 89. Thou, O Pandurang, hast a character that when anyone pleads with Thee for mercy, Thou dost become angry, but if anyone uses harsh words towards Thee, Thou favourest him. 90. How is it that Thou dost not consider me as Thy servant? Tell me this, O Lord-of-Pandhari. For whom else have I left desires for earthly riches, and brought about this ruination? 91. If a mother does not provide her child's demands, it has to wander afield. To whom should it relate its tale of sorrow when all the dear and near ones have forgotten it? 92. How am I now to praise Thee? How am I to proclaim the fame of Thy goodness? No longer does there remain to me the propriety of showing my face to men. 93. I have spent all my strength. Neither physical nor mental strength are of any use. Whatever Thou dost, that is what will happen, O Husband-of-Rukmini, Shri Vitthal."

Tuka Continues His Suicidal Fasting.

94. Praising God in this way with eyes closed, Tuka fixed his imagination on the *sagun* form of God, and steadied his heart at God's feet. 95. He made his bed on the slab of stone, near the *tulsi* altar before the temple. He refused to take fruit, or roots or water. He entirely lost all consciousness of body. 96. He was much insulted by people, and even his wife would not come to care for him. To begin with, she hated the idea of spiritual-riches, and

now on top of that came this state of things. 97. Others who had faith in God, and who came to listen to his Hari *kirtans* now and then, their minds were defiled by doubts, seeing Tuka's desperate condition. 98. As when a fruit has reached its ripe state it lets go of the stem, in the same way excess of love for God results in madness by the force of Shri Hari's' wave of mercy. 99. There were pious people who, one after the other, came and pleaded with Tuka, but he would not reply to anyone. His determination did not waver. 100. He had determined on this fasting condition before the door of the temple in order that he might starve to death. No one was certain whether he was dead or alive.

RAMESHVAR PUNISHED FOR HIS HATRED OF TUKA.

101. You, wise listeners, turn for the moment to Rameshvar, the Brahman, living in Vagholi. His hatred of *bhaktas* became intense. And God became angry with him. 102. Ravan and Kumbhakarna, haters of Ram, were carried to the home of Final-Deliverance, but there is no Deliverance for those who hate *bhaktas*. They rightfully belong to Hell. 103. To protect His *bhaktas* Shri Hari carries in his hands a club and a disk, and being the inspirer of the mind, brings calamity on those who are against His *bhaktas*. 104. Those who hate *bhaktas* lose their store of good deeds, and all forms of sin come there to dwell, finding a fit place in their hearts.

105. Rameshvar was a Brahman, who practised austerities. He was like the very sun. He had studied the four *shastras*, and in every way was entitled to the title of *Rajamanya* [Worthy of a king's respect]. 106. But he hated the *bhaktas* of Vishnu, thereby he lost from his store

of good deeds. One day he came to Poona to see and worship Shiva. 107. There was the wakeful deity, Nagnath. All Rameshvar's faith was fixed on His feet. 108. Rameshvar had chosen the most auspicious of days, a Monday, and Pradosh, the thirteenth of the fortnight. He had come to Poona, and the following event took place. 109. There was a yogi there, by name of Anagadsha, and this fakir was performing his austerities. Without knowing it, Rameshvar entered into his garden. 110. Rameshvar had two of his students with him, and when it was time for the morning bath, seeing a pool of pure clear water, they went at once into it. 111. While Rameshvar was bathing, Anagadsha, the *yogi*, happened to be at a distance. But when he heard the repetition of mantras (by Rameshvar) at the time of bathing, he pronounced a curse. 112. "He, who has befouled the water in which I perform my prayers, will feel his body burn with fire, and will not be able to obtain water to quench it." 113. As soon as the fakir had uttered this curse, Rameshvar's skin, where it was untouched by water, burned as it were being scorched. He said to his students, "What am I to do?" 114. When he attempted to come out of the water, his body seemed all the more on fire. He sent out piercing cries for help, to know what to do. 115. The students said to him, "The fakir must have used some *mantra*. Go as a suppliant to him immediately. Let us go at once." 116. But said Rameshvar, "I am of the highest caste, a Brahman, and this fakir is a Muhammadan, of low caste. I certainly will not go to him." 117. With this pride in his heart, he made the determination not to go, but when he attempted to come out of the water, his body seemed to turn to fire. 118. After four *ghatikas* had passed, he came out of the water. He kept his wet garment around his body that water might trickle from it. 119. His students carried a watering-pot, and sprinkled water over him. Said he, "Let us go back home. The pain in my body is intense. 120. It seems to me that I shall surely not survive from this pain." That his death should come from such a calamity gave him great concern. 121. He had this burning sensation all the time, whether he was lying down, sitting up, or walking. The austerities he had performed were of no avail. He could not understand what was the matter with him. 122. Seeing Rameshvar's desperate condition, people of differing opinions made their respective remarks. "The fakir used his *mantra.* It could have been nothing else." 123. The wise ones remarked in opposition to this, "He caused Tuka's *abhangs* to be sunk, and thereby the Husband-of-Rukmini has become angry. Anagadsha was merely God's instrument. 124. King Ambarish was a perfect *bhakta* of Vishnu. Durvas cursed him. Vishnu's disk then pursued Durvas. The same thing has caused this." 125. They all talked thus, but no one thought of a remedy. They simply remarked, "An earth-god (a Brahman) like Rameshvar lies suffering in pain." 126. While this disease was torturing, his body had no pleasure in son, house, wife or wealth. He then went to Alandi and before Dnyanadev's tomb sat down to fast. 127. To the Ajan tree he fastened a leaking jar, and sat under it. He said to himself, "My body is suffering this great affliction, I know not what Fate has for me."

God Comforts Tuka.

128. Now while these events were happening to Rameshvar Bhatt, the hater of *bhaktas,* let us turn to Tuka, and what events were taking place with him. He had re-

fused food and water. Now what did the Dweller-in-Pandhari do 129, but assume the form of a child, and in this form Shri Hari placed his hand on Tuka and comforted him. Said He to Tuka, "I am your helper and advocate. If I stand by your head, why need you feel concern? 130. Because Pralhad was constantly repeating my name, Hiranyakashipu, my enemy, persecuted him in many ways. He certainly hated his son. 131. When he pushed Pralhad over a precipice I, *the Infinite One*, bore him up with my infinite hands. The water of the ocean could not drown him, because I assumed the form of a tortoise and bore him up. 132. Hiranyakashipu, that great villain, threw his own child, Pralhad, into the fire, but the fire seemed to him pleasantly cool, and this because of the waves of my mercy. 133. The intoxicated elephants, which that demon Hiranyakashipu drove to trample upon Pralhad, seemed to see Pralhad as a lion, and they fled into the jungle. 134. Hiranyakashipu tried to have serpents bite Pralhad, but Pralhad seemed to them to be the King of Birds. Legs appeared on their underbodies, and they hastened into antholes. 135. In order that my *bhakta* Pralhad might die, Hiranyakashipu made him drink a virulent poison. But to Pralhad, who was repeating my names, the poison seemed like nectar. 136. And when he called me to his help I manifested myself as Narahari [Half man, half lion]. I tore the demon open with my claws, and preserved my servant. 137. There are innumerable such like stories of me, which you have often sung in your *kirtans*, and often heard. They are not untrue stories. In the Purans these heroic deeds are proclaimed. 138. I, the Supreme-Being-of-the-Universe, am sitting in the water holding your manuscripts to my heart. You will see with your own eyes what I mean to do."

Saying this he embraced Tuka to His heart. 139. And after these words (of comfort) God vanished out of sight. Or one might say that the bee, Shri Hari, became caught in Tuka's lotus heart.

140. As pious people, and as evil minded men also, frequently came to look at Tuka, they saw that he hardly breathed. His body lay there like a piece of wood. 141. He was unable to change the position of his body as he lay on one side. "He is dying from the wasting away of his body," said those who were revilers of Tuka. 142. One remarked, "His wife died in the famine, crying: 'Give me food, food.' And now the same thing is happening to Tuka. He is going to lose his life, dying of hunger." 143. But the pious people on the contrary said, "Shri Hari is protecting Tuka. Even without food and water for his body, a special lustre is to be seen. 144. If the Life-of-the-Universe had not been his helper, he would already have lost his life. We still hear the sound of his voice repeating aloud the names of God. Go near and listen." 145. Such were the remarks made by people, but Tuka's heart was now filled with joy. Outwardly it seemed to people that he was still holding to his fasting at the door of the temple.

Tuka's Manuscripts Float Dry on the Water.

146. Thirteen days thus passed. Let us now see what the Pervader-of-the-Universe did. The Soul-of-the-Universe appeared in a vision to many, and said to them, 147. "I have truly preserved Tuka's *abhangs* dry in the water. These manuscripts are now to come to the surface,

and float on the water. Go immediately and take them out." 148. Having seen this vision at night, as soon as it was morning they came there, and lo! and behold!! the manuscripts were seen floating on the water, just as a gourd floats on water. 149. Then with the loud shouting of God's names and the clapping of hands the crowd of *bhaktas* expressed their joy. Said they, "The Wearer-of-the-wild-flower-garlands [*Krishna*] has come to Tuka's help. This is a new thing, with which nothing can be compared." 150. There were some swimmers amongst these *bhaktas,* who dove into the deep pool of water, and passing the manuscripts from hand to hand took them out of the water, remarking, "The Lord-of-Pandhari has come to Tuka's help."

151. Then all the people came to the temple and reported the news to Tuka, and said, "It is because of your perfect sincerity of *bhakti* that has brought the Husband-of-Rukmini to your help." 152. And when the God-loving *bhakta* opened his eyes, he saw that the salvation of his manuscripts was true. He then and there composed seven *abhangs* of praise, in which the sentiment of mercy is especially contained.

Tuka's Heartfelt Confession.

153. Said Tuka, "O Husband-of-Rukmini, O Shri Vitthal, I have greatly transgressed. Affected by the gossip of men, I have indeed caused Thee trouble. 154. Thy thoughts, O Vithabai, have had to be in two places, one in protecting my body, and the other in preserving the manuscripts dry in the water. 155. Thou hast preserved

my life for thirteen days without food or water, and (for thirteen days) the papers have remained dry in the water. In this Thou hast shown an extraordinary miracle. . 156. O Helper-of-the-Helpless, O Pervader-of-the-Universe, I am indeed a sinner. I have also committed another great wrong in that I sat here at the door of Thy temple fasting (to attain my purpose). 157. That which was to happen has happened, and those things will never return. And now, O Mother Vitthal, I will not henceforth burden Thee. 158. Although all these evil men should combine and threaten to cut my throat, unless I did what would be a trouble to Thee, I will not do it. 159. I have this once committed a mistake, and I have burdened Thee, O Thou-of-dark-complexion. As I remember from time to time my transgressions, my throat chokes with emotion. 160. Thou, O Krishna, didst stand in the water, and in Thy love Thou didst keep my manuscripts dry. The saints praise Thy reputation as a helper. Thou hast made me experience its truth. 161. I have no authority to put Thee into trouble, but I did it to preserve my own reputation, without taking due thought. 162. At the slightest transgression of a child its father or mother are ready to punish it. I cannot, therefore, use them for a comparison with Thee. Thou art unique in Thy possession of a pitying heart. 163. Enough, enough of this worldly life! I am not able to hold in check my *karma,* so difficult. Steady my heart, O Husband-of-Rukmini, Guru-of-the-Universe. 164. Frequently in my heart arise many waves in the sea of infinite thoughts, and by connection with them, my heart becomes bound. 165. So now delivering me from my anxiety, come and dwell in my heart. I will then forever serve Thee with feelings of love. I want no other purpose in life."

THE FAME OF TUKA'S MANUSCRIPTS SPREADS.

166. When the manuscripts were taken out of the water dry, Tuka wrote seven *abhangs* in praise of God. They are extraordinarily filled with the sentiment of love. Saints drink it in with a sense of satisfaction.

167. For thirteen days those manuscrips had been lying in the water, but finally they were taken out dry. But now the pious people carried off the manuscripts in order that they might become widely known. 168. The Husband-of-Rukmini had personally preserved the papers dry, though in the water. The story of this spread from province to province, and gladly copies were made of them. 169. Just as in the case of flowers. They are in one place, but their fragrance pours out in the vaulted sky. So Tuka's fame spread from that time far and wide over this round earth.

RAMESHVAR BHATT IS HEALED.

170. Turning now to the story of Rameshvar Bhatt, we have seen that he had gone to the sacred city of Alandi, and was sitting fasting while his body seemed aflame. 171. He had tied a leaking jar to the Ajan tree, and sat under it day and night. He thus always had wet clothes on him. 172. Having this great desire in his heart (to be free from his pain), he prayed to Shri Dnyaneshvar, "Do this kindness at once to me of freeing me from the curse of the fakir. 173. Through this pain I am suffering intense torture. You are the visible *avatar* of Vishnu, descended in this *Kali yuga* to save the world."

174. In this manner Rameshvar Bhatt continued to praise Dnyaneshvar. Then by night a vision was given to him. You saints, please listen with reverence to what it

was. 175. (Dnyaneshvar said to him) "Amongst all the *bhaktas* the most excellent, the noblest, is the noble Vaishnava, the God-loving Nama. Tuka is his *avatar,* descended to save the world. 176. Because of your reviling him in your hatred, your store of good deeds has become depleted, and your faults are stored up (to trouble you) for ever. This is the reason for your bodily pain. 177. Now if with sincerity in your heart, you go to him as a suppliant, your terrible disease will disappear, and you will be saved from the ocean of your worldly existence. 178. Any one who shows hatred to a *bhakta* of Vishnu commits a sin that cannot be washed away, though one bathe in sacred waters. But go as a suppliant to Tuka; only thus can your suffering be relieved."

179. Such was the dream in which Dnyanadev appeared to Rameshvar. As soon as Rameshvar became awake, he felt repentance for his treatment (of Tuka). 180. Without the heat of the fever of this worldly life, repentance is not possible. Without repentance sin does not leave one. This statement is absolutely true. 181. When Shiva took in the poison his whole body was in a flame, then giving his undivided worship to Shri Ram, his body became cool. 182. But enough of too much talking. The use of too many illustrations will expand this book too much. Rameshvar felt repentant (as we have seen) as the result of seeing the vision. 183. He then wrote a letter, and gave it to one of his disciples telling him to go to Dehu and inform Tuka of what had happened. 184. Rameshvar thought to himself, "If I should go immediately to see him, God will afflict me with some other disaster, my transgression is so great. 185. I have heard the news of how the papers (of Tuka's manuscripts) were taken out

of the water dry, and immediately after Dnyanadev appeared to me in the vision of a dream and spoke to me." 186. Feeling the importance of that miracle, Rameshvar wrote the letter with fear and trembling. He used many words of praise of Tuka, and sent it at once to Dehu. 187. The disciple of Rameshvar told Tuka everything that had happepned. "The fakir Anagadsha has cursed Rameshvar, and he wishes to know what remedy there is for it."

188. When Tuka heard what had happened to Rameshvar, he felt pity for him. Said he, "This Brahman pandit is a man of fine character. I wonder what has caused this misfortune." 189. To Tuka enemy and friend were alike, so he had forgotten Rameshvar's past enmity. He saw the Lord-of-Pandhari in every object of the universe, and had the power to transform the mundane body into a divine one. 190. The noble Vaishnava's heart melted with pity as he read Rameshvar's pleading words. And then in the fulness of his compassion he composed an *abhang* and gave it to the disciple (to take back). 191. The disciple took the letter in his hand, and speedily arrived at Alandi. He gave the letter to his *sadguru,* and orally related what had taken place. 192. Rameshvar read the letter that Tuka had written to him. You wise and pious ones, listen to its contents, its extracted cream.

TUKA'S ABHANG TO RAMESHVAR.

193. If the heart is sincerely pure, enemies become friends. Tigers, serpents may come near one, but will never devour him.

194. If he is given poison, it will turn into nectar; if any one tries to harm him, it will only result in good; if he is spoken to with harsh

words, they will sound to him as very courteous.

195. If a mighty effort is made to give him pain, it will only give him the fruit of all happiness. The flames of fire will feel cool, if God, Merciful-to-the-lowly, is pleased.

196. If there is one feeling towards all, if there is love of others more than for one's self, God (Hari) will look on such with the eye of mercy, and in the heart there will be an experience of it.

197. Such was the *abhang* that Rameshvar read. And then behold! an extraordinary miracle took place. Listen to it, you pious people. 198. As Rameshvar read those words, "Even a volcano will become cool, if God is pleased," the burning sensation of his body from the curse of the Fakir Anagadsha at that very moment abated. 199. Rameshvar had been feeling that scorching pain continuously which had come from the curse of the fakir, but now the whole burning sensation ceased. It was indeed a wonderful experience.

200. Then repentant at heart, he came and fell prostrate before Tuka. His eyes filled with tears, and he exclaimed, "Blessed is the glory of the saints. 201. I have read all the Upanishads and the Vedanta, but there is no power in me that could preserve paper dry in water. 202. A *sadguru* who can save one in this ocean of a worldly life, such is Tuka." And with this sincere feeling Rameshvar now enjoyed happiness joined with love.

203. When Rameshvar was on his way to meet Tuka, Tuka became aware of it in his heart, and he said

to himself, "I will go and meet that distinguished Brahman as he comes." 204. And with this thought he at once started, and they met one another half way. 205. Rameshvar said to Tuka, "You are a supreme *bhakta,* a noble Vaishnava. I, a sinner, was unaware of this, and it was I who caused your manuscripts to be sunk in the water. 206. I did not understand the glory of your descent into this world in order to save the world, and so I persecuted you without reason." 207. To this confession of Rameshvar Tuka replied, "But I am one of low caste, and a sinner, and always wishing for mercy." 208. To this reply of Tuka's Rameshvar made answer, "The *abhang* which you wrote me in your own hand, has, indeed, brought to me the blessing (of discipleship). 209. And there is for me no going back to my home, leaving association with you." With this determination of heart, he fell at Tuka's feet.

210. The narrator of the next most interesting chapter is the Husband-of-Rukmini Himself. Having laid his hand of assurance on Mahipati, he is narrating the contents of this book.

211. Svasti! This book, the Shri Bhaktalilamrita, by the mere listening to it one's desires are supplied. Let the pious, God-loving *bhakta*s listen. This is the thirty-fifth interesting chapter.

CHAPTER 36.

Mahipati Would Sing only of the Saints.

Obeisance to Shri Ganesh.

1. Seekers after salvation in this sea of worldly existence perform austerities, but I intend to sing of the charac-

ter and deeds of God's *bhaktas.* I know nothing aside from them. 2. Some giving up absolutely all bodily desires, have made their way to the Himalayas, but I am going to be the bard of the saints, and sing in clear notes their praiseworthy deeds. 3. Some sit down to accomplish their purpose through the means of *yoga.* Some wander to sacred places, but my mind has no liking for anything save the acts of the saints. 4. Some by special pleading collect money, and perform *yoga* practices and sacrifices, but I have only this wish in my heart to sing the praise of the *bhaktas.* 5. Some having a delight in good deeds perform the Five-great-sacrifices every day. Some study the philosophic books, and then contemplate their contents. 6. Some restrain their breathing. Some see the same substance in all creatures. Some adopt a pure mental worship of God, and devote there their love. 7. Some, though in the body, reach a state of unconsciousness of body. Some go and sit in a forest. Some study metaphysical books, and proclaim their knowledge to the world. 8. Some through the *bhakti* of a *sadguru* hope to reach the fourth stage of Final-Deliverance. But the only desire that I have in my heart is to sing the praises of the saints. 9. If I have any wish aside from this, Thou, O God, who seeest the heart, knowest it. I have made a vow. Bring it to completion. Thou art the support of my life.

A Review of Chapter Thirty-five.

10. In the last chapter we had the beautiful stories of Rameshvar's persecution of Tuka, of how God, the Mine-of-Mercy, preserved all the manuscripts that had been sunk in the water, 11. of how by the curse of a fakir, Rameshvar suffered intense physical pain, and of how, when fasting at the tomb of Dnyaneshvar, he was told every thing in

a dream, 12. and then how with deepest repentance in his heart he at once started for Dehu, and how when accomplishing one half of the journey the two met one another. 13. Then how Tuka came to Alandi, and saw Dnyanadev, his friend. How when his good fame became known to all the people they came to see him. 14. The story of the dry manuscripts in the water spread from country to country. Pious people came from a distance to see Tuka. 15. Finally taking leave of Dnyanadev, the noble Vaishnava returned to Dehu. Rameshvar, learned in the six systems of philosophy, came with him. He was never far from him. 16. He had left knowledge, personal appearance, family pride, son, wife, property, money, honour, and reputation, and was clinging to the feet of his *sadguru*.

THE FAKIR WHO CURSED RAMESHVAR VISITS TUKA.

17. Anagadsha Bova learned the news from various sources that Tuka had effected the release of Rameshvar from his curse. 18. Said he, "Without his (Rameshvarbhatt's) coming to me as a suppliant, Tuka has made him well. I must go and see Tuka. I would like to know what sort of a miracle it was." 19. So thinking, the *Mahant* [chief of fakirs] started to where the *bhakta* (Chintaman Dev) of Ganapati lived. 20. The fakir went to the door of Chintaman Dev, and cried out, "Bring out your gifts". He had a large begging bowl in his hand. "Fill this up at once," he demanded. 21. Chintaman's steward over his grain cellars brought a great abundance of the materials for cooking, and put them in the begging bowl, but it did not fill it at all, to the wonder of every one. 22. Chintaman was sitting in the God-room. Some one came and told him, "A fakir has come into the front yard, with

a begging bowl in his hand. 23. We have put an abundance of food material in it, but it does not fill it at all." Chintaman strictly charged them not to send the guest away empty handed. 24. "Whatever grain we have in the house, put it in his begging bowl." With this command the steward 25. put into his bowl all the grain which the house contained. Still the bowl would not be filled up. Then he opened the grain cellars, 26. and poured into the bowl bushels and bushels of grain; but they were all contained in his bowl. Chintaman Dev now came out of the house, and made the Siddhis stand there, 27. and they filled with their hands the bowl, and the fakir now started on his way. He came at once to Dehu, and entered into Tuka's house. 28. Avali was cooking in her kitchen, when this fakir shouted aloud from outside, "Mother, bring some flour, and at once fill my bowl." 29. Avali said to herself, "What damn beggar has come! The beggars come to molest us when there is no grain in the house." 30. Ganga, the little daughter, took a handful of flour to give him. But Avali grasped her hand, and some of the flour fell on the floor. 31. To begin with the child's hand was small, and the mother had snatched some of the flour away. The fakir stood outside watching the fun. 32. Then the little daughter Ganga came outside, and put into his bowl a little bit of flour. But it filled the bowl to overflowing, and Anagadsha was astonished. 33. He attempted to show his occult powers, but they would not work on this occasion. So overwhelmed with astonishment, he began to question the girl. 34. "Is Tukoba your name?" Gangabai, hearing this question, said, "You talk like a fool. 35. Don't you know that my father, after his morning bath, is now sitting in the temple?" Anagadsha gaining this information said to himself, "I will go at once to see him." 36.

He went at once to the temple, and there saw the state in which Tuka was. He was the very image of the Everlasting Brahma, and in his heart no such thing as desire. 37. Anagadsha became filled with love for Tuka, and prostrated himself before him. He remained there a few days, listening to Tuka's Hari-*kirtans*. 38. Though the *kirtans* lasted until the fourth watch of the night, still he continued standing before Tuka. And Tuka, the noble Vaishnava, paid Anagadsha honour and reverence. 39. In listening to the stories told about Tuka, the fakir felt great pleasure. Finally he took leave of Tuka and hastened back to his hermitage.

TUKA AND THE WOMAN WHO WAS A SINNER.

40. The enthusiastic *kirtans* continued daily in Dehu, and large numbers of people came to listen. Suddenly one day a beautiful, handsome woman, with lustful feelings, 41. found Tuka alone, after one of his *kirtans*. Said she to him, "A desire has arisen in me to realize my wish. 42. For many days I have been watching for an opportunity, and to-day I have found you alone." The Vaishnava *bhakta*, hearing her say this, began to tremble violently. 43. Just as Shuka, the chief of Yogis, when he saw Rambha was disturbed in his mind, so it happened to Tuka. 44. Rising up, he composed two *abhangs*, with which he preached to her. "Every woman is to me like my mother. These are by no means untrue words. 45. The six enemies of the soul which live in our bodies, I have placed at Vithoba's feet. I have cast aside the great Siddhis; then of what use are carnal desires to me? 46. Mother, hasten away, Your attempts will all be in vain." Thus admonishing her, the Vaishnava *bhakta* went, and sat down alone by himself. 47. He gave himself to worship with feelings of love, and

now suddenly the sun arose. A crowd of people from distant villages assembled in the temple of Vishnu with shouts of "Victory! Victory!" and the loud repeating of God's names.

TUKA'S SECOND VISIT TO LOHAGAV.

48. One day some people from Lohagav suddenly appeared to take Tuka back with them. They had to use much persuasion with this God-loving *bhakta*, but it ended in their taking him back to their town. 49. The Vaishnavas who accompanied Tuka, and ranked high in honour and influence, were as follows. Rameshvar, the great pandit, a Brahman, who would not return to his home. 50. Then there was Tuka's younger brother, whose name was Kanhoba. The third, a Brahman named Gangaji Maval, who sang in Tuka's *kirtans*. 51. Then there was Santaji Teli [Oilman], a very God-loving man. He sat beside Tuka, and wrote down the *abhangs* as Tuka composed them. Blessed was his great fortune, that he should always be in the company of Tuka. 52. These above mentioned four were the principal ones, but many others later joined him, leading in the chorus of his *kirtans*, with emotions of love.

53. The God-loving *bhakta* approached near Lohagav. The inhabitants of the town came out to welcome him, and in sincerity prostrated themselves before him. 54. Those in whose houses Tuka performed his *kirtans*, they were full of supreme joy. They prepared various kinds of dainty food and feasted the Brahmans in their homes. 55. According as they were able, they feasted the Brahmans. The very wealthy gave a feast to a thousand Brahmans, and then had Tuka perform his *kirtans*.

The Conversion of Shivji the Coppersmith.

56. All the people of the town of Lohagav became pious, with the exception of one Shivji, a coppersmith, and a very bad man. He was a reviler, crooked, a miser, and a knave, but he was weak in this world's goods. 57. Tuka continued to tell all the people to go and invite Shivji to the *kirtans,* but he would never come, and instead, used insult and ridicule.

58. Now it happened that a certain Brahman, in order to pay off his debt, went to Alandi and sat fasting (before Dnyanadev's tomb). He had a debt of ten thousand rupees, and for this he rejected food. 59. After six months Dnyaneshvar said to him in a dream, "Go immediately to Tuka. He will at once free you from your debt." 60. The Brahman, hunting for Tuka, finally reached Lohagav. He said to Tuka that Dnyaneshvar had sent him. 61. The God-loving *bhakta* knew what was in the man's mind without his telling him, and said to the people of the town, "Beg here and there money and give to him. 62. Make use of some influence and get something from Shivji the coppersmith." The people not wishing to withstand Tuka's request, went to the house of the coppersmith. 63. Through supreme effort on their part he did give two copper coins. Tuka lifted up a pebble, and with it rubbed the coins. 64. They turned at once into gold, and he gave them into the hands of the fasting Brahman. But said he, "My debt will not be paid off by this amount." 65. "Well", replied the Vaishnava Tuka, "If there are any copper vessels here give them to me." The towns people were very surprised at this remark, being under the seduction of earthly joys. 66. The Brahman then showed Tuka the utensils for worship in his bag. At once Tuka applied the pebble

to them, and turned them into gold. 67. Now happy in mind, the fasting-Brahman returned to Alandi. And Tuka threw the pebble down into a well.

68. Now Shivji, the coppersmith, opponent of the *bhaktas,* and a knave, marvelled over the occurrence. Said he, "Tuka possesses a *paris* [Touch-stone]." And so immediately he began to perform acts of worship. 69. He thought to himself, "By rendering service to him, I shall be able to rid myself entirely of poverty." Therefore, he came to listen to Tuka's preaching, but his heart's desire was on something different. 70. Just like a *vrindavan* [Cucumber-like fruit], bitter within, but outside it looks like a sweet cucumber, so the coppersmith began to perform rigorous austerities for attaining desires, but his mind was placed on the hope of material gain. 71. For a whole year he listened to Tuka's Hari *kirtans,* and then suddenly The Husband-of-Rukmini was pleased. Listen to the reason for this. 72. The Coppersmith had sent thirty-six pack bullocks to Bombay to bring back tin. His agents loaded the bullocks for the return, but lo! and behold! it all turned to silver. 73. He then sent the bullocks back to those from whom he had purchased the tin. The merchant examined his accounts, and said, "That certainly does not belong to me." 74. He loaded the bullocks up again, and sent them back to Lohagav. Shivji was astonished, and immediately went and told Tuka. 75. The *sadguru* replied to him, "This has come about through your good fortune. God [Krishna] has come to your aid. Now use the money in good deeds." 76. He had a great well (with stone steps) built, to which the name is given, 'The Coppersmith's well.' He gave gifts of food to many, and made Brahmans happy with his gifts. 77. From that

time the coppersmith became one very indifferent to worldly things. He deserted his house and wife and all his worldly affairs, and was constantly with Tuka.

SHIVJI'S WIFE SCOLDS TUKA.

78. Because of this, his wife felt great hatred against Tuka. Said she, "He has made my husband crazy, and keeps him sitting by himself. 79. They perform *kirtans* all night long, and he will not let my husband come home even to sleep." She began to plan how she could take Tuka's life. 80. She heated four large brass vessels full of water to the boiling point, and set them aside in the house. She brought Tuka to the house, without his suspecting her cunning. 81. She seated the noble Vaishnava on a bathing board under the wall of the terrace. Then she emptied on him the boiling water. Tuka was scalded to his insides. 82. Then Tuka cried out for help, "Rush to my help, O God-Supreme. My body is all aflame." He then composed an *abhang*. Then suddenly, He, who is the resting place of His saints, came to his aid. .83. The boiling water that was scalding him, now seemed cool to Tuka. After this bath she gave him a light meal, but she mixed arsenic with it. 84. But all the joys and sorrows of His *bhakta* the Husband-of-Rukmini Himself bore. Tuka's condition was that of bodily unconsciousness, and the poison did him no harm. 85. When the God-loving *bhakta* left her house, the Lord-of-Pandhari showed His anger towards her. She became immediately a sore-covered leper, and she was in dire misery. 86. Just then Shivji, the coppersmith, returning to his house, found his wife fallen in a faint. He recognized at once the garland of flowers that had been used in the pavilion, and thought he, 87. "Last night there was the usual enthusiastic *kirtan*, and there

was a garland around Tuka's neck. She must have brought the noble Vaishnava here, and adopted this method of persecuting him. 88. Rameshvar Bhatt then said to him, "If you take the mud from the place where Tuka had his bath, and apply it to your wife's body she will be healed." 89. Shivji trusted what was told him, and did so, and God came at once to her aid. All her leprosy sores disappeared, and her health was restored. 90. From that day she also placed her worship at Tuka's feet. She was a constant listener at the *kirtans,* and she put away all hatred.

Tuka Meets King Shivaji.

91. Such are the many events in Tuka's life. Many had direct manifestations of God through him. The manuscripts that Rameshvar had caused to be sunk the Husband-of-Rukmini had preserved dry. 92. When the report of these good deeds reached King Shivaji he marvelled greatly. Said he, "I must call Tuka here and listen to his *kirtans.* 93. So he sent to Lohagav an umbrella, a horse and an officer to invite Tuka. They informed the Vaishnava *bhakta* of the king's message. 94. "The king," they said, "is very desirous of the pleasure of meeting you. Come along to where he is, and make yourself his helper." 95. When Tuka heard this message, he fell into the greatest distress. He cried, "O God-Supreme, Lord-of-Pandhari, why dost Thou entangle me in this? 96. The display of hypocrisy and honour are to me, like swine-dung. O Ocean-of-Mercy, Cloud-of-Intelligence, rush to my help and free me." 97. With such contents the Vaishnava *bhakta* wrote four *abhangs* and gave them to the officer. As the officer [*karkun*] was leaving, Tuka said to him, 98. "Sit on the horse that was sent for me." The other replied, "He is a

very fiery horse, and allows no one to ride him." 99. Hearing this about the horse, Tuka patted it and the horse became gentle at once. Such are the extraordinary deeds of saints. 100. The secretary reported the news to the king, and he marvelled. He read the four *abhangs* that Tuka had composed for him. 101. Seeing the nature of Tuka as indifferent to worldly things, the king thought to himself, "I will go to where he is with pleasure, and meet Tuka there." 102. The noble king, taking garments, ornaments, adornments, materials for worship, and gold coins, started on his way. 103. Along with him to Lohagav came his prime minister and those of very high rank. He saw at once that all the people of the town were pious people experiencing the joy of loving God. 104. Although Krishna was born at Mathura, still there was no limit to the joy felt by the inhabitants of Gokul. In the same way the inhabitants of Lohagav manifested their intense love for Tuka. 105. By night they listened to the deeds of Shri Hari. When the day dawned there was the ceremony of Gopalakala. There is no end to happiness, where there is mutual sympathy and love.

106. Shivaji the King arrived to visit Tuka, and together with his prime minister prostrated himself before him. 107. The king with his own hand sprinkled the fragrant powders, and put around Tuka the *tulsi* and flower garlands. The noble king then placed a platter full of gold coin before Tuka. 108. Seeing this royal wealth, Tuka was disgusted. Listen with reverence to the gracious words which Tuka uttered on that occasion.

109. "What need have I of stores of wealth. Vitthal alone is all I want. My soul has no other desires aside from Him. 110. I have heard a great deal of your high reputation, and now to-day I understand your generosity.

But how can you give with pleasure that which we Vaishnavas have no heart for. 111. If you were going to visit the sun why would you need a little lamp? Clouds pour their rain on the ocean, but it has not desire for the rain. 112. Why should the Himalaya mountains need the wind of a fan, O noble King? One might rub the sandal-wood paste on the moon, but it can have no desire for it. 113. Would the Ocean-of-Milk feel pleasure at the gift of a milch cow? If one should offer to the Gold-mountain some gold, would it take pleasure in that offering? 114. You have brought me this gift of wealth, but it is to me like cow-flesh. But I will tell you something which will be to your comfort. 115. Put around your neck a *tulsi* garland, and perform the ceremonies belonging to the eleventh day of the fortnight. Aside from this whatever money or things you may give me, it will seem to me like earth. 116. In my heart there is but one desire, that you should call yourself the servant of Vithoba." Hearing these words of Tuka's, the king was pleased. 117. The money which the king had brought to give to Tuka, he distributed among the Brahmans. At night he listened to the Hari *kirtan*, and the gracious words of Tuka. 118. There was first the verses of praise, and then the loud repeating of Hari's names. The sound of the cymbals, *vina* and drums filled the sky to the full. 119. In the joy of their delight, and in their supreme happiness they sang and danced. There was great clapping of hands, and snapping of fingers, and the enthusiasm was great. 120. The sole subject of the *kirtan* was that "Vitthal is our Mother and Father. Vitthal is our brother, friend and uncle. Aside from Him there is no object of our affection. 121. Vitthal is the close friend and relative. Vitthal is my wealth and property. Vitthal is my secret treasure, my dearest one, the resting place of my life. 122. Vitthal is my all, whether in my private thought or in my public life. If I should look at any one beside Vitthal, my eyes would burst and waste away. 123. If I should sing the praise of anyone aside from Vitthal, my tongue would immediately be paralyzed. If my heart cares for anyone beside Him, it will be to my reproach. 124. If I do not walk the path leading to Pandhari, my feet will immediately become lame. I have offered my body at the feet of Vitthal, and have discarded all worldly things. 125. Philosophers waste their words in vain, when used for other themes than Vitthal. And if they are uttered to saints and good men, they should not at all be listened to." 126. Tuka continued on that occasion to say to his listeners, "Worship Vithoba. Only thus will you, my father, be saved from this earthly existence." 127. After thus discoursing, he repeated with great enthusiasm the names of God. Veiled from human vision in the sky, gods looked down on the wonderful sight. 128. Vitthal was both speaker and listener, and, therefore, all sang, and all listened. And the king, listening to such a *kirtan,* felt his heart impressed with indifference to worldly things. 129. Said he, "At this very moment I give up my kingdom. I wish to sit in the forest worshipping Shri Hari." And with this the noble king took off his turban, and placed it on the ground. 130. Just as the sun was rising, the light of the wave-offering was waved, and the king after making his *namaskar* to Tuka, went into the jungle, and sat alone in silence. 131. He had told his Prime Minister, and others by no means to come near him. The king, now indifferent to worldly things, was experiencing the joy of loving God. 132. By day he sat in the jungle, at night he came into the town to listen to the *kirtan.* The Prime Minister wrote a letter, telling all that had happened, and sent it to the king's mother. 133. When Jijabai heard the letter read, she burst out crying before everyone. "Tuka has now destroyed our kingdom," she exclaimed. "This is not good news." 134. She sat in her palanquin, and came at once to Lohagav. When she saw Tuka she prostrated herself on the ground before him. 135. Then in the attitude of one pleading, and with eyes full of tears, she said, "My only son, through your *kirtans,* has become indifferent to worldly things, and sits in the jungle worshipping. 136. He has no son. Who will carry on the kingdom?" Hearing Jijabai's pleading words, Tuka said to her, 137. "When Shivaji comes to the *kirtan* I will say a few words to him. Let your mind be at rest, and worship Vithoba." 138. Hearing Tuka's words, Jijabai bowed before him, and said, "If you give me the gift of my son, how shall I ever be able to express my gratitude?"

139. As the Hari *kirtan* was performed that night the king came to *listen.* Tuka then at the proper moment explained to him the System of Salvation by good deeds. 140. Said he, "In order to be saved in this worldly existence, supremacy is given to the way of good deeds. One should follow his own religious duties. For him there is no other way. 141. (As says the Bhagavadgita) the duties belonging to others are good. But if on that account one performs them (instead of one's own), it will not prove a means of salvation. This is the teaching of the *shastras* on human duties. 142. If a fish leaves the water and jumps into melted butter, how can it live? A bird should not leave the air, and carelessly make its way into a hole in the ground. 143. Great rats and little rats will run into their holes. If they come out, they lose their lives. If serpents

eat food, that in itself causes their death. 144. Noble trees cannot walk. They grow where they sprouted. Will a human being, whose mind is fickle, so remain immovable? 145. An Arab horse does not know how to drag a plow. If a soldier sits on an ox, the battle will not be for him. 146. The reason for giving these many examples by way of illustration is because if any one fails to perform his special duties, he has nothing but a miserable death before him. 147. When God created the universe, He assigned to each one his duties. To Brahmadev he assigned the duty of creation. He kept for himself the preservation of the universe. 148. The duty of holding the earth up was assigned to the serpent Sesha, while Vasuki's duty is to keep it from moving. He arranged that the oceans should surround the earth, and stay within their limits. 149. He appointed the sun with its great fierce heat to give light to creatures. He appointed the moon to radiate coolness, and it performs that duty. 150. The Cold, Hot and Rainy Seasons at their own special times appear in power. And when one's life has come to its end, Death punishes the body. 151. This is truly God's command, and all act as He has appointed them. And they who transgress the teaching of the Vedas at once go to Hell. 152. A Brahman's duties are to observe Brahmacharya (celibacy), and learn the Vedas. Then having become a householder, he should turn his thoughts to the six duties of a householder. 153. When he becomes a Vanaprasth [forest-ascetic] he must continually conquer his sense desires. And by his discarding of every desire, he attains the highest form of *sanyas;* so the scriptures have said. 154. He who wholly forgets all his family and caste duties, he is known as a Paramahans [the highest form of asceticism]. These are the teachings of the *Vedas* for the Brahmans. They are the commands of Shri Hari.

155. I will now tell you the duties of a Kshatriya. Listen to them. To attack and conquer the enemy, and protect the subjects in the performance of their special duties. 156. Just as a lover of pleasure gains supreme happiness in providing for all his bodily parts, or as when a family man goes to his home and looks with pleasure on all connected with his home. 157. In the same way when a king sees his subjects happy, he himself becomes happy. There is no good deed greater than this for any one in whose heart there are noble thoughts. 158. In order to attain God the Kshatriya must make gifts, and never to deceive by body, speech or mind. 159. The principal and first caste is the Brahman, then come the Kshatriya, the Vaishya and fourthly the Shudra. There are many other castes, but they also must be faithful to the special duties of their caste. 160. In one's mind one should regard all with impartiality. One should see God in all creatures. No one should injure another, and in worship there should be love (of God). 161. When carrying on one's business, one should not speak an untruth. There is no sin so great as that of falsehood. 162. One should feel compassion for every creature. One should feed the hungry. One should never tell a falsehood, and one should always be repeating the names of God. 163. If one lives in this good way, he will be happy in this worldly existence. Why go into the jungle (for worship). God [Hari] will meet him in his own home."

164. Such was Tuka's preaching, and all the listeners were giving ear. The king's mind was intensely absorbed in it, and tears flowed from his eyes. 165. Then followed the loud repeating of God's names with love, and the lights for the wave-offering were lighted. They were waved around the Husband-of-Rukmini, and all fell pros-

trate before Him. 166. Sweetmeats were distributed to all the listeners, and recognizing Tuka's wish the king picked up his turban (which he had placed on the ground). 167. Then King Shivaji's mother fell at Tukoba's feet saying, "I see nothing with which I can return my gratitude." 168. For four days more the king remained there, and then suddenly a very strange thing happened. Listen to it, you good and pious people.

A Brahman Struck Dumb, then Cured.

169. There was there one Navaji, a gardener, a very pious man. While a *kirtan* was going on, he said to Tuka, 170. "For a moment or two I will stand up and lead, and you take rest, my Svami." And full of love for the names he was repeating, he danced as his mind inclined. 171. Repeating verses with the names of Vitthal, he danced with supreme joy. He clapped his hands in delight, and God filled his heart. 172. For full four *ghatikas* he carried on the *kirtan*. Perspiration flowed from his body, and then worn out he sat down. 173. Tukaram then arose to continue the *kirtan*, and the enthusiasm increased infinitely.

From that day Navaji, the gardener, did as follows. 174. He spun thread on his wheel, and used it in making garlands of flowers. And when the Brahmans were seated at the *kirtan*, he put these garlands on them. 175. When therefore, Navaji came to the *kirtan* the Vaishnava *bhakta* exclaimed, "Here comes our heart's rest." And as the Vaishnava *bhakta* thus spoke, the people there marvelled. 176. The man folded his garment in four folds and placed one end in Tuka's hand. Navaji then tucked up the garment and danced before the Vaishnavas. 177. He used (a sentence), "The things of Dvarka came gladly to Pandhari." It was too difficult for him to pronounce correctly. For "chojavit" he said "chodavit." 178. Hearing Navaji's blunder the whole assembly laughed heartily. But Navaji, with increased pleasure, continued his joyous dancing. 179. Now there was in the town a learned Brahman. He went into Navaji's garden for his bath. He made fun of Navaji. Said he, "You use words without following rules. 180. You always say, 'The things of Dvarka came with pleasure (chodavit) to Pandhari.' That mispronunciation will surely send you to Hell." 181. Hearing him say this, Navaji expressed himself very humbly. Said he, "I will not do so from to-day. You have taught me a good lesson." 182. Having created this confusion in Navaji's mind, the Brahman went back to his home. But lo! his power of speech was gone. He could not utter a single word. 183. He wrote on a slate what had happened, and sent it to Rameshvar, who amazed at the occurrence, reported it at once to Tuka. 184. Just at that moment a farmer brought a tender cucumber with the desire in his mind that Tuka should eat it. 185. Knowing his thought, the noble Vaishnava split it. He cut it into four pieces and ate three of them himself. 186. One remained uneaten. Rameshvar Bhatt suggested that he give of it as favours to all of them. To this the servant of Vishnu replied, 187. "It was not worthy for you, therefore, I ate it all." But he gave a half of the remaining piece to the man who had lost his voice. As he ate it a wonderful thing took place. 188. While eating this favour of Tuka's, he immediately began to talk. The piece that still remained he cut into small pieces and distributed them to all. 189. As each one put the piece in his mouth his mouth puckered, and hiding here and there, they spit it out. It was so terribly bitter.

190. That night when the *kirtan* was starting, Navaji the gardener came in. He said to Tuka, "I will not truly perform the *kirtan* to-night." 191. Tuka replied, "It was I who made the mistake. God was pleased with the expressions of your pure love." 192. Hearing these words of Tuka's, Navaji was made very happy, and then for four *ghatikas* he stood up, dancing in his love of God.

King Shivaji Departs.

193. As I have said above, King Shivaji continued to remain for four days. He continued to listen to the enthusiastic *kirtans,* and always with feelings of love (for God). 194. The king then came to Tuka to obtain leave to return to his own place. But he had a desire in his heart, and he wished for a favour from Tuka. 195. Said he to himself, "If our kingdom is to be freed from (the Muhammadan rule), the Svami will give me some bread. If a son is to be born to me, he will give me a cocoanut." 196. Knowing what was in the king's mind, Tuka gave him both, bread and a cocoanut. The king then made a prostrate bow and started back.

Tuka's Increasing Followers.

197. Kondabhat, a Puranic reader, came to be always with Tuka. Then there was Rameshvar, at first a bad man, but now a God-loving *bhakta.* 198. These two Brahmans were able to discuss the Vedanta philosophy. Besides these there were fourteen Vaishnavas, who left their worldly business, and remained with Tuka. 199. The people loved greatly to listen to Tuka's *kirtans,* so they followed and sought him out in a village where he had gone without telling them.

200. This book, the Shri Bhaktalilamrita, is a perfect ocean-of-milk. The Husband-of-Lakshmi, Recliner-on-the Serpent, is ever lying here. 201. Fortunate listeners, lovers of God, they are gods come to observe. With joy they drink the nectar of the stories of the saints. 202. Through them there is deliverance from birth and death. There will be no coming back whatever, for those who will experience that supreme deliverance [*sayujya*]. 203. He who is the Brother-of-the-helpless, Store-house-of-Mercy, Lover-of-his-*bhaktas,* Ocean-of-Mercy, has given Mahipati the assurance that he need not fear, and causes him to compose this book.

204. Svasti. This book, the Shri Bhaktalilamrita, by the mere listening to it supplies all the desires of the heart. Listen then, you God-loving, pious *bhaktas,* this is the thirty-sixth interesting chapter.

CHAPTER 37.

Description of the Image of Hari.

Obeisance to Shri Ganesh.

1. As the blue sky appears in the heavens, so is Thy beautiful lustre, O Shri Hari. Pearls and jewels glisten in Thy crown as if the sun had just risen. 2. Thy lovely lotus face is like a molten image made from pure nectar. The great eyes sparkle as pure lotus petals. 3. Thy two earrings are designed with jewels in a setting of gold made in the shape of crocodiles; they glitter in Thy ears when quiet, and oscillate when Thou art moving. 4. Like diamonds set in a row, so Thy teeth sparkle in Thy mouth. And the

brilliant lustre of the Kaustubha jewel is like that of the rising moon. 5. Thy dark hued body of the colour of a dense cloud is delicately rubbed over with thin sandal wood paste. Like the lightning flash does the brilliancy of Thy yellow robe appear. 6. On Thy wrist is the warrior's bracelet. The three wrinkles on Thy abdomen are beautiful in shape. The hair appears in tufts like a swarm of bees. Thou hast the beauty of the *Shrivatsa* mark. 7. The shape of Thy body is comely, and delicate. Around Thy neck is a garland of tender *tulsi* leaves. Both hands are placed on the hips, and Thy delicate feet are on a brick. 8. Thou who art the object of the *yogis'* contemplation, Thou who wast the divinity worshipped by Shiva, in order to protect the reputation of Thy *bhaktas,* hast assumed visible shape and recognizable qualities. 9. Thy beautiful form which I have brought before my imagination, I have described in words on paper. And now give me Thy assurance that I need not fear, and cause me to relate the deeds of the saints.

Tuka Feeds the Multitude by a Miracle.

10. In the last interesting chapter you listened to how King Shivaji, hearing of Tuka's great fame, came to meet him, and how the occasion brought him joy.

11. After four months had passed Tuka returned to his town of Dehu. And here a remarkable event took place, to which I ask you to listen. 12. Chintaman Dev, with the intention of going to Bhima-shankar, started with a band of pilgrims from Poona, and arrived at Dehu. 13. The Vaishnava *bhakta,* seeing him, prostrated himself on the ground with sincere reverence. In this meeting with one another, their hearts experienced joy. 14. The

pilgrims were out in the open, so the merchants had their tents pitched. They sat down with all provisions for sale around them. Chintaman then said to Tuka, 15. "Give us some favour, as we are here, you God-loving Vaishnava *bhakta.* If you can give us materials for cooking sufficient for all, our desires will be fulfilled." 16. Hearing this suggestion, Tuka was gratified, and going into his house, he brought out materials for cooking. 17. But Tuka brought only enough flour, dal, rice, and *ghi* for one person. But the whole pilgrim band came about him, and asked him for some favour [*prasad*]. 18. As Tuka observed their ardent wish, this God-loving *bhakta* became perplexed. So he prayed, "O God-Supreme, Husband-of-Rukmini, supply enough material for all." 19. As the Vaishnava *bhakta* was thus praying, the Lord-of-Pandhari came unseen; he had provisions sufficient for one man, but in distribution they were sufficient for all. 20. Chintaman Dev, seeing this extraordinary deed, marvelled. Said he, "How did this supply take place, seeing that the *Siddhis* did not come to this place." 21. With this thought in his mind, he lovingly embraced Tuka. And after the cooking was duely finished, they seated Tuka in the row with them. 22. They remained there one night, listening to Tuka's *kirtan,* and then as soon as it was dawn, the pilgrim band left (for Bhimashankar).

THE MIRACLE OF IRON TURNED TO GOLD.

23. There was another Brahman who lay fasting before Dnyanadev's tomb. Seeing his intense determination, the *sadguru* [Dnyanadev] appeared to him in a dream, 24. saying, "Go to Tuka, and come back with whatever he gives you." Having seen this vision, the man came to Dehu. 25 As he told the circumstances connected with

his dream, Tuka was disgusted. Said he, "Why has the Lord-of-Pandhari increased these hindrances (to my work). 26. I am a helpless, weak person. I do not know how to manifest the skill of a *Siddhi.* These fasting people come to me so frequently. He [Dnyanadev] alone knows the meaning of his actions. 27. However, he said to this Fasting Brahman, "Go to Lohagav at once. There is one Shivji, a coppersmith, there. Take without remark whatever he gives you." 28. The Brahman agreeing, started immediately for Lohagav. When the coppersmith heard his story he wondered at it. 29. On that day it happened that there was a feast to Brahmans in Shivji the coppersmith's house. After which, there was the usual giving of *pan supari* and favours, with which all were made happy. 30. After the feast was over, the Brahman was taken into the house by Shivji, and the latter lifting up four iron harrows, placed them on the Brahman's head. 31. Said he, "Go at once to Dehu, and show these to Tuka." The Brahman, in great perplexity of mind, thought to himself, "What am I to do with these things? 32. I performed austerities before Dnyanadev in order that my poverty might entirely end. However, wealth is not in my fate. So what can he do?" 33. There were two mountains he had to pass, Kanhe and Reke. Here he threw down three of his iron harrows. 34. The Brahman kept one, however, on his head and came to Dehu. Tuka, the noble Vaishnava, was sitting alone by himself. The Brahman stood before him. 35. The God-loving *bhakta* asked him whether Shivji had given him any alms? As he showed the harrow to Tuka it turned into gold. 36. Then said Tuka to him, this gift is from Dnyanadev. See that you tell no man, and with this carry on your worldly affairs. 37. After these words of the noble Vaishnava, the noble Brahman left, taking the gold with him. He hastened to the place where he had thrown down the three harrows. 38. He had placed them where there was no passing by of men, but as he sought for them, they were not there, to his great surprise. 39. "Well," said he, "Whatever was in my fate has come to pass." Thus persuading himself, the Brahman made his way home.

Tuka Quiets a Fierce Dog.

40. Here is another deeply interesting story. At the junction of the Mula and Bhivara rivers (there is a sacred bathing place). Tuka went from Dehu to bathe in that sacred water. 41. Along his path there was an uninhabited stretch of country. On it were herds of sheep. There was here a fierce dog, which no one could control. It even killed men. 42. If a man came along that path, it would seize his throat, and drink his blood. Many complaints were made, but the dog could not be controlled by any one. 43. Tuka had to go by that path. Suddenly the dog rushed straight for him. But Tuka felt neither concern nor fear. The dog came near him. 44. Just as it was about to seize Tuka's throat, the God-loving *bhakta* said to it, "There is no bark in me, and why do you keep it in yourself?" 45. At these words of Tuka's, the dog at once became quiet. It lay on the ground perfectly still. The shepherds even came to where he was. 46. And as they looked, there was the dog lying on the ground, and looking like a pet cat. It did not bark at any one, and they thought it most strange. 47. But Tuka, continuing his worship, loudly repeating God's names with love, went on his way, and bathed by the bank of the Bhima river.

Tuka Cures a Dumb Boy.

48. On an island in the river, there was a temple to Shiva, and the noble Vaishnava sat there alone. He brought before his mind for contemplation the Husband-of-Rukmini, and sang of his deeds in his *sagun* form. 49. When it was noon he went to beg for food to Ranjangav. He arrived at a Brahman's house, just as he was making his offering to the Fire. 50. The householder was very happy in his heart when he saw with his eyes the *bhakta* of Vishnu. He served food to Tuka, and then said to him, 51. "I have a son eight years of age. But he is dumb. Up to now he has not spoken a word. The putting on him of the sacred thread has, therefore, been delayed, for he is not able to repeat the Gayatri *mantra.*" 52. Tuka then brought this boy near him and said to him, "Say Vitthal, Vitthal." And with this *mantra* of the saints the Brahman's son began to speak. 53. The Brahman had Tuka remain with him, and on the next day the ceremony of the sacred thread took place. All said, "The deeds of the saint are most extraordinary. He makes the dumb to speak."

The Fierce Dog Follows Tuka Home.

54. As Tuka was returning home by the same path, the shepherds said to him, "The dog has ceased to be of any use to us. Take it away with you." 55. As the Vaishnava continued walking, the dog came following him. On the eleventh day of the fortnight (the day for fasting) the dog would not eat. And it was always listening to the *kirtans.*

Tuka's Son-in-Law and His Reading the Gita.

56. Tuka's son-in-law, living at Yelvad, said to Tuka on one occasion, "Tell me something to do regularly," and

fell at his feet. 57. Recognizing his sincerity, Tuka gave him the Bhagavadgita to read. As he began his regular reading of it, it pleased the Lord-of-Pandhari. 58. One day the astrologer of Khed came to his house, and said to him, "You are not reading the Gita correctly. You will certainly go to Hell." 59. Malaji Gade accepted the astrologer's words and said, "From now on I will not read it." Putting Malaji into this perplexity, the Brahman went back to his home. 60. Now in a dream the Lord-of-Pandhari appeared to the astrologer, and gave him a punishment. Said He to him, "My heart was being pleased there, and you needlessly put a doubt in Malaji's mind. 61. Now go to his house, and set him to reading the Gita. Thus only will your good be served, and I shall have nothing against you." 62. Seeing this vision, the Brahman was terribly frightened. So that very morning he went to Yelvadi, and told Malaji to continue his reading of the Bhagavadgita. 63. Malaji replied to him, "I am a dullard; and, therefore, I will not read it." The Astrologer remained, therefore, with him for four months showing him how to properly pronounce the Gita, by repeating it again and again. 64. The Husband-of-Rukmini hungers for sincerity of heart. With all their wisdom the *Vedas* became weary in their attempts to adequately describe God. The pious repeat it mispronouncing the words, and in rude fashion, but God greatly loves these pious *bhaktas*.

Rameshvar Changes the Puranic Text.

65. In the chapter of the Bhagavat Puran, on the child-pranks of Krishna, it is related in jewelled words, that Krishna, with his dirty face [mukha-malina] was taken up by (his mother) Yashoda, and carried on her hip. Tuka used those words. 66. When Rameshvar Bhatt saw

this he changed the words of the text with his own hand, so as to alter the story as told in the Sanskrit, and made the text read, "The Supreme-Being of the Universe with his sad face" [mukha-mlana]. 67. But the Lord-of-Pandhari appeared to Rameshvar Bhatt in a dream, and said to him, "You have altered Tuka's quotation, and substituted your own idea. 68. What trouble did I have that made my face sad? In my childhood, if I ate dirt, my face would naturally become dirty. 69. In every avatar of mine, Tuka has been my companion, and surely he has described me exactly as he saw me (in the Puranic story)." 70. As soon as the Lord-of-Pandhari had given Rameshvar Bhatt this vision, he vanished out of sight. Rameshvar awoke and marvelled. 71. After that he changed the text back with his own hand to correspond with Tuka's version. And when all the saints were seated at the *kirtan* he confessed the whole affair to them.

Tuka Visits Shiva's Temple at Kothaleshvar.

72. Once in the month of Chaitra (April), Tuka started on a pilgrimage. He had a desire to see Shiva's Peak. 73. He took two Vaishnav companions with him, Gangaji Maval the Brahman, and secondly Santaji Teli. 74. As they walked along the path, they were engaged in the worship of God. Wherever they lodged for the night they performed a *kirtan*. On the seventh stage of their journey the mountain peak came in sight. Then with sincerity of heart they prostrated themselves on the ground. 75. On the summit of the high mountain, Kothaleshvar, The Husband-of-Parvati [Shiva] dwells. At the base of the mountain is the sacred town of Singanapur. There is a pond there. 76. Because there was no water on the mountain, they bathed in this pond. Tuka's companions

then said to him, "Let us now go up, and visit Shiva's temple." 77. To this the Vaishnava replied, "Let us first feed Shiva, and then we shall visit Him when His hunger is satisfied. Let us complete here the hindering duties." 78. Learning Tuka's wish they prepared a meal for four persons. Suddenly the Lord-of-Kailas [Shiva] in the form of Digambar appeared. 79. A crown of matted hair adorned his head. His whole body was covered with ashes. His body could not contain its own lustre. In his hand was his begging bowl. 80. He said to Tuka, "Give me a meal here. I have been hungry for many days, waiting to see you." 81. To this request of the guest the Vaishnava *bhakta* replied, "I surely will." And giving him a seat, he prostrated himself before Him. 82. When the cooking was finished Gangaji arranged four plates. But Tuka said to him, "Let our guest have his meal first, and then we three will eat afterwards." 83. Hearing Tuka's suggestion, Gangaji served the food on one plate only. The Lord-of-Kailas, seeing Tuka's loving devotion, ate the meal. 84. They had prepared food for four persons, but the guest ate it all. Then belching (to express his satisfaction) he gave them His blessing. 85. He drank a gourdful of water. He accepted the water for washing his hands, and eating the *pan supari* for the cleansing of the mouth. He said to Tuka, "All this will be to your good, Tuka,." 86. Thus expressing Himself, the guest, went on up to Mount Kothaleshvar.

Gangaji Maval was astonished and said to Tuka, 87 "Your suggestion was a good one, otherwise the guest would have remained hungry." He then sent Santaji in haste into the town to bring the needed cooking materials. 88. Because flies swarmed over his vessels he covered them with a cloth. He came back quickly with the needed materials, when suddenly a wonderful thing took place. 89. In order to do the cooking Gangaji uncovered the vessel, but lo! All things there were wholly perfect. 90. Then both companions recognized the fact that the Lord-of-Kailas had eaten in the form of a guest, and that they had a direct vision of Him, because of their being in the company of a saint. 91. The divine favour was served on their plates, and the three ate with feelings of love. They then climbed up the mountain, and made their worshipful visit to Shiva. 92. Full of love, they performed a *kirtan* by the chief door of the temple, and full of love to God, repeated in various forms the *kavadi abhang.* 93. After remaining there five nights, they returned to Dehu. Though Tuka was in the body, yet he became one unconscious of body, which is an extremely strange thing.

A Man Possessed with a Devil is Cured.

94. One day the Vaishnava *bhakta* repeated an *abhang* in his *kirtan,* containing the thought that if one were to repeat God's names while walking along a path, at every footstep a sacrifice would be made to God. 95. Now there was in the *kirtan* a pious Brahman from Lohagav. He believed what was told him, and said to himself, "This is not an untrue statement." 96. So at every step he took, he tied a knot in a string. A year passed in this way, and then an extraordinary event took place. 97. There was a distinguished Brahman, but he was possessed with a Brahman-devil. He went to Harihareshvar, and rendered special service to the god there. 98. The devil, then manifesting himself in the man's body, said to him, "If you will give me the good deed of one sacrifice, I will leave

you, and I also shall be free." 99. The Brahman listened to this proposal, and he became much concerned in mind. He said to himself, "I have no means sufficient to perform a sacrifice." 100. The noble Brahman then wandered from country to country and said to people, "If any one has performed a sacrifice, give me at once that good deed." 101. He saw in his wanderings many great cities, but nowhere was he able to achieve his purpose. Then as he wandered and wandered he suddenly found himself in Lohagav. 102. Here also he pleaded, "If any one has performed the good deed of a sacrifice, give it at once to me as an act of benevolence." 103. Now the man who, whenever he walked along the path repeated God's names, and because at every step a sacrifice was offered to God, tied knots in a string, heard the story of the man possessed with the Brahman-devil. 104. He called the man possessed with the devil to his house. Here he cut off one knot, washed it in water, and made the man drink the water. 105. The power of God's name is extraordinary. The devil left the Brahman. But he fell unconscious to the ground, and for three hours lay there like a corpse. 106. All the inhabitants of the town gathered around him to see the strange sight. Said they, "Tuka's words are true. Our eyes have witnessed their truth." 107. The noble Brahman, who had been grievously possessed by the devil, was now happy, and many witnessed the miracle. His own heart melted with emotion.

Illness Prevents Tuka's Pilgrimage to Pandharpur.

108. Such was Tuka's Character, Knowledge, Indifference to worldly things, and Goodness, and in addition his *bhakti* out of love to God. Alone by himself he worshipped God.

109. In the months of Ashad [July] and Kartik [November] he never failed to make a pilgrimage to Pandharpur. But one day suddenly a physical illness appeared. 110. His body became extremely weak through chills and fever. Said he, "A great hindrance has come preventing my going on a pilgrimage. What shall I plan to do?" 111. When a calf sees its mother it lows. The Chakor bird is all in a tremble when it does not see the moon. Just as the *chatak* bird loses its strength when not seeing a cloud, so Tuka was sad at heart. 112. Just as a fish out of water is in distress; just as an infant cries when its mother is away; or, just as when a miser loses his money, he has no peace of mind, 113. just so when Tuka failed to go on the pilgrimage to Pandhari, his heart was full of regret. But he could not walk a single step, and so he was sad at heart.

114. Now the people who had listened to Tuka's *kirtans* with his love of God, and had given themselves to the worship of God, were on their way to Pandhari with fourteen banners. 115. These pilgrims came to Dehu to get Tuka to go with them. Instead, Tuka wrote twenty-four *abhangs,* and sent them as a letter to God at Pandhari. 116. The God-loving Tuka came out to see the pilgrims on their way. His throat choked with emotion, as he wrote his letter.

TUKA'S LETTER TO THE GOD AT PANDHARPUR.

117. "Dear Vithabai, I have no strength in me, with which to plead with Thee. But assuming boldness, I claim friendship at Thy feet. 118. The Vedas and Shastras do not know Thy whole extent. The great *rishis* composed the Purans, but even they did not know the whole

of Thy deeds. Then how can I, a sinner, describe Thee? 119. May the Husband-of-Rukmini accept my uncouth words, just as they may happen to be. On the brick are Thy two beautiful feet. On them I lay my head. 120. O Pandurang, Thou art the life of an infinite number of dull and strengthless beings, and how is it that Thou hast forgotten me? 121. Why wilt Thou send the invitation? Therefore, I am disturbed, and for ever wasting away in my heart, O Merciful-to-the-lowly, O Vithabai. 122. If Thou hast so reserved a heart; then why didst Thou give birth to a child? He, whose the child is, will alone accept the burden. To others he is a trouble. 123. If the young doe does not see the mother doe, she glances anxiously in every direction. That is my condition Thou knowest, O Lord-of-Pandhari. 124. When a cloud passes over, the chatak bird, because of its thirst, cannot sorrow enough. Such is the sorrow I feel. How am I to recount the many reasons. 125. If a mother should abandon her infant child, it would seem to people a pitiful sight. But such is my condition, O Husband-of-Rukmini. Thou knowest it. 126. When a miser loses his money, he is in a frenzy day and night. And so I am in disquiet, as Thou, O Krishna, knowest. 127. A fish out of water is all in a flutter. Death has it in its grasp. That is my condition also, as saints and other good people will tell Thee. 128. The step on which one treads does not know how to rise up alive. So at this time, O Shri Hari, may I be in relation to Thee, prostrate at Thy feet. 129. Or, as when a cane is dropped, it falls lifeless on the ground, so I, O Krishna, fall prostrate at Thy feet; 130. or, as when a mother does not grant her child its whim, it rolls noisily on the floor. Such is my prostrate falling before Thee. All the pilgrims will tell Thee this. 131. I have asked the saints to enquire of the Lord-of-Pandhari, what wrong has Tuka done, that he should suffer this separation from Thy feet. 132. If Thou wilt have mercy on me, O-Husband-of-Rukmini, I shall come running, I shall meet with the saints and other good men, and dance with joy in the *kirtans* to Thy praise."

133. Such was the sad letter Tuka wrote, and then fell prostrate at the feet of the saints. His throat choked with emotion, and tears flowed from his eyes. 134. The noble Vaishnavas gave and received the *namaskar* of each other, and then shouting aloud the name of Vitthal the pilgrim band started on its way. 135. The pilgrims started on their way to Pandhari with fourteen banners in their hands, but because of their separation from Tuka, they did not start to walk rapidly.

136. And so Tuka, whose heart loved God, walked slowly, slowly after them. Said he, "O Pandurang, why hast Thou become weary of me?" 137. As Tuka thus spoke, the pilgrims were choked with emotion. The pilgrims then took final leave of Tuka, and arrived at the sacred city of Pandhari.

Tuka's Letter Delivered to God.

138. When these servants of Vishnu, with cymbals, *vina* and drum made a very loud noise dancing in their *kirtans,* performed in the enthusiasm of their love of God, it seemed that every divine sound had gathered there. 139. As they saw Pandharpur they were full of delight, and these noble Vaishnavas made their *namaskars* to one another. 140. They embraced one another, and then waved wave offerings before the Husband-of-Rukmini. They bathed in the Chandrabhaga, and then paid their respects at the tomb of Pundalik. 141. They danced in

joy, and went round the sacred town. They then went to the great door of the temple, and prostrated themselves in sincerity of heart.

142. The twenty-four *abhangs,* which Tuka had composed, and written as a letter, were read to the God by the pilgrims as they were singing the God's praises at the Eagle-platform. 143. To begin with, Tuka's words were full of love of God, and they were sung by the noble Vaishnavas with reverence. As the pious listened to them, tears flowed from their eyes. 144. After this service of praise, they waved the wave-offerings over the Husband-of-Rukmini. They bowed prostrate with love, and then went to render worship to Vithoba. 145. Listen to the names of those who brought Tuka's letter. There was the learned Brahman Rameshvar Bhatt, who was absolutely devoted to Tuka. 146. Then there was Gangadhar Maval Kaduskar, and the noble Vaishnava Santaji the Oilman. Besides these there were very many pilgrims. But why fill up this book with their names?

147. They took the letter in their hands and went into the inner sanctuary. And there they saw the Husband-of-Rukmini standing on the brick. His lotus hands placed on his hips made a charming sight. 148. As they saw the Supreme-Brahma in visible form [*sagun*] they immediately embraced Him. They placed their heads at His feet, and then looked up into His face. 149. They placed Tuka's letter before Him, and told Him of its contents. "Tuka is not physically well," they said, "and is not able to walk as far as here. 150. But he has written a letter to Thee, O Lover-of-*bhaktas,* O Statue-of-Compassion. But Thou Statue-of-Intelligence art the Seer-of-the-Heart, and it is not necessary to tell Thee of this." 151. Hearing

this message of Tuka's, Krishna was choked with emotion. And calling Rukmini to His side, the Giver-of-Eternal-Life said to her, 152. "Tuka is my special *bhakta*. He is not in good health, and, therefore, is unable to come here to Pandhari. Instead, he has sent a letter. 153. Let us, therefore, go there personally to express our concern for him." To this suggestion of Krishna's, Rukmini replied, 154. "Pious people have come here to visit you, you Supreme-Being-of-the-Universe. If your visible form is not seen by your dear *bhaktas,* they will be troubled. 155. I propose that you send (your vehicle) the eagle, and bring Tuka here." Shri Hari listened to His wife, and gave his orders to the Eagle. 156. Krishna said to the Son-of-Vinata [the Eagle], "Go quickly to Dehu. Seat Tuka on your back, and bring him here to see us." 157. At this command of Shri Hari, the eagle accepted the order with the bow of his head, made a *namaskar,* flapped his wings, and started. 158. In less than the twinkling of the eye the eagle arrived at Dehu, and there was Tuka, the God-loving noble Vaishnava, still standing outside of the town. 159. The Vaishnava *bhakta* was standing just where he said farewell to the pilgrims. He was without the least bodily consciousness, and was waiting for the pilgrims' return from Pandhari. 160. In thinking of the Lord-of-Pandhari with love, his own body had changed into the divine form, although he disliked the Advaita (Non-Dual) philosophy, this God-loving, noble *bhakta* Tuka. 161. Just like the trunk of a tree, that neither walks, nor moves in the least, so Tuka's body seemed to be there on the path. 162. The eagle saw him, and was astonished. But slowly descending to the earth, he said gently to Tuka, 163 "On account of your absence the Husband-of-Rukmini is feeling very grieved in His heart. 164. As your body is without strength, and, therefore, unable to walk to Pandhari, I have been ordered by the Husband-of-Rukmini to come and bring you." 165. At these words of the Eagle's Tuka was moved with emotion. He read the letter sent by God. Listen to it, you pious *bhaktas* of His. 166. "So long as Vaikunth [Vishnu's Heaven] and Kailas [Shiva's Heaven] last, you, Tuka, may live. And you alone have authority over my glory, manifested in the animate and inanimate. 167. You are not able to bear this separation from me, and it is the same with me, therefore, I have sent the eagle today to bring you here. 168. So sit on its back, and see again the sacred city of Pandhari. It will make me happy. Do not at all refuse."

169. The Vaishnava read God's letter, while tears flowed from his eyes. He then said to the Eagle, "How can I do this improper thing? 170. You are my Lord's noble vehicle, and I am but the bearer of His sandals. The toe-ornament, even if made of gold, is not to be worn on the head. 171. Tell Him of my condition, and bring the Lord of Pandhari here." Thus saying, the God-loving Tuka fell at the Eagle's feet. 172. Recognizing the wish of his *bhakta,* the Lord-of-Birds started back, and quickly reaching Pandhari, made his obeisance to God. 173. He told Hari all the events of his flight. "Tuka would not sit on my back, but is standing outside of the town waiting for Thee." 174. The Supreme-Being of the Universe, listened, and was moved with emotion, and said then to Rukmini, "Let us go now and see Tuka."

175. After a few days had passed the Vaishnavas went to Gopalpura. Performing the ceremony of kala, they wagged their heads joyfully. 176. After this great celebration the assembly of pilgrims broke up. They asked leave of

the God, saying to Him, 177. "O God-Supreme, Husband-of-Rukmini, Thou shouldst go to visit Tuka." Thus pleading for Tuka, they started on their way home. 178. By continued travelling, all the pilgrims finally reached Dehu. And lo! there was Tuka standing in the very same spot where he stood when he accompanied them a short way as they started for Pandharpur. 179. He had his hand on his forehead, constantly looking for their return. The noble Vaishnavas were astonished, and exclaimed, "No one else has such fixed determination. 180. In performing his Shri Hari *kirtans* his whole body has become Brahma Itself, and still he does not let go his feeling of love for God. Which other Vaishnava is like him? 181. The King [Shivaji] fell at his feet, and said to him, 'Accept the gift of a town,' but Tuka would not take it, for his mind is always free from desire. 182. While he was looking at the iron harrow, it turned at that moment into gold, but his wife does not wear so much as a broken jewel. He regards gold as defiling. 183. Wherever his footstep falls there the eight *Siddhis* are ready to serve him, but he does not reserve in his house sufficient grain for a single day."

184. Turning now to the pilgrims as they returned from Pandhari, they saw Tuka, and fell prostrate before him. 185. Among them was Rameshvar the Brahman, who called himself the disciple of Tuka. The bodily-unconscious Tuka prostrated himself before him, for he had not the least personal pride. 186. Seeing one's own disciple whom he considers as his god, he alone deserves to be called the guru of the world, and has attained perfect knowledge, and his mind becomes tranquil in the contemplation of the non-Dual. 187. As when the sea receives a stream of filthy water it regards it as but part

of itself. When the stinking hingan wood, and the fragrant sandal-wood fall into the fire, both are alike to the fire. 188. So were Tuka's feelings of love. He did not keep in mind what was to be reverenced, and what was not to be reverenced. So although Rameshvar regarded himself as heart and soul a servant of Tuka's, still Tuka regarded him as God.

189. Such was Tuka's loving devotion. With what am I to compare the incomparable Tuka. He who increased the glory of *bhakti*, and the Perfect-Being was subservient to him.

190. Turning again to the pilgrims, when they returned they fell prostrate before Tuka. They embraced one another in mutual love. 191. The pilgrims gave him some of the favours (they brought from Pandharpur), which he received with delight, and said he, "Is all well with Shri Hari? He has abandoned me here far from Himself." 192. They told Tuka the whole of the events connected with the celebration at Pandharpur, and added, "The Husband-of-Rukmini is coming to-day to visit you." 193. Tuka's ears having heard this report, he at once tied the auspicious knots in his garment. His desire to meet God there was very great. His exclamation was, "O Thou Supreme-One of the Universe, come quickly." 194. Thus exclaiming, the noble Vaishnava placed his hand to his forehead, and waited with courage, pleading in pitiful tones.

Krishna comes to see Tuka.

195. Recognizing Tuka's determination, the pilgrims entered into the town, each one going to his own home,

and engaging in his usual business. 196. But Tuka remained standing in that same spot from which he had sent the letter to Pandhari. Later the servant of Vishnu composed nineteen *abhangs,* 197. which all of you, saints, must make an effort, and bring them to your mind. Tuka continued waiting, saying, "Why does not the Husband-of-Rukmini come? 198. Of which of Thy *bhaktas* art Thou accepting the worship, O Thou-of-the-Eagle-banner? It is there that Thy love has become entwined, and Thou hast forgotten me. 199. Or perhaps, some one has put Thee in difficulty, so that Thou art busy there, O Krishna. And Thy mind has forgotten about me. Thou hast abandoned me in the jungle." 200. In such words the God-loving Tuka brought the thought of the Lord-of-Heaven to his mind.

Suddenly the Eagle's wings flashed in the sky as the Friend-of-his-*bhaktas* approached. 201. The Lord-of-Heaven, riding on his Eagle, suddenly descended to the earth. The light from his yellow garment was brilliant, so that the sun paled before it. 202. His delicate form was beautiful. His two hands on his hips made a pleasing sight. Crocodile shaped earrings adorned his ears. Hari's glorious face was entrancing. 203. On his neck was the divine *kaustubh* jewel and the garland *Vaijayanti.* Peacock feathers adorned his crown. The *tulsi* garland around his neck was a pleasing sight, to see which gave one's heart a sense of rest. 204. Krishna, along with Rukmini, now stood before Tuka. The four-armed Mine-of-Mercy at once embraced Tuka. 205. Then suddenly Tuka came to consciousness, and opening his eyes, behold! there stood before him the Supreme-Being-of-the-Universe, in visible form [sagun]. Tuka clasped His feet. 206. Just as a mother clasps to her heart her infant child, so He clasped Tuka to His heart in His love. And in that same way the Life-of-the-Universe caressed and called to Tuka.

207. The next interesting chapter has the Husband-of-Rukmini for its narrator, but Mahipati pleads with his listeners to let their hearing be sincere.

208. Svasti. This book, the Shri Bhaktalilamrita, by the mere listening to which all the heart's desires are supplied. Listen you pious, God-loving *bhaktas.* This is the delightful thirty-seventh chapter.

CHAPTER 38.

God the Real Author; Mahipati His Instrument.

Obeisance to Shri Ganesh.

1. Victory to Thee Husband-of-Rukmini, Dweller-on-the-bank of-the-Bhima, Existent-Intelligence-Joy, Mercy-in-visible-form! Thy praise is universal. The *Purans* sing aloud of Thy great deeds. 2. The *Vedas* and *Shastras* describe Thy character, but even they cannot fathom Thy glory. That being so, how can I, dull of mind and ignorant, describe Thee? 3. I have no cleverness or skillfulness in me. I have not read much. I lack ability to compose. Needlessly perhaps a fear has seized me, but do Thou bring this book to its completion. 4. Depending on Thee, O Krishna, I have taken my pen in hand. So remaining always in my heart, give my mind its thoughts. 5. I am narrating the deeds of the saints, but the responsibility is on Thy head. If by accident any

faulty word occurs in my work, do Thou, O Infinite-One, fulfil it. 6. In the roaring whirlwind of the Three-fevers, there may come innumerable hindrances, but if so, send Thy disk (to destroy them), and carry this book to completion unhindered. 7. I have accepted this seemingly impossible wish, O Husband-of-Rukmini, but the completion of the book is in Thy hands, and, therefore, I, Mahipati, plead with Thee.

God Dines at Tuka's House.

8. In the last interesting chapter there was related how Tuka did not have the opportunity (of going to Pandhari), so sent a letter to God, and the Dweller-in-Pandhari came to see him. 9. He met Tuka in his *sagun* form, and in his embrace drew him close to His heart. And Tuka embraced His feet. The universe could not contain their joy. 10. Krishna then took Tuka by the hand, and they came to his house. It was an old dilapidated hut. Strong winds blew through it from every direction. 11. The Dweller-in-Heaven said to Tuka, "I am hungry. I wish for a full meal, so prepare it quickly." 12. Tuka counselled with his Avali. "God-supreme has come to our house. Having first purified your heart, give Him to eat." 13. She cooked some cereals, some greens and bread, and when served on a plate Shri Hari sat down to eat. 14. He who will not partake of the sacrifice offered by great *rishis,* He ate with the utmost courtesy the simple food in the home of his *bhakta.* 15. He who found fault with the sacrifices, He, looking at the love of the Bhil woman, ate greedily and eagerly the *bor* fruit she had tasted. 16. Duryodhan had prepared an abundance of dainty food, but Krishna would not go there. Instead, he hunted for Vidur's house, and there ate cooked cereals.

17. Thus is God closely tied to *bhakti*. The Omniscient-One recognizes his Vaishnava *bhaktas*. And so seeing Tuka's sincerity, and without the desire of gain, see Him eat the simple food at Tuka's! 18. The Life-of-the-Universe satisfied his appetite with the food supplied by sincerity. Tuka then offered Him in his love the *tulsi* leaf for the cleansing of his mouth. 19. Thus, after fulfilling Tuka's desire, God vanished out of sight. Or shall I say that He became a bee, and seated Himself in the lotus heart of His *bhakta*?

Tuka and the Philosopher.

20. Here is another interesting story. There was a Brahman philosopher. He had made a copy of the Viveksindhu (by Mukundaraj), and was accustomed to read it with delight. 21. He had heard of the good fame of Tuka, but he despised him in his heart. For, thought he, "If God dwells in the heart, why wander about in search of Him?" 22. So saying, the noble Brahman thought to himself, "After Tuka hears the reading of the Viveksindhu, I shall understand his inner thought." 23. So the Brahman came to Dehu and sought for Tuka. He found the Vaishnava by the bank of the Indrayani, repeating the names of God. 24. As soon as he saw Tuka, both bowed to one another. The Brahman made his request known very courteously. 25. "I want to read to you here the philosophical book called the Viveksindhu, composed by Shri Mukundaraj. Kindly listen." 26. In order to show the Brahman respect, the God-loving *bhakta* said, "I will do so." He then drew his blanket about him so as to completely cover himself. 27. Said he to the Brahman, "If I see every thing around me, my thoughts

go everywhere. So I am going to close my eyes, and you may continue your reading." 28. Hearing Tuka's reply, the noble Brahman began to read the book. He also explained it as he read along. But Tuka said not a word. 29. The Brahman continued reading the book for about three hours, until it was finished. But all this time Tuka never uttered a word. What did the Brahman then do? 3/. But lift up (a corner of) the blanket, and there was Tuka doing an unexpected thing. He had placed his fingers in his ears, and was wagging his head as he repeated the names of God. 31. The Brahman was irritated by this, and said to Tuka, "I have come here walking from a long distance. I have been reading this book for three hours. I have made a useless effort. 32. I have sought this meeting with you, with the thought that I might get some ideas from you. But here you are with ears closed, and without bodily consciousness. You have no desire to listen." 33. The noble Vaishnava hearing him say this, replied by an *abhang,* which he repeated to him, adding, "In order that I may fix my mind on the name and form of God, I have abandoned my home, and use the jungle. 34. I have adopted the principle of concentrating my thought on the name and form of God, but I am afraid the evil eye will affect my love. Thereby my heart will become free from desire. And this is the same thing as the 'I am Brahma,' of the philosophy. 35. For this reason I will never listen to the *Advait* doctrine [Non-dual]. It would mean separation between God and his *bhakta.* One should not make that vain attempt. 36. With their mouths they proclaim this philosophy, that all men are Brahma in form, and then they will sell their lives for a *kavadi,* and quarrel in the market-place. 37. If everything is Brahma, then why sorrow over loss and gain?

To one, who is a follower of the Brahma without qualities, words in such a case cease to have any meaning. 38. Therefore, if any one refutes the doctrine of God and His *bhakta,* he will fall into Hell. God has instituted limits, and we must walk according to them. 39. Suppose a man does become a devotee of the Advaita philosophy, still God's power is without limit. The Brahma-knowing man has no power of creation, preservation and the destruction of the universe. 40. We are able to comprehend the three Gods, so long as they are *sagun* (recognizable through qualities). That is the limit for us. One should not preach the Advait doctrine." 41. While the Vaishnava *bhakta* was thus talking, the Brahman felt the truth of it by his own experience, and his heart turned at that very moment to the worship of God in His *sagun* [visible] form. 42. With great pleasure he sang and listened to what the saints of old had said in their pleading words. He was converted through and through.

Tuka Changes a Brackish Well into a Sweet Well.

43. One day the chief citizens of Lohagav came, and took Tuka back with them, in order that they might listen to his inspiring *kirtans.* 44. They prepared various dainty foods, and arranged for a Brahman feast. As night fell, the *kirtan* began, that had for its subject Salvation from the sea of this worldly existence. 45. The night of the Holi festival ended, and now the sun arose.

There was a well there of brackish water. No one drank of its water. 46. Tuka suddenly took a bath in that well with his clothes on. Immediately the water became sweet. That wonderful miracle still stands. 47. It is called the Coppersmith's well at Lohagav, and is there to this day. In this way the Dweller-in-Pandhari increases the fame of his *bhaktas.*

A Woman Feeds Tuka a Bitter Squash.

48. There was there a Brahman, a Vaishnava *bhakta,* whose heart was devoted to Tuka. As he listened to Tuka's inspiring *kirtans,* he sought to give up all worldly business. 49. His wife, a very graceful, beautiful woman, conceived a dislike of Tuka. Said she, "He has made my husband crazy. I will now put him to the test." 50. Her husband was away in a neighbouring village, and she cooked a bitter squash. She then invited Tuka to her house, saying, "Come and dine here to-day." 51. The Vaishnava *bhakta* had conquered his tongue. He had made it his fixed principle not to know what was sweet and what was bitter. And this was, because of his unconsciousness of body. 52. "This vegetable is very tasty," he said, and she served him some more. But as Tuka left, the Lord-of-Heaven became wrathy. 53. All over her body there appeared clusters of swellings. She took medicine, but they did not disappear. She was reaping what she sowed. 54. Those who hate God continually (by that very contact) reach final salvation. But for one who hates a *bhakta* there is eternal Hell, whose torments they can never escape.

Tuka's Miracle of the Unfailing Oil.

55. There was a Brahman in Lohagav, who was a supremely pious man. He invited Tuka to his house at one of his Monday night celebrations. 56. There was only the man and his wife there. No third person assisted on the occasion. The oil in the lamp suddenly failed, and the couple were much concerned. 57. The

wick was dry. Who will go to the bazaar? The God-loving *bhakta* seeing their distress said to them, 58. "You have an empty bottle in the house. Look and see whether it may not contain some oil." The lady of the house looked, and behold! she saw much oil in it. 59. She brought it at once and poured oil in the lamp, and both were rejoiced. Where there is the state of God and *bhakta* being one, there the *Siddhis* are all ready to serve. 60. So long as the couple lived so long the oil never failed.

Tuka Turns Iron into Gold.

Here is another miracle. Listen to it, you pious people, with reverence. 61. Before the *Patil's* door, there was a stone slab. And Tukaram used to sit on it. Suddenly a mendicant with his begging bowl came there on his rounds, and danced before Tuka. 62. For a whole month he made his rounds of the town. As the begging-bowl man wandered among the houses of the town, he received some pieces of iron. 63. These he brought with him when standing before Tuka, and saying to him, "Fill my bowl". The noble Vaishnava said to him, "What have you really received to-day?" 64. In answer the man piled on the slab the pieces of iron which he had with him. They suddenly turned into gold. "Fill your bowl with them and go," said Tuka to him. 65. The beggar, greatly delighted, took up the gold at once and left. There were people there of avaricious minds. They were astonished, and rubbed iron on the slab, 66. but it did not change into gold. "This is evidently not a touch-stone," they remarked. "The man with the begging bowl had good fortune on his side, and so he obtained this wealth." 67. That slab, touched by Tuka's feet is still there to-day.

TUKA RAISES A DEAD SON TO LIFE.

Still another event occurred, which, if saint or *sadhu* hears it told, becomes absorbed in it. 68. One day the Vaishnava *bhakta* was performing a *kirtan* in Lohagav. A pavilion had been erected, and many flags fluttered on every side. 69. People had heard of Tuka's great fame, and a crowd of two thousand had assembled from other towns. All of the town itself, young and old, sat listening with reverence. 70. The astrologer of the town was an extremely pious man, and regularly listened to the *kirtans.* His son was suffering from a very serious disease. At times he fainted away. 71. The Brahman would leave his son at home, and come to listen at the *kirtan,* for, said he, "That which is to be, cannot be escaped." Indifferent to things around him he sat listening. 72. After three hours of the night had passed the angels of Yama (God of Death) took the child away. The wife lifted the corpse, and brought it into the Hari *kirtan.* 73. She said to Tuka, "If you will bring my boy to life at once, then only are you surely a Vishnu *bhakta,* otherwise you are a hypocrite. 74. My husband thinks only of you, and from the day he began to do so, we have been suffering loss, and disaster. You have poured water (destroyed) on your own worldly affairs, and have made our condition the same as yours."

75. With this interruption in the midst of the *kirtan* all minds were perplexed. Just as when one is eating some dainty food off a plate some one should mix poison with it. 76. Seeing the trouble he was in, Tuka closed his eyes, and brought Pandurang before his imagination, by concentrating his mind on Him. 77. Then he prayed, "Victory, victory to Thee, O God, Lover of Thy *Bhaktas,*

Supreme-Lord-of-Heaven, Pervader of the Universe, Omniscient-One, Dweller-at-Pandharpur, Shri Vitthal. 78. In former times Thou didst perform many wonderful deeds, the glory of which the Vashnava *Bhaktas* sing. Now here in this place prove them to be true, making the evidence that of our experience. 79. A confusion has arisen in our worship, and what could be a worse death than this? Take the disk in Thy hand, and put an end to this interruption, O Vithoba. 80. If Thou wilt not come here, then I truly will not preserve my own life." While the God-loving *bhakta* was saying this, many tears flowed from his eyes. 81. While Tuka was thus pleading for help, the Lord-of-Pandhari at once appeared. He awakened Tuka, saying, "Why are you troubled? 82. You, who are the chief jewel among *bhaktas,* have with you the life-giving nectar. When yuo repeat it in the *kirtan,* the life of the child will return." 83. When Shri Hari gave him this assurance, he was very happy. He then opened his eyes, and awakened his hearers. 84. Said he, "Clap your hands, and snap your fingers, and all of you shout the name of Vitthal. Thereby great hindrances are removed. Have no doubt of this." 85. Thus requested by the Vaishnava *bhakta,* all the audience began to worship. The loud noise, as if in visible form, seemed to have descended to the earth. 86. Cymbals, the *vina,* and drums sounded in tune with the shouting of Vitthal's names. Great was the sound of the clapping of hands, and snapping of fingers. The enthusiasm was unlimited. 87. For three hours in this manner the audience carried on their worship. And Tuka, losing his illusion of body, became one unconscious of body. 88. The Lord-of-Pandhari then performed a miracle. You fortunate hearers, listen. Life returned into the corpse, that had been placed in the midst of the *kirtan.*

89. The child sat up in the Hari *kirtan,* and began to worship with feelings of love. His mother was near him, and she fell at Tuka's feet. 90. The whole audience rejoiced, shouted, "Victory, Victory," and clapped their hands. The custom of repeating Hari's names became more and more established.

Two Sannyasis Make Trouble for Tuka.

91. After the above event had taken place, the night had advanced six hours. Just then the distinguished Sannyasi, Shripad, came into the *kirtan* and sat down before Tuka. 92. The noble Vaishnava was just then establishing the principle of the repeating of God's names with the worshipful spirit. "The Name of God is the cream of all ways of salvation. The Name is the supreme Brahma. 93. Before beginning any work, one should repeat the Name of Keshav, Narayan. If there is any failure in any great work, the failure will be repaired by the repeating of Vishnu's names. 94. In performing marriages of bride and bridegroom, they look for thirty-six points in the horoscope, but in the end the marriage will not be properly performed without the repeating of the names of the Husband-of-Lakshmi. 95. All is done well in the ancestor worship, but at its close there must be the offering to God. In fact without the use of Hari's names, there is no way of performing good deeds." 96. The God-loving *bhakta,* after thus discoursing, shouted aloud the name of Vitthal. There were two villainous *sannyasis* there, who spoke to one another depreciatingly of Tuka. 97. "We should never listen to the name of God uttered by the mouth of a *Shudra.*" And these evil-minded *sannyasis* after these remarks got up quickly and left. 98. They

had shaved off their tuft of hair, but their pride had increased ten-fold. And those who hate the *bhaktas* are on the way to hell.

DADU KONDADEV OF POONA HEARS THEIR CHARGE.

99. Dadu Kondadev Mokasi was in Poona at that time, and the complaint of the two *sannyasis* came before him. 100. Full of anger, they threw down their staves and begging bowls on to the ground. They beat their foreheads, and made their complaint. Listen to it. 101. "Tuka is a grocer of the *Shudra* caste. He is carrying on improper deeds. He has seduced the pious people, and set them to repeating God's names. 102. He has increased the glory of *bhakti,* but has declared the way of good deeds of no value. And although he is a *Shudra,* still Brahmans make obeisance to him. 103. You are the ruler in this part of the country, and so we have come at once to tell you. Aside from you, who is there to take our part? 104 So call Tuka here, and speedily punish him. If you refuse to listen to us, we shall commit suicide right here." 105. Seeing their intense determination, Dadu Kondadev replied to them, "Let your minds be at rest, I will call Tuka here. 106. After you and he have discussed the matter, whoever loses I will punish" Thus informing the *sannyasi* Shripad, he sent messengers at once to call Tuka. 107. He wrote to the Brahmans of Lohagav to come under penalty of fifty rupees. He explained the circumstances in a letter, and what the *sannyasis* had reported. 108. The messengers of Dadu Kondadev quickly arrived at Lohagav. He collected all the Brahmans, and gave the letter into their hands. 109. Seeing this disaster, the timid felt the rising of fear. "What will the outcome be," said they, and violently trembled.

110. When Tuka heard of it, he gave a comforting assurance to all the Brahmans. "If the Lord-of-Pandhari is at the head of our affairs, why should we be anxious?" 111. The Government servants said to the Brahmans, "Pay down at once the fifty rupees security." "Let us at once go there," said all the Brahmans. 112. Although the officer strongly insisted, still Tuka's reputation was great in the public mind, for even the King Shivaji came and bowed prostrate before Tuka, and was seen by every one doing so. 113. Then with cymbal, *vina* and two drums and four persons to lead in the chorus, and a procession with uplifted banners, they walked along, performing a *kirtan* as they proceeded. 114. The Brahmans, and all the people of the villages through which they passed came out to see the strange sight. They arrived at Poona in due time, and encamped at the junction of the rivers. 115. They all bathed. Some completed their regular religious observances, and then sitting down, they listened with reverence to Tuka's *kirtan.* 116. In order to pay their respects to Tuka, other crowds came from distant villages. And when all the multitude was gathered together it looked as if an army had encamped there. 117. They listened gladly to the performance of the *kirtan,* and the inhabitants of Poona began to come to pay their respects. And in many forms the pious people brought the materials for their worship in their platters. 118. They brought bananas, cocoanuts, dates, fragrant powders, *tulsi* and flower garlands. These they placed before Tuka, and in sincerity bowed before him. 119. Dadu Kondaji Mokasi went on the terrace of his house, and looking here and there enquired of his servants, "Whose army is it that is seen in the distance?" 120. "The inhabitants of Lohagav have come to the junction, and

Tuka, the Vishnu *Bhakta,* is performing a kirtan. The people of this city also are going together to pay their respects to Tuka." 121. Hearing this information, Dadu Kondadev was deeply moved. Said he, "I also will at once carry there some offerings, and pay my respects to Tuka." 122. Thus saying, the town official started on his way. Just then he met the two *sannyasis,* who said to him, "What is this that you are doing, Ruler? 123. You are in every way our support, and we trusted to this. And now you are going to pay your respects to Tuka. Our hopes are now in vain." 124. To this objection of the *sannyasis* the official replied, "It is necessary that I should go with the people to pay my respects to Tuka. 125. After meeting with him at this time, I shall bring him along into the town. Then if at that time, you win in the discussion, I shall see that he is well punished. 126. But if he wins over you, there will be no limit to my punishment of you. Be at peace in your minds, and consider well what you do." 127. With these words to the *sannyasis,* he took the materials for his offering, and accompanied with many. distinguished citizens came to meet Tuka.

128. With cymbal, *vina* and drum the *kirtan* was full of the enthusiasm of love of God. The servant of Vishnu danced, and there was no limit to the joy of all. 129. As he sang of the various deeds of Shri Hari, his throat choked with emotion. Tears of joy flowed from his eyes at which even the wicked were moved. 130. Listen with reverence, you wise *bhaktas.* A naked Yogi, with his mass of hair on his head appeared in the *kirtan.* 131. A brilliant divine light made his body shine, and moreover his body had been rubbed over with divine ashes. He lovingly embraced Tuka, and prostrated himself before

him on the ground. 132. He said to Tuka, "I have had a great desire to see you, and now my wish has been gratified." This is all he said. 133. With these words to Tuka, the Yogi departed by way of the sky. The people who were sitting in the *kirtan* saw this wonderful sight. 134. They said to one another, "He must be the Dweller-in-Kailas [Shiva]." Some said, "He must be Dattatreya," but no one had exact knowledge. 135. The *sannyasis,* who were present, although they wanted to say something, yet they even were puzzled at this sight. 136. A divine affluence had been poured on them, and their troubled minds were quieted. Said they, "Blessed is Tuka, the God-loving Vaishnava, the Keeper-of-Heaven is his helper." 137. They continued singing aloud the names of Vitthal in their love for Him. Then they lighted the lamps for the wave offering. They waved them over the Husband-of-Rukmini, distributed favours, 138. also the dates, bananas, sugar and various other things. Said they, "This is a blessed distinguished day, on which all have been saved."

Dadu Kondadev Receives Tuka with Honour.

139. Dadu Kondadev now came near to Tuka, and spoke to him in a humble way. "Come into the city, and make me one who has a protector." 140. Seeing his earnest wish, the Vaishnava *bhakta* assented. The *sannyasis* became anxious. Said they, "The prospect does not look good. 141. We told him all in order that Tuka might be disgraced, but his fame has only been increased thereby. What plan shall we adopt now?"

142. Dadu Kondaji took Tuka into the city, and choosing a beautiful great palace gave him a place in it.

143. He paid high honour to the Brahmans of Lohagav, who had brought the security with them, and provided them with all they needed for their meals. 144. A merchant of the city also provided for their necessities. On that day he dined two thousand Brahmans in the same row as Tuka. 145. At the third watch of the day (afternoon) the *kirtan* began. "Now," said Dadu Kondaji to the *sannyasis,* "start your discussion with Tuka. 146. Whoever loses in the debate, I shall seat him on an ass." The *sannyasis* replied, "We shall win in our debate with him in a moment's time." 147. The *sannyasis* brought with them such rascals and crooks as they could find. Just as when one crow hears the voice of another, all of one feather come flocking together. 148. Or, as when a dog's voice is heard, all the dogs of the town begin to bark. Or, as Kumbhakarna acted as a support to the Vishnu hater, Ravan. 149. Or, as Duryodhan's dearest friends, Shakuni and Shishupal protected him. So, pundits skilled in debate were gathered to assist the *sannyasis.* 150. They sat down in the *kirtan* with that one purpose in mind. But there was no such thing as hatred in Tuka, and he bowed to all. 151. The *sannyasis* sat directly in front of the speaker with much ostentation. They did so with hatred for the Vishnu *bhakta,* but thereby wasted the good deeds that belonged to them.

152. Shouting aloud the name of Vitthal, Tuka began the *kirtan,* and awakened all the people to their duty to worship the Lord-of-Heaven. 153. "Mighty Death is devouring our lives as hours, minutes and seconds pass; just as a cat devours the rat the moment it leaves its hole. 154. Just as when one performs the fasting ceremonies, connected with the elevenths of the month, and then starts to cook sweet potatoes. As soon as they are cooked the

hungry man seizes them, so Death lies in wait for the body. 155. Or, as the fish in the water is unaware of the standing crane in apparent meditation, one does not know when it will swallow the fish. So one does not know the mysteries of Death. 156. Whatever one sees, that meets with destruction at the end. In order to prevent this, one must go as a suppliant to Shri Hari. 157. If one does not worship Shri Hari, he will never escape the circle of births and deaths. Many means may be employed, but the coming back to this earthly existence cannot be avoided. 158. If one repeats the names of God [Shri Hari], either with some desire in mind, or without any special desire, Yama [God of Death] will not be able to trouble him, for the Being-of-Supreme-Goodness is his protector. 159. Ajamil, the Brahman's son, fell in love with a low caste woman. By it he accumulated in his existence here a mountain of sin. 160. Even the chief sacred watering places trembled with fear at the thought of being touched by such an one. The seven Hells also feared to receive him. He was out of the reach of penances. 161. But suddenly a great *rishi* met him by accident. He repented, and told the *rishi* his story. 162. Hearing his story, the good man said to him, 'You have perfect affection for your son. His name is Narayan [a name of God]. Use it in your loving caresses.' 163. Giving him this suggestion, the good man, went off to a sacred watering place. As Ajamil went out to die, he called out to his son, 164, 'Come near to me Narayan.' And the Lord-of-Heaven took mercy on him. He sent his heavenly Chariot of Light, and caused him to enjoy Final Deliverance. 165. The prostitute [Pingala] was taken to Heaven while she was calling her parrot by the name Ragho [Ram.] When Gajendra [the elephant] was in distress from the crocodile, the Supreme-Being-of-the-Universe Himself delivered him. 166. A little frog was put into a pot and a fire was kindled beneath the vessel. It called to Krishna through some good deed done in its former birth, and the water ceased to be hot. 167. A voice from heaven said, 'Take the young frog out of the boiling pot. The water will at once get hot.' All the people heard this. 168. Vishnu's chariot of light came at once, and changed the frog's body into a heavenly body. It has been given a place in Heaven for ever, by the Saviour of the world. 169. Kali-yuga and Death are hard to overcome, but Shri Hari's name is the Saviour. If any one says, 'There is greater means of salvation,' that fool is deceived." 170. Thus discoursing, the God-loving *bhakta* smiling, shouted every now and then the names of God. And the whole audience joined in a great shout of Vitthal's name. 171. With the noise of the clapping of hands and the snapping of fingers there was the shouting from the excess of joy. People forgot differences and dualities, and they saw God every where.

172. While the *kirtan* was continuing with such joy, a most extraordinary thing occurred. The two *sannyasis,* standing up, made obeisance to Tuka. 173. Dadu Kondadev said to them, "Svamis, how is it you do this improper thing? You have made a *namaskar* to Tuka, and yet you blame Brahmans. 174. How is it that you are now falling at his feet? I will now apply the punishment. The guilt of falsehood has fallen on your own heads, and yet you came to me for justice." 175. The *sannyasis* replied, "The light that shines from Tuka is like the form of God. In him we have seen before us the Four-armed-one [Krishna], therefore, we bowed to him in love." 176.

The Ruler, with rage in his heart, said, "You evil-minded hypocrites, you made me make the Brahmans of Lohagav give security. Why did you do so? Tell me." 177. He persisted in his resolve. He had two asses brought. Now said he, "Shave the hair of their heads so as to make five stripes, and take them around the town on the asses." 178. When Tukaram realized what was happening, he prevented it. Said he, "One should not pay disrespect to (those who wear the mendicant's) garments. The Lord-of-Pandhari will not honour it." 179. When Tuka said this to the Ruler he quieted down, otherwise there would have been no one to prevent his determination.

DADU KONDADEV'S JUSTICE.

180. Listen now to an illustrative story thrown in here. While Dadu Kondadev was eating lunch one day, his wife stepped outside. 181. The salt and the greens were within reach, so he took them with his own hand. His wife in fun said to him, "You have done a very improper thing. 182. My authority rules here (in the dining room). How is it you took this food with your own hand? You preach to others to obey the law, and how is it you have done this improper thing?" 183. Hearing his wife's charge, he at once called a soldier. And said, "Cut off my hand at once. It has committed a great offence." 184. Just then a distinguished Brahman came in, and told him on scripture authority that if one cuts short the sleeve of his coat, it is the same as cutting off one's hand. 185. Accepting this explanation, he followed it the rest of his life.

A hired woman was brought before him for having stolen some flour. 186. She denied having stolen it. The hand-mill being lifted up they found a quarter measure of grain underneath it. They hastened to impale her. 187. But he brought the nether stone and said, "I have found the unjust thief." He then impaled the handmill, and all the people looked on. 188. Such was his rigorous justice; but he had no liking for any thing false. But in the case of the *sannyasis,* Tuka's word was his limit, so that he did not administer punishment.

189. While telling the story of the saint, I have introduced in its midst these side stories. Let not the audience be wearied by them. I have spoken for the sake of illustrations.

190. The Vaishnava *bhakta* carried on his *kirtans* with shouts of "Victory! Victory!" They lighted the lamps for the wave offering, and waved them over the Husband-of-Rukmini. 191. Tuka danced, and the loud sound of the shoutings of Vitthal's name was distinctly heard. The little bells tinkled sweetly on his feet, while the noise of the shoutings filled the sky. 192. And as Tuka gazed at the listeners, they seemed to be in the form of Vitthal. All differences seemed to disappear, and Shri Hari appeared in the whole universe. 193. While Tuka was in this condition of unconsciousness of body, he brought to his imagination God's visible form. He lovingly fell prostrate before it, and then the favours were distributed.

194. The dust of the saints' feet touch the earth. I, Mahipati, worship that dust. While distributing the favours some fell to the ground. Picking them up, I gladly eat them.

195. Svasti. This book, the Shri Bhaktalilamrita, by the mere hearing supplies all the desires of the heart. May the God-loving *bhaktas* always listen to it. This is the thirty-eighth interesting chapter.

CHAPTER 39.

MAHIPATI'S PERSONAL CONFESSION

Obeisance to Shri Ganesh.

1. Thou, O Pandurang, hast personally conducted an infinite number of the dull-minded across the sea of this earthly existence to the other side. I am one who has been left behind. So, be Thyself my ferry boat. 2. I am not able to perform the baths, the devotions, ancestral worship, repetition of *mantras,* austerities or Thy worship according to established rules. 3. *Yoga* practices, and sacrifices, I cannot perform. My body is weak. I have not visited sacred places. Thou knowest this, O Vithabai. 4. If I ought to give gifts to those worthy of them, I have not much of money or grain to give. I lack more than most in goodness. My mind is terribly evil. 5. O God, I have not been a disciple of a *sadguru,* nor have I served the saints. In every way I am lame. This Thou knowest, O God. 6. If all sins could be collected together I would be a statue made out of them. I have committed many forbidden things. I confess all this to Thee. 7. I am wholly a sinner in every way. My own heart bears witness to this. But Thou, O Shri Hari, look now to Thy reputation (as a Saviour), and ferry me across the sea of this life.

KING SHIVAJI'S SECOND VISIT TO TUKA.

8. In the last chapter there was told how the two *sannyasis* saw Tuka in the form of God, and in sincerity bowed before him.

9. The Ruler wrote to Shivaji a report of what had happened from its beginning to its end. The king then

came to Poona and paid his worshipful respects to Tuka. 10. King Shivaji worshipped him in the various customary ways, and bowed at his feet. The *Bhakta,* unconscious of body, began his *kirtan.* 11. There were cymbals, *vina,* and drum, and fifty voices led in the chorus. As they shouted the sweet name of Vitthal, the sky was more than filled with the sound. 12. To begin with, it was a Hari-day, a festival occasion, and an auspicious day, and the king was eager to listen. Then there was the eloquence of the God-loving *bhakta.* What could there be lacking in that enthusiastic performance?

13. Now the Muhammadan Governor at Chakan was informed of what was going on. He sent two thousand *Pathan* soldiers to apprehend King Shivaji. 14. The Hari-*kirtan* was being performed in a very extensive building in the city of Poona. The King seated himself to listen. Suddenly the cruel enemy arrived. 15. The king learned of what was taking place, and requested Tuka to give him leave to go. All the audience was thrown into confusion, and all the enthusiasm vanished. 16. Realizing the trouble they were in, Tuka pleaded with Vithoba for His help. He composed and repeated four *abhangs,* which all good people should study. 17. He pleaded with God to have mercy (on others). "As for myself I have no fear of death. If others suffer pain, my eyes cannot bear the sight, 18. and that this interruption should come to our worship, what could be a worse death than this? And so, O Vithoba, by Thy mystic powers deliver us from this trouble." 19. Hearing this plea, the Cloud-of-Mercy gave Tuka his assurance. "Continue your *kirtan* in joy. I, the Life-of-the-Universe, am the king's protector."

20. The furious Muhammadans were outside the building. They said to themselves, "We are not able to recognize King Shivaji among those inside. Let us, therefore, kill all listeners and speakers, then the king will naturally be found amongst them. 21. While those evil minded men were thus taking counsel, the Husband-of-Rukmini performed a clever trick. He himself became Shivaji the king, and started to run with haste. 22. In the Muhammadan army there were spies, and they recognised the king. "Here is our enemy," they cried, "seize him quickly." And so saying, the *Pathans* rushed after him. 23. The Supreme-one-of-the-Universe, in his illusory form, would be seen for a moment, 24. and as the soldiers caught up with him, and were so near that they were about to seize him, when they said, "Our sight has deceived us." Then the Recliner-on-the-Serpent [Krishna] would be seen just in front of them. 25. The moment they would say, "He is not here," he would appear near them. But just as they were about to seize him, they saw nothing. In three hours he led them forty miles into a jungle of thorny bushes. 26. Just as the Life-of-the-Universe at the time he became the Krishna *avatar* fled in fear from Kalayavan, and then as he hid himself in the Muchukund cave, 27. in that same way now Krishna became invisible in this jungle. The moon had now set, and darkness filled the sky. 28. The Muhammadans were unable to find a path, and their clothes were torn by the thorns. Their beautiful horses also ran away, and those poor fellows became miserable indeed.

29. In the meantime the God-loving *bhakta* was singing and dancing in his glorious *kirtan*. Listeners became lost in attention, and the enthusiasm became extraordinary.

30. "Krishna, Vishnu, Hari, Govinda, Achyuta, Ananta, Root-of-Happiness, Supreme-Being, Satchidananda, Shri Mukunda, Guru-of-the-Universe." 31. Such were the names used in his singing, and with feelings of love he pleaded with God. His throat choked with the emotion of love, and tears streamed from his eyes. 32. Thus for four watches of the night the loud shoutings of their loving worship continued, and as the sun was rising they waved the wave offering over the Husband-of-Rukmini.

33. That the enemy voluntarily went off was a surprise to the king. Said he, "I escaped death to-night, because I sat among saints." 34. The king then took leave of Tuka, and went to (his fort at) Sinhagad. As he left he asked for some favours. Tuka gave him with his own hand a handful of horse dung. 35. The king took it in his garment, and placed it in his office. His heart was full of joy. Said he, "My good fortune has begun to rise."

THE GOLD COIN AND THE AVARICIOUS BRAHMAN.

36. Such were the events that happened in Poona at that time. Then all the people took Tuka with them, and returned to Lohagav.

37. A man by name of Kondoba, surnamed Lohakar, was a sincere follower of Tuka. He used to lead in the choruses in an unusual way, which gave delight to the Vaishnavas. 38. He used to constantly remark to Tuka, "I have the desire to go on the great pilgrimage. Every householder respects your word, so help me to beg for the expenses of the journey. 39. I have nothing with which to pay for the expenses, but a word from you will accomplish the deed." Such is what the Brahman was continually saying to Tuka. Now what did that Vaishnava do? 40. He put his hand under his seat, pulled out a golden coin,

and gave it to the man. Kondoba was perplexed what to say, but he hinted that it would not bo sufficient for his purpose. 41. But Tuka said to him, "Constantly make change with the coin, and keep one copper coin in your purse. 42. On the next day it will become a gold coin. However often you make change with it, always be careful to keep one copper coin. 43. Spend the money in worthy objects, and fully complete your pilgrimage. When you come back, give me back my coin." 44. Kondoba the Brahman was astonished, but said to himself, "I will at once this very day test this miracle." He changed the gold coin and kept one copper coin. 45. He purchased eagerly the materials he needed, and made popped corn, cakes and sweets. He bought ghee, sugar eagerly, that his tongue might taste sweet things. 46. Having made abundant preparation, the Brahman came to tell Tuka, and said he, "I made change with the gold coin and have seen the miracle, Svami." 47. The Vaishnava *bhakta,* hearing him, said, "Let no one know of this thing. Accomplish your purpose and when you come back return me my coin."

48. The noble Vaishnava then composed three *abhangs,* and sent them as letters by the hand of the Brahman. Listen you wise and pious, to the substance of those letters. 49. He wrote one letter of request to Vishveshvar, the Lord-of-Kailas [Shiva]. He wrote one to the river Bhagirathi, and one to the Vishnupada. 50. "The arrangement of the universe seems most wonderful, and Thou Mahadev, pervadest it in the form of soul. Therefore *bhaktas* give Thee glory, through Thy name of Vishvanath [Protector-of-the-Universe]. 51. Have mercy at this time on one who is lowly, poor and helpless. Again and again I place my head at Thy feet. 52. My heart

is easily satisfied, and Thou dost not lack anything. Tuka asks a favour of Thee. Send it please, O Shiva."

53. In his letter to the River Bhagirathi he said, "Hear my request, O Mother. Thou art the supreme mistress of all sacred waters, O Mother. 54. By the mere sight of Thee the greatest sins are washed away. Therefore, I bow with love at Thy feet. 55. Those who in sincerity bathe in Thy waters receive the heavenly enjoyment, and the experience of Final-Deliverance. They say that Tuka is patronised by the saints, and he sends Thee these word-flowers."

56. The noble Vaishnava sent a pleading letter to the great seat of Vishnupada at Gaya. "With my own hand I offer my body at Thy feet. 57. My Gaya-ceremonies have been completed. I have paid back what I owed my ancestors. My deeds have been well performed, and the burden of Egoism has been removed from me. 58. Thy name alone, I, Tuka, proclaim aloud to the world that there is only one name Harihar. And this letter of three *abhangs* is written by me as the result of the joy I experienced."

59. Kondoba Lohakar took these letters in his hand, and bowed down lovingly to Tuka. Then he started immediately on his great pilgrimage (to Benares). 60. As he went along he would change the gold coin, and keep one copper coin tied up in his garment. He continued to spend more and more, so that people began to wonder. 61. They said, "He has no money. From whence does he meet these expenses? As in a hole dug in the sand, the water does not fail. 62. The amount of water looks small, but as one draws it out there is no lack. And such was Kondoba's confidence in Tuka that he told no one about the mystery. 63. Thus continuing his journey, he arrived at Benares.

He bathed in the Bhagirathi, and gave her his message. 64. "O Mother, mistress of all sacred waters, Tuka has sent you a letter." While he was thus speaking a wonderful thing took place. 65. From the broad expanse of the water Bhagirathi put up her friendly hand. There were jewelled bracelets on her arms, and shone as if the sun was just rising. 66. On the bank there were great crowds, and seeing the miracle all wondered. Said they "Bhagirathi has come in person." So all hurried to bathe. 67. Some brought gold coins as offerings, and lovingly put them in her hand. Some gave her foot ornaments, garlands of jewels, jackets, and women's garments. 68. They worshipped her in this way, but the Mother-of-the-Universe would not take them. Suddenly Kondbhat bethought himself. 69. He took Tuka's letter and waded into the water. The moment he put the letter in Bhagirathi's hand, she closed her hand upon it. 70. And after letting the people see this wonderful sight, the hand withdrew into the water. As they saw this, all the dwellers in the sacred city were astonished. 71. Said they, "Bhagirathi preferred Tuka's word-flowers, he, whose manuscripts the Husband-of-Rukmini saved from the water."

72. Kondbhat remained happily in Benares for four months. He had learned to repeat Tuka's *abhangs,* and he repeated them to Vishveshvar [Shiva]. 73. As Shiva heard Tuka's pleading in jewelled words, He wagged his head. *Bel* leaves and flowers fell from the sky, and people saw them. 74. Thus both Bhagirathi and Shiva showed wonderful miracles. All the pilgrims were astonished at what they saw.

75. Kondbhat then went to Gaya, and paid off his debts to his ancestors, and through Tuka's favour, he

spent his money in a worthy cause. 76. Thus having completed his pilgrimage, he commenced his homeward journey. His heart was full of joy, but he thought to himself, 77. "I asked Tuka to help me to beg my expenses, but instead, I received this great accomplishment. It is like one hunting for some medicinal plant, and lo, he finds a dew-drop of nectar. 78. Or, as when one desiring a pool of water should see the ocean before him. Or, as if one was wishing a milk-giving goat, and then should find a wish cow at his house. 79. Or as if one trying to commit verses to memory, should find his tongue blessed with the gift of gracious poetry. Or as when one in the intensity of the summer heat should suddenly see a snow mountain (the Himalayas). 80. Or as when one has a great wish for a lamp, the sun should appear out of the darkness. Or wishing one could have a vision of God in a dream, one should meet Him in actual visible form. 81. So I had wished for an opportunity to beg for travelling expenses, and instead, Tuka had lovingly given me this great accomplishment. 82. Now if he asks for the gold coin back again, I should not give it to him." With this avaricious thought, he came to see Tuka. 83. Tuka was sitting outside of the town of Lohagav alone by himself, and in a state of unconsciousness of body. Kondoba Lohakar came, and fell at Tukâ's feet. 84. Said he, "By your favour my pilgrimage has been accomplished." The noble Vaishnava bethought himself, and asked that his coin be returned. 85. Kondbhat replied, "I have truly lost the gold coin." "Very well," was all the answer Tuka gave him. 86. Kondbhat hastened to his home, and searched for his coin. It was not in the knot he had tied in his garment. He was shocked with amazement. 87. Said he, "When I at noon performed my bath the coin was in my garment. The knot is the same as before. How could the coin have slipped out? 88. If I should now go, and tell Tuka, I have already told him that I lost it. My lie has yielded its fruit." So saying, he was greatly troubled. 89. For one thing he incurred the anger of his *sadguru*, and so he failed in his selfish plans for a livelihood. Failure came from both sides, and so his mind was in commotion.

Tuka's Sincere and Simple Life.

90. Enough of these thoughts. Many have lost through the snare of avarice. Some hold up their hands (until withered). Some take the smoke of five fires. 91. Some drink only milk. Some live in great forests. Some grow a great mass of hair on their heads, and cover themselves with ashes. 92. Some fasten a swing to a tree and there adopt eighty-four sitting positions. Some remain dumb, never speaking a word, and write on a slate their wishes. 93. Some study the Vedas, and perform the ceremonies for the householders. Some become pandits, and engage themselves in disputes with their opponents. 94. Some become Haridas, and preach deep wisdom to many. Some become *sannyasis*, others say they are servants of Vishnu. 95. Then there are Jangams, Jain *sannyasis*, fakirs, kanphades and naked mendicants. Some call themselves followers of the terrible path [*Aghorpantha*]. How can I mention all these sects? 96. I have seen all these, but I have not seen one among them who was without desire. But Tuka was not like them. He was absolutely indifferent to every thing. 97. Although all accomplishments were possible for him, yet he kicked them away, and having subdued the six enemies of the soul worshipped the Husband-of-Rukmini. 98. Although the king Shivaji urged it upon him, yet Tuka would not

accept any gift of land, nor would he accept a *wadi* or a house, garments or jewelry. 99. He ate very moderately, and with every mouthful would repeat God's name. By day and night he performed *kirtans,* and there was no interruption to this rule. 100. Fourteen other Vaishnava *bhaktas,* throwing aside the snares of this worldly existence, attached themselves to Tuka, and led in his *kirtan* choruses. 101. Without telling them he would slip away, and go to various towns. Then they would have to hunt for him, and finally all would come after him. 102. If anyone asked the noble Vaishnava where he was going on this occasion, he would reply, "I am on my way to the city of Heaven." Such was his customary reply. 103. If anyone asked him a question, he never replied except in the form of an *abhang.* His tongue delighted in the repetition of God's names, and his body became completely Brahma.

TUKA'S BODY SHINES LIKE THE SUN.

104. On one occasion the Vaishnava *bhakta* was performing a *kirtan* at Lohagav. His whole thought was on the name and form of God, and he lost all bodily consciousness. 105. The loud music of the cymbals, *vina* and drums was as if all divine sound had come in a great flow. The names of Vitthal were shouted, and more than filled the sky. 106. And as the listeners saw the condition of the leader in his loss of bodily consciousness, they also lost bodily consciousness.

The man whose duty it was to pour oil in the lamp, he also lost his bodily consciousness. 107. Every one was wholly absorbed in worship. He put no oil in the lamps, and they went out. But now a most extraordinary wonder took place. Listen to it you good and pious people.

108. A bright light shone from Tuka's body. Listen to some interesting illustrations which in my opinion explain this appearance. 109. While the fœtus is in the mother's womb, its light appears on her body. Or whatever a poet experiences in his mind he expresses it in words outside the mind. 110. Or, again, as when in a house with glass windows, a lamp is lighted, its light falls outside, although there is no opening whatever to the house. 111. So the Eagle-bannered-One sat joyfully in Tuka's heart, and His light spread in all directions. So at least I think. 112. Vishnu who is the theme of the poems of the greatest of poets, in whose crown are ten million suns, who is the lover of His *bhaktas,* that Lord of the Universe, He stored Himself in the heart of Tuka. 113. And that is why the light from his person fell powerfully on the *kirtan.* They actually saw this light. And this because of their great good fortune.

114. In order that the world might be saved these *bhaktas* are *avatars.* The *kirtan* ended at the third watch. The wave offering was then waved over the Husband-of-Rukmini. 115. Then as the noble Vaishnava sat down it suddenly became dark. The audience came to their bodily consciousness, and all the lamps were lighted. 116. But not any of the oil had been used which had been brought for the lamps. The oil jar was as full as it was before. All wondered greatly.

God and Tuka Converse.

117. The pious people of Lohagav had the great good fortune of serving Tuka. In listening to his impassioned *kirtans* even they, as it were, robbed love from him. 118. Just as the Krishna *avatar* took place at Mathura, but the Dark-complexioned-one spent his active life among the

cowherds of Gokul. Living in Vraja he took his part in the festivals. So I think it happened to Tuka. 119. The world-renowned noble Vaishnava was now held in high and growing respect.

Without saying a word to any one, Tuka hastened back to Dehu. 120. He went immediately to the temple, and looked at the image of Pandurang. Choking with emotion he bowed before Him prostrate, just as a stick lies fallen on the ground. 121. The impression of that form was stamped upon his heart, so that when he was outside the temple he could see God's *sagun* form. His heart could not contain the love he felt. It overflowed from him. 122. Tuka said to God in pleading words, "Thou must accept me. This is my chief thought. I have truly no other thought, O Vithoba. 123. I have stained both parties, and brought shame on God and on the relationship of God and *bhakta*. My heart bears witness to this. 124. I am bound by a powerful chain, O Vithabai. Attachment to the things of this world has grown in me. Deliver me from this, O Merciful-one. 125. When people give me to eat, they cook all kinds of dainty food for me. And I find physical enjoyment from it. Thou, Lord-of-the-Intelligence, art a witness of this. 126. Many faults find a place in me. Drowsiness and laziness are increasing in me. I beg of thee in the name of the saints to take me to Thy Heaven [Vaikunth]." 127. While Tuka was thus pleading for mercy, the image of Pandurang smiled, and said, "Your heart's desire will be gratified. I, Krishna, am Thy protector. 128. When your body comes to its end I will not let Death [Kala] even look at you." As the Supreme-Being-of-the-Universe thus spoke to Tuka, Tuka's throat choked with emotion.

TUKA AND THE BIRDS.

129. On a certain occasion Tuka went to Alandi. In the assembly hall with great reverence he prostrated himself before God. 130. There were birds picking up seed under the Ajan tree. When they saw Tuka, they flew away. 131. When the God-loving *bhakta* saw this his hair stood on end ((from distress). Said he, "If my mind recognized no difference, why did the birds fly away? 132. The idea that I have conquered the six enemies of the soul, and by courageous endeavour I am a noble Vaishnava, and that the three worlds seem myself, is all in vain. 133. My body has become like a corpse, and I have not the least bodily consciousness, but although that is my condition, it seems to me to be all in vain. 134. I have placed the cow-dung-cakes of Indifference-to-worldly-things around my body, and kindled them with the fire of Brahma. I have turned my back on this worldly life. Now all this seems to my mind to be in vain. 135. This body of mine is a jar broken at Vithoba's feet. I have destroyed all desires of my heart but all that seems to-day to be in vain. 136. I made the funeral farewell ceremony to family, name and form. I have offered this body of mine to whom it belongs. Such has become my condition. But all this seems to me to be in vain. 137. Although the measure of my life is not yet complete, it has turned to ashes of its own accord. A light has been lighted within me, even by Pandurang, the father of the Universe. 138. I have thus described my condition from experience, and still birds fly away from me from fear of me. So I have spent my words in vain." Thus thinking, he felt great sorrow in his heart. 139. Then concentrating his mind, he contemplated the Lord-of-Pandhari, and said, "O Merciful-to-the-Lowly,

Compassionate-One, Protector-of-the-Helpless, O Vithabai! 140. A blind man takes hold of a seeing man's hand, and walks along the path, but sees nothing at all. He walks along, putting his weight on God. 141. While walking the good path that leads to the Supreme-spiritual-riches, I have stepped into a side path. O Merciful-to-the-Lowly, O Pandurang, do Thou Thyself protect me." 142. Thus saying, the God-loving *bhakta* stood perfectly still. He did not let his body move in the very least. He did not even let eyelid meet eyelid. 143. Said he, "When the birds will come, and sit on me without fear, then only will I be comforted. Otherwise my life is in vain." 144. With this strong determination, he stood perfectly still for an hour and a half. He did not even breathe. The Soul-of-the-Universe knew this. 145. But now the Lord-of-Pandhari found Himself in difficulty as he saw Tuka's determination. Said He, "I must plan some way of meeting so the birds will come, and sit on him without fear, then only will 'I grant to *bhaktas* their desires.' If I do not grant Tuka his desire, my word will prove false." 147. The Soul pervades every creature, so He, Mercy-in-visible-form, entered Tuka's heart. And so with no fear in their hearts, the birds came and sat on Tuka. 148. The God-loving *bhakta* moved his body, but the birds did not fly away. Just as when a violent wind shakes a tree the birds are not afraid of the tree. 149. Tuka felt supreme joy, and with loving thought composed an *abhang.* I will quote the first line in this book. Listen. 150. "I had never seen all creatures come together as if they were one. But Thou hast granted me this my great desire. Thou didst it as a mother gratifies her infant child." 151. So wording his *abhang,* and prostrating himself before Dnyanadev's (tomb) with feelings of love, Tuka felt happy.

152. If the listener will now look back, and remember the past events, he will recollect that without telling any one, Tuka came to Alandi. 153. The fourteen Vaishnava *bhaktas* (who led in the choruses), searching for Tuka here and there, arrived at Alandi in their hunt. 154. Tuka, the noble Vaishnava, was sitting by himself under the Ajan tree, and birds were sitting every now and then on him. 155. As they were looking at this wonderful sight, they all came near him. Then the birds all flew away. Blessed was that occasion, on that auspicious day.

Tuka Performs a Kirtan by Dnyanadev's Tomb.

156. In the sacred city of Alandi on this occasion Tuka performed a *kirtan* at Dnyanadev's tomb. 157. Cymbals, *vinas* and other instruments had gradually been assembled there, and the loud music fell on the listeners' ears. 158. "Krishna, Vishnu, Dark-as-a-cloud, Achyuta, Narahari, the Best-Being, Advocate of Thy *bhaktas,* Home-of-Goodness, give me love of Thee in my worship. 159. So long as life lasts, so long I will perform Hari *kirtans.* Shorten my life at such time (as it pleases Thee) but let not the members of my body grow weary (to perform). 160. I can think of no sin greater than to forget Thy name. Shiva was burning with poison, but by repeating Thy name, He became immediately cooled. 161. The Muni Narad wanders over the three worlds singing Thy name. He carries his Brahma-vina on his shoulder, and always with love of Thee in his heart. 162. Dnyaneshvar had composed those noble *abhangs,* called the Haripath. And this the noble Vaishnava Tuka used to sing with love and reverence. 163. The clapping of hands, the sharp snapping of fingers, the sound of bells and other ankle ornaments made the music. There was not the least difference in the

harmony of drum and *vina*. 164. Thus the whole sky was filled with the manifestations of their joy. Gods even came, and in joy looked on the wonderful sight. 165. In invisible form the gods showered flowers. Everything seemed like the Pervader-of-the-Universe giving to the listeners joy with love.

166. Well enough of telling of Tuka's condition. Even a poet's ability has a limit. The *kirtan* lasted until the fourth watch of the night, then they waved the wave offering over the Husband-of-Rukmini. 167. They broke their fast on the twelfth of the fortnight, and then they were ready to go back to Dehu. They took leave of Dnyanadev, and afterwards arrived at Dehu. 168. Such was Tuka's state of mind that he was without enmity towards every creature. That is why the birds without fear sat on his body.

Tuka Visits Chintaman Dev at Chinchvad.

169. From the mouths of many, Chintaman Dev of Chinchvad heard about Tuka. So he thought he would invite Tuka, and see his miracles with his own eyes. 170. He, therefore, sent a man to Dehu in a friendly spirit, telling him to be very humble before Tuka, and to bring him back with him. 171. He assented, and came to see Tuka. The Vaishnava *bhakta* was performing a *kirtan*, and in listening he found rest for his soul. 172. He wished to give Tuka Chintaman Dev's message, but he was not in the state of one with bodily consciousness, so he continued to listen to his *kirtans* day and night, with mind always full of joy. 173. Chintaman waited three days, and still his man had not returned. So he said to himself, "I must go myself and see Tuka." 174. Thus thinking, Chintaman Dev started immediately. As soon as Tuka knew this through

his inner sight, he said to himself, "I must go and meet him." 175. Without telling any one, the noble Vaishnava started to go. When he had gone one half the way he was met by the noble Brahman. 176. As Chintaman embraced Tuka, he felt very happy, and said, "Blessed! blessed is this auspicious day, I have met the Vaishnava *bhakta.*"

177. They sat down where they were, Chintaman remarking, "I am glad we are alone. In your thought all creatures are one, and so the birds came and sat on you. 178. If a straw scarecrow so much as moves, the birds seeing it, fly away, but on you they sit without fear. I am impressed by this extraordinary condition. 179. You seem in the form of a man, but aside from that there is nothing with which to compare you. In your loving *bhakti* you have spoken so extraordinarily that the Best-Being has become subservient to you. 180. Nevertheless, Tuka, who are you really? Tell me the truth. Give me evidence of actual experience, and remove my doubts." 181. To this request of his worshipper Tuka showed a miracle. He split the skin of his thigh, and there was nothing but pure cotton in it. 182. There was no bone, or flesh, or blood. It was like carded cotton. Chintaman Dev saw this with astonishment, and said to himself, "Tuka is not a human being. 183. To save the world he has descended into this mortal world as an *avatar*. On the outside he looks like a man, but one should call him God." 184. Thus praising him, Chintaman prostrated himself before him, but Tuka grasped his feet and exclaimed, "O Svami, it is not proper for you to prostrate yourself before me. 185. I am of the *Shudra* caste, I am but the servant of all the saints." Thus saying, he grasped Chintaman's feet in love. 186.

Just as when the child Krishna ate dirt, and then showed to his mother the universe in his mouth, and then the good Yashoda bowed before him, and in childish manner Krishna cried, 187. and said, "I am your child, why do you fall at my feet, my good mother?" So was it with Tuka. He never thought of his own honour. 188. With his own hand he gasped his skin and showed the cotton to Chintaman Dev, but when the latter prostrated himself before him, he said, "It is wrong for you to do so." 189. Just like the extraordinary deeds of Vishnu, so the saints show the same deeds. There is not the least difference between God and His *bhakta.* 190. Air and motion, or the sun and its rays, the sea and its waves, these are not two different things. 191. Thus praising Tuka, Chintaman Dev took him by the hand, and led him that night to Chinchvad, and there listened with love to his *kirtan.* 192. The *kirtan's* music continued during four watches of the night, to the enjoyment of the noble Brahman. Then as the sun was rising the wave offering was waved over the Husband-of-Rukmini.

Tuka's Divine Nature.

193. Thus with love for Tuka, the worshipper of Ganapati [Chintaman Dev] kept him there three nights, and listened to his recitation of Hari's deeds. 194. Chintaman prepared many kinds of dainty food, and made a feast to Brahmans out of love for them. He seated Tuka in his own row, and ate lovingly with him. 195. After the eating, there were distributed the *pan supari,* fragrant unguents and flowers. A garland of flowers was placed around Tuka's neck, and all lovingly bowed to the Vishnu *bhakta.* 196. The Vaishnava Tuka then took leave of Chintaman Dev, and returned to Dehu. He who was an

avatar in a human body, the beloved of the Lord-of-Heaven. 197. In worshipping God Pandurang with his enthusiastic love, he himself became Pandurang. Thus they became two, so that He could enjoy the pleasure of worship. 198. If God alone exists, who is to have a longing, and for whom? There might be a heap of fruit fallen on the ground, but there is need of one to eat them. 199. A mirror may be bright, but it needs some one to look into it. Various may be the fragrance of flowers, but unless there is some one with a nose, they are useless. 200. So if there were no *bhaktas*, who would know of God's glory? So although He worships Himself, He makes two parts in the act [God and *bhakta*]. 201. The fourth *mukti* is the chief over the other three, so it is declared in the Bhagavat. To prove this to be true, Tuka descended as *avatar* to this earth. 202. He who performed his musical *kirtans*, had conquered the difficult *Kaliyuga.* Therefore, his body had become immortal. His whole body was Brahma in form. 203. There have been great good men on this earth, but they left their bodies here. But Tuka, though Brahma in form, yet possessed a human body. This is a profoundly strange thing.

204. In the next interesting chapter we shall see how the Merciful-to-the-lowly, the Supreme-one-of-the-Universe took Tuka suddenly, and in his love carried him to heaven.

205. He who is Achyuta (Unchangeable), joy itself, and the root of joy, who takes form voluntarily, Satchidananda, has given me, Mahipati, the blessing of assurance, and will gladly make him narrate the story of his *bhaktas.*

206 Svasti. This book, the Shri Bhaktalilamrita, by merely listening to it the desires of the heart are gratified. May the God-loving pious *bhaktas* listen to it. This is the thirty-ninth interesting chapter.

CHAPTER 40.

Tuka's Bodily Ascension into Heaven.

Mahipati's Preface to Chapter 40.

Obeisance to Shri Ganesh.

1. All rivers could run dry, and then be filled with nectar, but the deeds of God and His *bhaktas* have no known limit. 2. All the sprouts of grass on this earth might be fully counted, but in trying to describe the unsearchable attributes of the Lord-of-Heaven, the mind loses its reason. 3. A swimmer, even without a pumpkin raft, might swim across the sea, but no one is able to recount the sublime praiseworthy deeds of the Lord-of-the-Ocean-of-Milk. 4. One might fasten a violent whirlwind in a bundle, and keep it in his house, but O Krishna, in singing of Thy heroic deeds, one's voice comes to its end (through weariness). 5. The leaves in eighteen loads of plants might be counted, but the mind is not sufficient to describe Thy heroic deeds, O Lord-of-Heaven. 6. Great poets wtih great ambitions sing Thy praises, O Recliner-on-the-Serpent, but they do not know the whole of Thy glory. 7. The *Vedas*, *Shastras* and *Purans* tell without ceasing of

Thy attributes, but no one has demonstrated that Thou art just as Thou art described. 8. Each one, according to his understanding, unceasingly sings Thy praises, and among them let there be myself, this dull minded Mahipati. Remember this, O Krishna. 9. The cowherds made garlands of wild flowers and placed them around Thy neck. Seeing their loving endeavours, Thou, O Dark-complexioned-One, didst wear them jauntily. 10. In the same way, O Shri Hari, accept my uncouth words, so that the listeners' hearts may become crowded by the waves of love. 11. By giving to Tuka his feelings of love, Thou, O Lord-of-Pandhari, didst an extraordinary thing. Thou didst remove the conditions belonging to the Kaliyuga, and death, and made his body a spiritual body [Brahma body]. 12. Thou didst send the friend of *bhaktas* into this mortal world in order to save the world. Thou didst bring him to an equality with Thyself, and so Thou dost experience the joy of the relationship of God and *Bhakta*.

THE VISIT TO CHINTAMAN AGAIN DESCRIBED.

13. In the last chapter the interesting story was told of Tuka's going to Alandi, and of the birds sitting on him, although that seems an impossible thing. 14. Then how Chintaman Dev at Chinchvad heard of that event, and at once invited Tuka to come to Chinchvad. Then how he slashed his thigh open, and showed nothing but cotton inside. 15. Chintaman could see no bone, flesh or blood which made him exclaim, "One should not call him a man. He seems to be the Supreme-Brahma in a *sagun* form." 16. Then how in astonishment he asked Tuka, "The five elements have ceased to exist in you, then what is it that I see? 17. Such is my perplexity. Tell me

who you really are." Tuka replied in an *abhang* which I will quote in this book.

Abhang 1. Tuka is less in size than an atom, yet is as large as space.

2. I have swallowed and dropped the body that has the form of this illusory worldly existence.

3. I have swallowed and dropped the group-of-threes (Knower, Known and Knowledge) and the light shines in my body.

4. Says Tuka, "Now nothing remains of me, except sufficient for benevolent deeds."

18. With this answer of the Vaishnava *bhakta*, Chintaman Dev realized what it meant. Said he, "One must not call him man. He seems to be the Supreme-Brahma in visible form. 19. Evidently I have in my possession the good deeds of an infinite number of births, and therefore, I have the privilege of worshipping him." 20. Thus praising him, the Vaishnava *bhakta*, he prostrated himself before him. Tuka remained there for a night, and then returned to Dehu.

A Counsel Takes Place in Heaven

21. The Dweller-in-Heaven, Shri Hari, took counsel with his *bhaktas* in heaven. "I cannot endure my life here without Tuka," he said. 22. "I have sent him into the world of mortals to save the world, it is true. He performs *kirtans* day and night, in order to fasten his love on my *sagun* form. 23. By the power of my name *Kali* and

Kala have become his servants. Now who will bring him here?" Such was the question put by the Life-of-the-World. 24. "Death has not the slightest power over him, and it is in Tuka's heart to always remain in the world of mortals. 25. It is not in his mind to go to his final home. Death has no power over him. What plan shall we adopt?" 26. Thus questioned by the Husband-of-Lakshmi, all the *bhaktas* fell at his feet. Then with hands joined palm to palm, they expressed their opinion to Shri Hari. 27. "We propose some great disaster, so as to make Tuka disgusted with the world, and thus make it possible to bring him here from the world of mortals." 28. To this opinion, given with reverence, the Lord-of-Heaven assented. Said he, "Where Tuka's love is especially attached, that is the place to bring about some disaster. 29. The noble Brahmans of Lohagav, besides women, Shudras, and children, and adults listen to Tuka's *Kirtans*, day and night turning their hearts to the love of God. 30. After a lapse of time I should make their minds disgusted with worldly life, and lodge them in Vaikuntha so that they will be united with me. 31. Through the service they render to Tuka they have all become wealthy in the world's goods. Now disgust them with their worldly life." Such were the thoughts of the Life-of-the-World.

THE EFFECT OF DISASTER ON TUKA'S MIND.

32. Turning now to Tuka, the people of Lohagav took Tuka back with them from Dehu. He spent a whole month there performing *kirtans*. 33. Suddenly by the wish of Shri Hari, a foreign enemy came and plundered them of all their property. Those on whose hearts the teachings of Tuka were well stamped, they made no complaint what-

ever. 34. Those whose minds were attached to both worldly and spiritual riches, they mourned over their loss day and night. Said they, "The enemy has robbed us of our wealth, what are we to do?" 35. The Vaishnava *bhakta* then preached to them. He said, "If the whirlpools of the three kinds of affliction have taken away your wealth, you should not grieve over them. 36. That which was to take place has taken place. Why vainly trouble yourselves over this? Our bodies are not our own, then to whom belong our money and property?"

Abhang 1. Take no troublous thoughts over what is lost.

2. But say that it has been offered to God; and this is service done without effort.

3. If anything is burnt by fire, or a theft is committed; (say that) the doer of them is Narayan (God).

4. Says Tuka, "This need not be paid for, God admires but (sincere) words."

37. Such was the *abhang* that the Vaishnava *bhakta* composed at that time. And at the same time he said to Pandurang, "Take me now to Heaven. 38. Don't leave me in this world of mortals; I abjure Thee in the name of Thy *bhaktas*." With these words of indifference, he came back to Dehu.

The Effect of the Disaster on the People's Minds.

39. To begin with, the people of Lohagav were already attached to Tuka, so that when the enemy plundered them of their money and property, it aroused in them a spirit of indifference to worldly things. 40. Said

they, "Our property has gone. Let it go. All perishable things of this world are in vain." So in order to get the advantage of Tuka's *kirtans,* they came to Dehu. 41. Moreover, people from all the villages at a distance came to see Tuka. And as they listened to Tuka's *kirtans,* they were absorbed with interest. 42. There were musical instruments and banners of various kinds. Cymbals, *vina* and drum gave out their sounds. There were fourteen leaders for the choruses, who sang with love. 43. Every time inspired and *extempore abhangs* were used in the *kirtans.* All were eager to hear what might come out of Tuka's mouth.

Discussions about Tuka continue in Heaven.

44. Shri Hari, the Lord-of-Heaven, Husband-of-Lakshmi, thought to Himself, "I must go to the world of mortals and bring Tuka back with me." 45. Indira replied, "O God-supreme, send the chariot of light [*Viman*] by the hand of Parshad. And giving Tuka a celestial body, have him brought here." 46. To this suggestion of the Daughter-of-the-Ocean the Supreme-Being replied, "I think I shall bring Tuka here along with his body. 47. And in connection with this I will tell you an ancient story. In my Krishna *avatar,* when I returned to my home, Uddhava would not return. 48. He had conceived a great attachment for the *Sagun* God, and for that reason was very sorrowful. I then preached to him in the Bhagavat, and sent him to Badrikashram. 49. Coming back to my home, I found that Kali had greatly troubled the people. All were committing sin, and the way of *bhakti* had disappeared. 50. There was no more performance of good deeds, no more sacrifices. The whole of the Bhagavat

dharma [The Law of God] had disappeared. No one was now seeking after the world to come. 51. I then commanded Uddhava to descend as an *avatar* to the earth, there sing in praise of my good deeds, and save the world. 52. He then said to me, 'I am disgusted with a life in the womb. I will not go to the world of mortals, and leave Heaven.' 53. Because of this decision of his, I provided another way. Without being born I put him in a shell, and set it adrift on the Bhimarathi river. 54. Damashet, a tailor, and his wife Gonai, were both at the time in Pandhari. They were worshipping me there, and I was pleased with them. 55. He asked a son of me. I went and told him in a vision that I had given Uddhava in *sagun* form to be his son. 56. 'When you go to bathe in the Chandrabhaga a shell will come floating down the river. Take the infant on to your lap, and in your love take care of it.' 57. When Damashet saw the vision he was greatly rejoiced, and remembering the vision, he sat by the Chandrabhaga's bank. 58. Suddenly the *avatar* Uddhava came floating down on a shell. Damashet took it at once on his lap, and then went into his house. 59. He said to his wife, 'The Recliner-on-the-Serpent has become pleased with us, and has given us a son in *sagun* form. Take it on your lap.' 60. As Gonai heard Damashet's words, her breasts filled with milk. 61. After twelve days had passed he called the child Nama. When he was seven years old he brought an offering into the temple. 62. I had seen Pundalik's love for his parents, and as Pandurang, I became an *avatar* on the earth. I seemed to people a stone image, but my love attached itself to Nama. 63. When he said to me, 'Here is my offering, eat it,' tears filled my eyes. I then with love ate the food he had brought for an offering. 64.

When in his seventh year Nama made the stone image speak. There are also many other stories which I will briefly tell you. 65. Dnyanadev asked my permission and went with Nama on his pilgrimage. He was not able to bear the thought of separation from me; and sobbed bitterly. 66. Muhammadans gave great trouble, and killed a cow before Nama. He called on me lovingly to help him. 67. In a moment I raised the cow to life, and with my hand I gave Nama the assurance of my help. As the noble Vaishnava was returning an event took place in Marvad. 68. Both Nama and Dnyanadev were suffering from thirst. The lord of the *yogis* [Dnyanadev] took the form of a gnat, and so drank the water (of the well). 69. Nama did not know that trick, and so with feelings of love he called on me for help. I will tell you the wonderful thing I did. 70. The water in the well was down very deep; but it came boiling up to the very top. When Dnyanadev saw this he fell at Nama's feet. 71. Before the temple of Avandhya Nagnath, during the night devoted to Shiva, Nama performed a *kirtan*. Many came to listen, and that made the Brahmans angry. 72. They told Nama to go behind the temple, and there perform his *kirtan*. Hearing this command of the Brahmans, he felt perplexed. 73. The servant of Vishnu felt grieved, still he went behind the temple, and stood performing his *kirtan*. I turned the stone temple around. It stands in that same way to this day. 74. As Nama's wife, Rajai, had insufficient food and clothing, she was much distressed. Then I gave her a bag full of gold coins, but Nama had them forthwith looted (by the Brahmans). 75. While Nama was one day performing a *kirtan* he made a vow before the saints that he would compose one billion verses in Marathi. Then he began his gracious compositions. 76. Into whatever country he went on his pilgrimages he composed verses in their language. No one can count the number of his verses, but myself. 77. Four million, nine hundred and forty million, and nine hundred thousand were the number of his verses at the end, but he was not brought to Vaikuntha until he had seen death. 78. The vow of composing ten million verses remained incomplete, and, therefore, Tuka is Nama's *avatar*. He has changed his body into a spiritual body, and is experiencing the joy of the singing of my name. 79. I had already said to Uddhava, 'Become an *avatar* in the world of mortals, and you will have neither birth nor death.' It is necessary to make this true. 80. In his first *avatar* he came floating on a shell, and became Nama, without being born. And now I must bring Tuka together with his body, by escaping the calamity of death."

81. Thus the Lord-of-Heaven explained to Lakshmi, while all the saints were standing near. The Vaishnavas then shouted, "Victory! Victory!," and their hearts could not contain their joy. 82. They descended to this round earth sitting in the celestial chariot of light. Krishna, along with the saints, arrived near the town of Dehu. 83. The Life-of-the-World met Tuka, and in His love embraced him saying, "Without you Heaven seems to be a barren place. 84. You have performed kirtans in ways that are excellent, and have honoured the name of Vaishnava *bhaktas*. This is the way of salvation for all beings, and it is unnecessary to begin on other means." 85. On the eleventh day of the bright fortnight of the month of Phalgun [March] the Lord-of-Heaven came to take Tuka to His heaven [Vaikuntha].

Just then Rukmini fell at His feet, saying, "I have one request to make at your feet. 86. Let the scene of Vaikuntha be exhibited on the bank of the Indrayani river. That Tuka should be given there a feast, together with all his fellow *bhaktas.* 87. Just as at the time of Dnyanadev's self-imposed death, Nama cherished a seemingly impossible wish, and then Thou didst hold events never seen before, so do it now." 88. Understanding Indira's wish, the Life-of-the-World assented. Then by means of his mystic power He showed a remarkable miracle. 89. The Architect of the universe quickly came, and erected an illusory City of Heaven, where the eight *Siddhis* stood ever ready to help with hands joined palm to palm. 90. There were necklaces in four folds of pearls, and there a remarkable feast was provided. The gods came round to see the wonderful sight. 91. The cowherds danced merrily, and their joy was hilarious. The pleasure of that happiness accompanied with love will be known later through personal experience. 92. In looking at this joy, the *yogis* had to stop their contemplation. They had to change their sitting posture, and look at God's *sagun* form, 93. and say, "Blessed is Tuka's love. He has made the Best-Being subservient to him. He has bewitched Him whose limit the *Vedas* even do not know. 94. Uddhava, Akrura, Ambarishi, dwellers in Heaven with their celestial bodies, they also have come here to sit in the same row as Tuka in the feast." 95. The great *yogis,* Sanak and others, Narad, Tumbar, and Shuka, the chief of the *yogis,* were all seated by Krishna in one row. 96. The Eagle-bannered-One felt delight in honouring His *bhakta.* Every necessity was fully provided for the use of his saints, and with an attitude of reverence. 97. Fragrant powders and celestial flowers were used by the Life-of-the-World in honouring His *bhakta*. Lakshmi served the celestial food which even Brahmadev and other gods desire. 98. The Lord-of-the-World performed the Sankalp ceremony. The saints ate the divine food to their full satisfaction. As soon as they had washed their hands, He with His own hands distributed the *pan supari.* 99. Gods came, and in their wonder at the scene showered down flowers, saying, "Blessed is this world of mortals, where the Lord-of-Heaven has descended." 100. From the eleventh day of the fortnight the feast lasted for five days, but no one of the mortals even heard it, aside from Tuka himself. 101. All came regularly to Tuka's *kirtans* with minds absorbed in them, but they knew not of the extraordinary deeds of the Gods that were going on. 102. It happened to be a great festival called the Shimga, but no one spent their time in play and throwing of dirt. They introduced no dramatic performances, dancing or buffoonery, for indifference to such worldly things had become impressed on their minds. 103. Truth alone seemed to them worth-while, and they had no liking for the untrue. They were all pious, God-loving people, and listened with pleasure to Tuka's *kirtans.* 104. Peace and indifference to worldly things manifested themselves in them, with compassion for all creatures. They worshipped the Lord-of-Pandhari with love, through the influence of the world-*guru* Tuka.

105. Tuka, the *avatar* of Nama, had now become known all over the world. Men and women came to see him, and great crowds gathered there. 106. This chief jewel of *bhaktas* had descended for the salvation of the world. Blessed is this bank of the Indrayani in the precinct of Dehu, that sacred place. 107. God dwells with his *bhaktas*. At God's feet are all sacred waters, and Vaish-

nava *bhaktas* always live by the sacred waters. 108. I think there is no sacred place greater than this, for it was here that the Recliner-on-the-Serpent [Vishnu] came to honour Tuka's devotion.

God's Conversation with Tuka

109. After the Holi festival, on the night of the month of Phalgun [March] on the first day of the dark fortnight the Lord-of-Heaven said to Tuka, "Listen to what I have to say to you. 110. To-night for the four watches perform your *kirtan* with joy, and then come with me to see the city of Heaven." 111. Thus speaking to his dear *bhakta,* he lovingly embraced Tuka closely to his heart saying, "In hearing of your good deeds that call forth praise, the world is going to be saved. 112. In the Three-worlds there are an infinite number of great *avatars,* and there are an innumerable number of great men, but I can see no one but you, who on earth can attain sameness with me. 113. You have given me in sacrifice in body and soul, having imprisoned lust and anger, and having restrained the fickle mind. 114. Even after you have attained the spiritual position, you even put that far aside, and maintain the relationship of God and bhakta, and in your worship, well expressing your love. 115. You followed me as an *avatar,* in every *avatar* of mine as my dear friend and companion. I can see nothing with which to repay you. 116. I put before you great accomplishments, and you kicked them aside. You will not have Deliverance, nor the Highest Deliverance. Now what am I to do? 117. There have been many *bhaktas* in the past, there will be many in the future, but I have never seen any one with a heart so free of desire. 118. I am

going to take you tomorrow to the home in Heaven bodily." As Krishna thus spoke to him, Tuka rolled at His feet. 119. Said he, "O God, hear one thing. You will confine me to one place in Heaven, while my wish is that I should perform *kirtans* day and night. 120. But there is a Heaven on earth here on this earth, the famous Pandharpur. Why take me so far away? I will not go to Heaven." 121. The Mine-of-Mercy, understanding Tuka's heart, said, "Come for once at least as far as Heaven, and you will realize the great glory for which it is praised. 122. I will at that time show you my glory on the Ocean-of-Milk. Just as I am the pervader of the animate and inanimate so also are you. 123. If you continue in this world, forever, their devotion for you will not be perfect. Therefore, put aside your determination, and come, O chief of *bhaktas*." 124. After this pleading by Pandurang, Tuka finally acceded to His request.

Tuka Expecting Bodily Ascension to Heaven.

He began the performance of his *kirtan,* with the music of cymbal and drum. Vitthal's name was shouted, and with exclamations of Victory, Victory! there was clapping of hands. 125. The sky could not contain the sound as the *kirtan* seemed like the roaring of ocean waves. 126. In the enthusiasm of their loving worship no one possessed bodily consciousness. The overwhelming sound came in streams, and it appeared as if the music was divine. 127. Tuka then composed an *abhang* which he repeated. I quote it here in this book for the help of the reader. Have no doubt about it.

Abhang 1. (1) I shall fill the philosopher with a longing wish. And make the man delivered (from rebirth) drop his thought of self.

(2) In the *kirtan* one attains a spiritual body, and the fortunate one makes God his debtor.

(3) I will make the man who depends on austerities drop his pride. I will make those ashamed who depend on sacrifices and gifts.

(4) I will bring laziness to the wanderer to sacred places, and make Heaven a place of bitter experience.

(5) I will make this world blessed. And (people will say) "We are fortunate to see Tuka."

2. (1) Through death one loses one's body. Give earnest thought to this.

(2) All sorrow is taken away, being the natural state of our experience.

(3) One has had to labour too hard to even look at it, but the substance of it is in one's hand.

(4) Says Tuka, "What need of pity. And in what is life indifferent?"

3. (1) The body has become like a corpse, and has noticed its place in the cemetery.

(2) Lust, anger, and illusion cry day and night, saying "Alas, alas, for rule and law."

(3) The dungcakes of Indifference to worldly life have been placed about the body, and the great fire has been kindled, to attain the Brahma life.

(4) The jar is upturned and broken at one's feet, and the great sentence (I am Brahma) is heard.

(5) I have said the funeral farewell to family, name and form, and I have offered my body to whom it belongs.

(6) Says Tuka, "I am naturally saved. The light is lighted, O Pandurang."

4. (1) I have seen my death with my own eye. It was incomparably holy.

(2) The three worlds were filled with joy, with the experience of perfect spirituality.

(3) For a time I had a place in me for pride, but in good time I abandoned it.

(4) The defilement of birth and death is gone, I am far from it through my fear.

(5) God has given me a place to live. Placing my confidence in Him, I remain at His feet.

(6) Says Tuka, "Whatever He has given, is evident in this world. What He has taken away, He has taken away Himself."

128. Listeners were astonished at Tuka's doctrine, but the gods sitting in their chariots of light listened with

delight to his *kirtan*. 129. Kapil Muni also, who might be called the statue of philosophic knowledge, listened with joy to Tuka's *kirtan*, and all smacked their lips. 130. Said they, "May I lose the snare of words, and have my mind fixed immovably on God." 131. He who is the *avatar* of the three Gods, free, but still living, the *guru* of the world, Dattatreya, he also left his spiritual state, and in reverence remained at the *kirtan*. 132. There is no one devoted to austerities who is the superior to Shiva. He also forgot Shiva-hood and listened eagerly to the *kirtan*. 133. Those who through sacrifices and gifts are now sitting enjoying the happiness of heaven, they listened to the *kirtan*, and understood its teaching, and they felt ashamed of their (sacrifices and gifts). 134. They began to call the *guru* Purandhar, they became disgusted with the joys of heaven. They wished to remain many days in this world of mortals to drink in the honey of *kirtans*. 135. Those who wander with the speed of the wind, and have seen the holy places of the three worlds they also with love enjoyed the sweetness of Tuka's *kirtans*. 136. Said they, "Tuka, by the singing of God's names, has made his own body a spiritual body. Blessed, blessed is this Vaishnava Tuka. He has made the Lord-of-Pandhari subservient to him." 137. Sanak and the others who live in heaven praised Tuka in the same way. The listeners' hearts were all impressed by the *kirtan*, and called themselves blessed and fortunate. 138. And the good men in his world of mortals said, "The good deeds of an infinite number of births are in our possession, and, therefore, we have seen Tuka. 139. Blessed is our good fortune, for because of it, we have seen the Vaishnava *bhakta*." And He who is the subject-matter of the *Vedas* and *Shastras*, He was openly listening to Tuka's profound teachings. 140. The minds of the listeners became concentrated, and their whole body turned into an ear, and had their minds intent on what came out of Tuka's mouth. 141. Tuka on that occasion, while performing his *kirtan* with love, composed an *abhang**. Listen to it with reverence you, who are wise.

142. The *kirtan* thus continued four watches of the night. As the sun was arising the wave offering was waved over the Husband-of-Rukmini. 143. And Tuka danced with feelings of love, while repeating the names of Vitthal. None of the people had any bodily consciousness, and as they danced they experienced joy. 144. And Tuka's last words by which the world can be saved, those gracious words I am going to quote, and they should be committed to memory.

1. Listen O pious ones, whoever you may be,
2. Cast aside association with philosophers and worship Pandurang.
3. Seek not the many opinions of men, they will drown you certainly.
4. The servant Tuka in this *Kaliyuga* is going, after taking his leave of men.

145. After repeating these words he shouted aloud the name of Vitthal. The Lord-of-Heaven then said to Tuka, "Come now to Heaven. 146. You have become an *avatar,* and saved the world. Now come, and see the city of Heaven. I have brought the luxurious Pushpak chariot of light [*Viman*]." 147. As the Supreme-being of the world thus spoke, Tuka embraced His feet. They suddenly went from there leaving in the world his good deeds.

---

*Not translated.

148. Tukaram sent word to his wife at home, "I am going to the city of Heaven. Come along with me." 149. Tuka then composed eleven *abhangs* of instructions to his wife, which it was necessary for him to make true. 150. So that as he was going to Heaven he called Avali. Let the saints listen with respect to the reply she gave. 151. "I am five months with child, and the buffalo at home is now giving much milk. Our family consists of small children, and who will look after our affairs after us?" 152. At this reply the Vaishnava *bhakta* felt surprise. Said he, "Still she does not lose her affection for her home. Maya is an everlasting force." 153. The Vaishnava *bhakta* was calling her to Heaven, but Jijai said that she would not come. But it is not her fault. Listen to what was a customary thing. 154. The Vaishnava *bhakta* used to go as he might wish to any town, and if any one asked him suddenly where he was going, he would reply, "I am going to Heaven." 155. So it is not Avali's fault, for she said to herself, "The crazy fellow is going to some town or other." Therefore, she sent her reply that she had no leisure to come. 156. Tuka then repeated his last words in the Hari *kirtan* to his fortunate listeners. "Now I am going to my home in Heaven, never to return."* 157. Thus saying, he made God a *namaskar*, and shouting God's names, he started outside. 158. All the listeners at that time had their hearts overflowing with love, and listening to his words of indifference to worldly things their eyes flowed with tears. 159. But no one knew that he was going to his heavenly home bodily. All thought that he was going to some holy watering place. 160. People said to one another, "He has become weary of us. He must be going to the Himalaya mountains. What shall

*Abhang not translated.

we do?" 161. Others said, "Tukaram must be going to visit Badarikashram, because of our false deeds. We do not understand the true meaning of *bhakti.*" 162. A third said, "Since Tuka has become indifferent to worldly things, he calls every place he goes to 'My heavenly home.'" 163. Still others thought he must be going to Benares, and they pleaded earnestly that he would remain, reverently falling at his feet. 164. One said, "The Brahman Rameshvar, skilled as a speaker among pandits, will plead with Tuka, and cause him to remain. He will not listen to any one else." 165. Such were the remarks passed from one to the other by the men and women who were sitting in the *kirtan.* Suddenly Tuka shouting aloud God's name came out of the temple. 166. He went to the bank of the Indrayani and there in his love composed an *abhang.** I will quote it. Listen to it you pious people.

TUKA'S BODILY ASCENSION INTO HEAVEN.

167. Having repeated his *abhang* an extraordinary miracle took place. Gods sitting in their chariots of light began to shout, "Victory! Victory!" 168. With supreme joy Narad and Tumbar began to sing. And the Lord-of-Kailas [Shiva], bringing Parvati, also came. 169. Brahmadev, Vishnu, Shiva, all three, looked on the scene from their chariots of light. The *apsaras* and Gandharvas sang songs. The sky could not contain the sound. 170. The great *yogis,* Sanak and others, Dattatreya, Kapil and the like, Lord-of-the-rishis, Yaksha, Guhyak, and Kinnar [celestial beings] all came to view the scene. 171. The very distinguished *bhaktas* of the past ages, and all the saints belonging to the *Kaliyuga* came in their celestial

*Not translated.

bodies, riding in chariots of light, with their attention fixed on Tuka. 172. And as they were contemplating the Lord-of-Pandhari, Tuka's body seemed to them a spiritual body. He seemed a statue of Intelligence, with all the illusion of Maya gone. 173. They exclaimed, "He bears the name of noble Vaishnava, and has descended as an *avatar* to this world of mortals. Through his *kirtans* he has saved the world." 174. Suddenly the gods along with Indra shouted aloud the names of God, and the light from the Pushpak chariot of light filled the sky. The sun itself was less in brilliancy. 175. People had come along with Tuka. The dazzling light made them close their eyes. Just as when an intense flash of lightning is seen in the sky, every one closes his eyes. 176. So by the dazzling brilliancy of the Chariot of light the eyelids of all closed. And Tuka, sitting in the chariot of light, went up to Heaven.

The Peoples' Grief at Tuka's Departure.

177. The pious, God-loving, Vaishnava saints could see the path through the sky. The sky was more than filled with the sound of bells while the Gandharvas sang, repeating aloud the names of God. 178. As the brilliant light of the Pushpak chariot of light came now from a distance, people could open their eyes and look. Tuka was no where to be seen on this earth. Their grief was intense. 179. Said they, "While we were in the act of looking at the beautiful jewel in our hand, it slipped away." The children went and told Jijai, and she came beating her breast. 180. Now a great crowd gathered from distant places, and also of the men and women of the town. It was an ocean of sorrow with swollen waves. How can it be described in a book? 181. Just as when Krishna left the Gokul, the inhabitants of Vraja sorrowed, so it happened now, when

Tuka was no longer to be seen. 182. All eyes longed to see the shapely form of the Sagun Tuka, and so they looked in every direction, but Tuka was not to be seen.

183. It was then 1571 of the Shaka era [A.D. 1649] in the *sanvatsar* [sixty-year circle] called Virodhi, in the month of Phalgun [March] on the second day of the dark half of the month, at the full moon, when it was four *ghatikas* [24 minutes = 1 ghatika] of the morning. 184. It was at that time that the world-*guru*, the Vaishnava *bhakta*, Tuka disappeared, and the pious God-loving *bhaktas* deeply sorrowed. 185. Gangaji Maval read from his note book the *abhangs* that Tuka composed at the time of his departure. The ground was sprinkled by his falling tears. The love he felt could not be contained in the three worlds. 186. Avali weeping exclaimed, "He sent to call me, but at the time I thought it was not true (that he was really going to leave) and so I remained at home. 187. When the flame of his life of indifference to worldly things touched me, it burnt up my body, and now while we were looking at him, he has left us and gone. 188. If I had at least known that he was really going, I would have hung on his garment, and gone with him, but now I am with child, and have to care for an ignorant child, and with household affairs on me, how can I go?" 189. Thus saying, she fainted and fell on the ground. Her two young sons, Mahadev and Vithoba, also were weeping.

190. Perhaps the Vaishnava *bhakta* will return, and so they watched and wailed. They remained until sunset, and then returned to their homes. 191. The crowds that had come from a distance to see Tuka, they also melted away, but the fame of that event spread throughout the three worlds. 192. The report spread from land to land,

that the Lord-of-Pandhari had come for Tuka, and taken him bodily to Heaven. And this was thought to be extraordinary. 193. Those who witnessed the event, they declared it to be true. Doubters regarded it as false. The illusion of Vishnu's uncontrollable Maya could not be controlled by anyone.

Life at Dehu after Tuka's Departure.

194. It was from the town of Dehu that Tuka passed to his home in Heaven, and here his fourteen Vaishnava disciples decided to remain. 195. They were Rameshvar the Brahman, learned in the six systems of philosophy. Kanhaya, the brother of Tuka, Gangaji Maval Kaduskar, Kondoba, the Brahman from Lohagav, 196. Santaji Jaganade, the oilman, who was Tuka's writer. There were nine other Vaishnavas, who had good thoughts awakened in them. 197. These fourteen disciples did not return to their homes, for they said, "Only if the *sadguru* shows us again his feet, shall we preserve our lives." 198. Kanha, the brother of Tuka, also sorrowed deeply He composed an *abhang** with its appeal for mercy. Listen to it with reverence you pious people. 199. While Kanhaya, Tuka's brother, was thus pleading, the other thirteen noble Vaishnavas sat there listening. 200. For three days and nights they sat by the bank of the Indrayani. They spent their time thinking of Tuka, and they felt a disgust for the worldly life. 201. Some continued looking in all directions. Some looked up into the path of the sky, and then on the fifth day at early dawn, a thing happened, to which listen.

*Not translated.

TUKA'S CYMBAL AND BLANKET FALL FROM HEAVEN.

202. Tuka was always accustomed to carry cymbals in his hand, and he always wore a blanket. These fell down from above. 203. From this they became sure that the *sadguru* had now become a dweller in Heaven. Therefore, they bathed in the Indrayani, and came to the temple. 204. Pious people now began to come from a distance to see the cymbal and blanket, saying to themselves, "This is seeing Tuka," and their eyes filled with tears. 205. Kanhaya then said to Rameshvar, the Brahman, "That day should be appointed as the holy day. If there is any scriptural authority on the matter, tell us." 206. Rameshvar replied, "Listen, Tuka, who was without dependence on religious deeds, and without the experience of bodily death, has gone to the abode of Shri Vishnu. 207. It was in Phalgun, the dark half of the month, and on the second day that the *sadguru* became a resident of Heaven, but his cymbal and blanket came down on the fifth, as a word of greeting to us. 208. So this day, the fifth, is the auspicious day on which to feast the Brahmans, and assemble the Vaishnavas and begin the *kirtan*. 209. Even if he had suffered bodily death, still he would have had authority over religious deeds. I have nothing to say regarding the deeds of the world-guru. 210. The uncontrollable Vaishnava Maya cannot injure him. While in the body, he became a spiritual body. 211. Tuka, who became Nama's *avatar* in this world of mortals, showed men wonderful deeds, and restored the worn out way of *bhakti*." 212. To this reply of Rameshvar's the saints shouted "Victory! Victory!" and then they began a great celebration on the fifth day of the dark half of Phalgun. 213. They prepared dainty food, and seated the rows of Brahmans

in the temple. They lovingly showed them reverence, and then served them the feast. 214. The Vaishnava *bhaktas* performed their *kirtans* on the fifth and sixth. On the seventh day, there was a celebration full of joy.

TUKA'S THREE SONS.

215. Tuka had two sons, their names were Mahadev and Vithoba. Tuka's wife was with child, and her nine months were now completed. 216. Then Avali gave birth to a son, the very statue of *bhakti,* knowledge, and indifference to worldly things. They gave him the name of Narayan, and all the saints felt joy.

217. Day by day he grew in stature, and Shivaji, the noble king, came to see him. He gave him the income of four villages, and built the temple of Vithoba. 218. Although money and property came to him in plenty, still his mind turned to indifference to worldly things. He had the Brahmans come and plunder his house, and he went off to Dvaraka. 219. He left his wife and child, and went on the great pilgrimage to Benares. He brought back eleven *kavadi* loads (of water) and worshipped Shri Rameshvar. 220. Many of Tuka's abhangs he had committed to memory, and the noble Vaishnava, Narayan Bava, now performed enthusiastic *kirtans.* 221. Although Mahadev and Vithoba were older than he, yet they submitted to his authority. Tuka's greatness fell easily on him. 222. So although Tuka had become a resident of Heaven, having gone there bodily, still by his favour he gives a sight of himself even to-day to the pious ones.

TUKA GIVES VISIONS OF HIMSELF.

223. To begin with, when Kanhaya pleaded for compassion, Tuka graciously gave him a vision of himself in

a dream. 224. Then there was Kanada, a Lingayat grocer, who lived in Sudumbara. He had been of great service to Tuka, being indifferent to worldly things. 225. Then there was one by name of Gaba Shet, a man of supremely good character. He abandoned all worldly affairs and business, and had associated himself with the good Tuka. 226. Then one day he came with hands joined, palm to palm and made this request. "When I come to die, I want my Svami to give me a vision of himself". 227. Realizing his loving sincerity, the Vaishnava *bhakta* assented. And after Tuka had gone to Heaven bodily a thought came to the grocer. 228. He privately told the saints his secret, that Tukaram had promised him that at his death he would give him a visit, and the time for this was near. 229. After some days the time of his end came. He immediately sent some men to Dehu, 230, with instructions to bring Rameshvar Bhat, the learned Brahman, Tuka's brother Kanhaya, and his youngest son, Narayan. 231. The noble Vaishnava seated them, and worshipped them in the customary way. Suddenly Tukaram appeared in their midst; the grocer bowed before him. 232. With his own hand he applied the fragrant paste, and put a garland of flowers around Tuka's neck, exclaiming, "You have had mercy on a miserable sinner, and given him a vision of yourself." 233. While thus speaking with his lips the people who heard him were astonished. All saw the grocer put the garland on Tuka's neck. 234. There was no peg in the wall so that the garland seemed hanging in space. The Vaishnavas shouted, "Victory! Victory!" and loudly repeated the names of God. 235. While repeating the names of Vitthal, Gaba Shet left his body. All exclaimed, "Victory! Victory! He has had a vision of Tuka." 236. Just as in the case of the *avatars,*

Ram and Krishna, whose avatarhood has ceased according to the teaching of the Purans, and yet they give direct visions of themselves to their *bhaktas,* taking *sagun* forms. 237. So although Tuka had gone to reside in Heaven he showed to men deeds like those shown by Hari. Yet his visions were reserved for the pious. Many can bear witness to this. 238. Niloba Gosavi of Pimpalner, and Bahinabai, wife of Gangadhar, were visited in a dream by the noble Vaishnava and given the *mantra* (that made them disciples). 239. That *avatar,* full of deeds, the friend of the universe, and *sadguru,* Tuka, is associated with me. Always remaining in my heart, he has raised the foundation of this book.

Laudation of the Bhaktalilamrita.

240. This beautiful book, the Bhaktalilamrita, is a moon of the full-moon day. The pious are the *chakor* birds that gaze on the moon and drink its nectar beams. 241. The evil minded, the wrong thinkers, like thieves, do not like its bright light, therefore, with hatred they revile this book, having no faith in their hearts. 242. Wrong thinking is the root of sin, and it has led many into trouble. If one has laid up good deeds, then there should be faith stamped upon him. 243. Those who make use of the Bhaktalilamrita are the saints, the good, the God-loving *bhaktas;* and the Brother-of-the-Helpless, the Husband-of-Rukmini, ever stands beside them. 244. Hari dwells in their hearts, and gives their minds waves of joy, and making Mahipati His instrument, He has expanded this book.

245. Svasti. This book, the Shri Bhaktalilamrita, with its life of Tukaram, so full of his love (of God) is for the God-loving pious *bhaktas* to listen to. This is the fortieth interesting chapter.

APPENDIX I.

GLOSSARY OF MARATHI WORDS USED IN THE TRANSLATIONS AND OF WORDS WHOSE TRANSLATION PRESENTS DIFFICULTIES

It might have been possible to have used fewer Marathi words in these translations, but where there is no English word that exactly expresses the Marathi word, or where it requires a whole English phrase to express the meaning of a simple Marathi word, it has seemed to me better to keep the Marathi word, so familiar to India, and let the English reader learn its meaning by its context, or by the following glossary. English literature is already enriched by many Marathi words. I see no reason why it should not still further enrich itself.

There are certain words, that are untranslatable except by a long explanation; others, where even the English word conveys only a part of the Marathi meaning. I have translated these words and expressions as best I could, but it seems worth while to include some of these words, in a glossary in order that the reader, familiar with both languages, may understand why I have used the special English word or words, sometimes in opposition to Dictionary authorities, even Molesworth. Usage has to be considered, as well as etymological meaning. The glossary will furnish the examples that have suggested the above remarks. I have used Molesworth's definitions freely, as carrying authority.

A

Abhang. A particular metrical composition in praise of the Deity. It is the popular meter of the poet-saints in their hymns of praise; the *abhangs* of Eknath, the *abhangs* of Tukaram, etc.

Avneda-bhakta. A bhakta who has the conception of no-difference (*abheda*) between the *paramatma* and the individual *atma.* Abheda-bhakti is the worship of God in harmony with the conception of the identity of the *paramatma* and the soul (*atma*) of the worshipper.

Acharya. Head of a religious order or sect.

Adhela. A copper coin worth half a pice.

Agnihotri. The priest who maintains the sacrificial fire.

Amrita. Nectar. The drink that prevents death.

Anugraha. Favor, grace, kindness, instructing in mystical verses of incantations.

Anushthana. Performance of certain ceremonies and works in propitiation of a god.

Arati. 1. The ceremony of waving around an idol, guru etc., a platter containing a burning lamp. 2. The platter and lamp waved. 3. The piece of poetry chanted on the occasion of the ceremony of waving expressing praise or worship.

Ashrama. 1. The abode of saints and rishis. 2. The word is also applied to four conditions of living, the *Brahmacharya,* or the period of chaste youth, and study; the *Grihastha,* the householder in his married and secular life; the *Vanaprastha,* who as age comes on passes his worldly cares over to others, and goes into the forest for meditation, and the fourth the *Sannyasi,* who entirely abandons all worldly cares, delights and passions, and is wholly absorbed in contemplation or the worship of God. These four *ashramas* are considered the ideal life for a Brahman.

Atma. The soul, the soul of the universe, the human soul, the vivifying principle, the self, the ego. For clearness the soul of the universe is spoken of as *parama* (supreme) *atma*, to distinguish it from the individual *atma.* The two, however, in Vedantic philosophy being identical. *Brahma,* or the *Parama-atma,* partially defined as *satchidananda* (existence, intelligence, joy) is the sole existing substance. The universe, as it appears in animate and inanimate forms, with their special names, is but the form in which the *atma,* the *paramatma,* or *Brahma* manifests itself. The human soul, or *atma,* is, therefore, only a form in which the *paramatma* appears. The great sentence, *aham-bramhasmi,* I am Brahma, is the conscious acceptance of the philosophic postulate of the oneness of the soul of the universe with the individual soul.

Avatara. Etymologically it means, "one who has descended." A divine *avatara* is the coming down to earth of such a divine being, as for example, Vishnu in the form of Krishna, or Rama. In Indian mythology, as well as in all popular conceptions, these *avatars* are for the sake of combating some evil condition or conditions in this world, or, to save the world from its sin and misery.

Human *avatars* are also recognized (*manava avatara*), that is, a good man who has died, reappears later in some other good man, to carry on, or to complete, the work of the former. Eknath is spoken of as an *avatar* of Dnyanadeva, and Tukaram as an avatara of Namadeva. Or Eknath, for example, is spoken of as an *avatar* of God, making him, therefore, both divine and human.

B

Bachnag. Poisonous root of the Gloriosa Superba.

Bhajan. 1. Adoration or worship. 2. Repeating the names of God as an act of worship. 3. A hymn, or verses sung in the worship of God.

Bhakta. 1. A worshipper, votary, or follower of; one devoted or attached to. While the above definition is etymologically correct, in usage, by the poet-saints, there is connected with it a moral idea. A *bhakta* implies a really pious man. A hypocrite is not a *bhakta,* though technically and outwardly he might appear to be one. 2. A special religious class devoted to the religious life.

As the different manifestations of God, and the various *avatars* appeal differently to different minds, there is a personal choice as well as the traditional, or family choice of the special manifestation of God. There is, therefore, a *Vishnubhakta,* a *Shivabhakta,* a *Haribhakta,* a *Ramabhakta,* a *Vitthalbhakta,* and so forth.

Bhakti. Literally, worship or adoration. It is the attitude of the *bhakta* towards God. It always implies a moral idea of sincerity and purity of worship, accompanied with love. Again and again the poet-saints affirm that there can be no *bhakti* without sincerity and love. *Bhakti* is, therefore, more than mere worship, which can be so easily a mere outward form. *Bhakti* must be the true feeling of the heart, of reverence, and love of God, whether expressed in outer forms of worship, or in the mental worship (*Manaspuja*).

Bhaktimarga. Bhakti-marga, the way of *Bhakti.* Three ways are recognized for the deliverance of man from the succession of births and deaths, with their sins and sorrows, and with their good deeds and joys, as well. The *Dnyanamarga* (The Way of Knowledge) holds the highest place in the minds of philosophers, because when by true Knowledge Ignorance disappears, all causes of sin and sorrow disappear. The *Karma-marga* or Way of Works is recognized by the poet-saints as a way, but a very hard way, and a very dangerous way. In the case of both of the above ways the danger is pride, and with pride comes a fall. The safe way, the sure way, the easy way, for all high or low, is the *bhakti-marga,* in which a man throws himself on the mercy of God, *bhakti* on man's part, and mercy, forgiveness, and salvation, on God's part. With *bhakti* sincere, and the consequent gift from God of *moksha* (salvation, deliverance), a return to this earth is avoided, and there is eternal life in the presence of God. Because it is a sure and easy way for all, the poet-saints give the *Bhakti-marga* the highest preference. Although, the word etymologically does not imply it, the usage of the poet-saints in strongest terms emphasizes the moral side of *Bhakti,* not only sincerity in *Bhakti,* but a pure ethical life is essential to the very idea of *Bhakti.* Eknath's writings are especially emphatic on this importance of internal and external moral purity.

Brahma. The One substance of which all existing things consist. *Brahma* is the substance of which all things exist. Existing things have forms and names (*nama* and *rupa*). That they exist and have *forms* and *names* is as real as is the real substance of *Brahma.*

To consider these forms, however, as different from *Brahma,* making a duality, is due to *ignorance,* that ignorance personified being called *maya* (which see).

Brahmachari. A Brahman who deserves the strictest chastity for a time or for life from a religious motive.

C

Chakor. A bird that is said to subsist on moonbeams. This idea is very frequently used in poetic figures and illustrations.

Charitra. Actions, deeds, proceedings, exploits, history.

Chataka. A bird said to drink only from the clouds, hence always eager for the rain. The idea is very frequently used in poetic figures and illustrations.

Chipla. A musical instrument, consisting of two sticks rattled together.

Chul. A fireplace. In its simplicity it may be three stones so arranged as to have the fire between them, and the pot or pan resting on them, or a semicircular erection on earth to contain the fire in its cavity, and support the cooking vessel on its rim.

D

Dakshina. Money or presents given to Brahmans and others on special occasions.

Darshana. Literally, sight, seeing, looking. In the religious usage of the word there is, however, much more than the physical sight, seeing or looking. There is an implication of respect, reverence and worship. There is no English word corresponding with this use of *darshana.*

Dasara. A festival commemorating the period of the year when the Maratha Kings started out on their campaigns.

Dhotar. The garment worn by men, consisting of a long piece of cloth wound around the body, tucked in front at the waist and also behind, taking the place of the European trousers.

Divali. The annual festival of lights.

Dnyana. 1. Knowledge in general. 2. Knowledge of a specific and religious kind, that which is derived from meditation and the study of philosophy; which teaches man the divine origin and nature of his immaterial portion, and the unreality of corporal enjoyments, sufferings and experiences, and the illusoriness of the external and objective universe; and which sanctifying him during life from earthly attachments and fleshly affections, accomplishes for him after death emancipation from individual existence and reunion with the universal spirit. In some parts of India the word is pronounced *gyana.*

Dnyanamarga. The Way of Knowledge. (See *Dnyana*).

G

Gayatri. A sacred verse from the Vedas, repeated by Brahmans at their morning and evening devotions.

Ghatika. A period of twenty-four minutes.

Ghat. 1. A mountainous range dividing countries. 2. A pass or difficult passage over a hill. 3. Quay, wharf, stairs, landing place (on banks of rivers or tanks). Hence applied by washermen, tanners, dyers, Brahmans, etc., to their respective places of resort.

Ghi. Clarified butter, also known as *tup.* The butter is melted, thus removing the water that may be in it, and then preserved in jars.

Guna. 1. A quality, attribute, affection, or property whether of matter or mind; a power, faculty, excellence, virtue; a property inherent or an affection supervenient in the most comprehensive sense. 2. The constitution of created things, as comprised in three *gunas; satva* (existence, truth, goodness, brightness etc.); *raja* (energy, passion, action etc.); *tama* (evil, darkness, ignorance etc.). All created things are a mixture of the three, *satvaguna, rajoguna,* and *tamoguna,* and therefore, are spoken of as *saguna,* (possessing these *gunas,* and Brahma, the *paramatma* is *nirguna* (unpossessed by these qualities). In God, in good men, in good things the *satva* predominates. In evil men or spirits or demons the *tama* predominates. The *rajoguna* is in all as the activity of either the good or the evil, or both. In God all is *satva,* because it is the *satva that is in activity* (*rajoguna*). In man there is a mixture of the *satva* and *tama,* and the activity (*rajoguna*) makes man a mixture of good and evil, sometimes the good predominating, sometimes the evil.

Guru. A religious teacher; one who instructs in the *Shastras.*

H

Harbara. A vetch, gram. Cicer arientinum.

Haridas. Servants of Hari [Vishnu]. Worshippers of Hari. Wandering singers who praise the deeds of Hari.

J

Japa. The repeating of *mantras* or the names of God. A rosary may be used so as to know the number of times the *mantra* or names have been used. As this outer form requires an inner reality, *japa* stands also for meditation, for worship, for prayer, indeed for the true spiritual life of a man. The correlative of *japa* is *tapa* (which see). *Tapa,* literally, religious austerity, is also extended in meaning to comprise the outer religious life of a man. *Japa,* his inner religious life and *tapa* his outer religious life.

Jiva, Shiva. When Jiva and Shiva are thus used together Jiva stands for the Individual atma, and Shiva for the Universal atma.

Jondhala. A cereal plant or its grain. Hulcus sorghum.

K

Kadaba. The stalks with their leaves of the *jondhala,* or *jivari,* Hulcus sorghum, used for fodder.

Kailas. The Heaven of Shiva.

Kakini. A weight of shells equal to 20 cowries.

Kaliyuga. The present, fourth age of the world, the evil age. Its duration is considered to be 432,000 years, after which the world is to be destroyed. The present year A.D. 1926 corresponds with the *Kaliyuga* 5027. The initial year is 3101 B.C. The four *yugas* are the *Kritayuga, Tretayuga, Dvaparayuga* and the *Kaliyuga.* The four *yugas* together make a *Mahayuga* (Great *yuga*) 4,320,000 years. It is this evil *kaliyuga* that has necessitated the frequent *avatars* to check evil, and to save mankind from its effects.

Kalpa. A day of Brahma, 432 million years of mortals.

Karma. 1. An act or a deed. 2. Religious action, ts sacrifice, ablution, etc. 3. Destiny; destiny being only the allotment, to be enjoyed or suffered in the present life of the fruit of good and evil actions, performed in former lives. 4. Deed or action. As all actions through the laws of cause and effect determine the actions in the next life. Karma is equivalent also to fate.

Karmamarga. The law of works; the road to heaven through observance of rites and ceremonies and performance of virtuous deeds. (See Dnyanamarga, Way of Knowledge, and Bhaktimarga, Way of Devotion). The way of deeds. One of the three ways of Deliverance: Dnyanamarga, Karmamarga, and Bhaktimarga.

Katha. A story, fable, exploits of gods or heroes related with music and singing.

Kavad. A bamboo lath provided with slings at each end in order to contain baskets, jars, etc. and carried on the shoulder. Used for carrying water, vegetables, etc.

Kavadi. A cowrie. A shell used in making small change.

Kirtan. Celebrating the praises of a god with music and singing. Reciting the names of the deity. In practice, however, it is a religious service of song. The leader has a topic which he delivers in song. He is accompanied with a chorus leader, and musical instruments. Following their leader the audience may break out in ecstatic repetitions of the names of God, or of the lines of a chorus.

Kshetra. A sacred spot, a sacred city, a place of pilgrimage; also the human form.

Kulkarni. A village officer who keeps public records and keeps the accounts of cultivators in their relation to Government.

M

Mahant. 1. The chief or head of an order of Gosavis, Bairagis, etc., a religious superior. 2. Applied to the head or leading man among pandits, devotees, etc.

Mahabharata. The great epic relating to wars of the Pandavas and Kauravas, ascribed to Vyas as author.

Maharashtra. The great nation. The old name of the country occupied by the Maratha people, now included in the Bombay Presidency.

Mana. Mind. According to Western psychology the mind is the soul itself viewed as thinking or imagining. Mana, however, is regarded as an organ (indriya) of thinking and imagining and not a part of the pure Atma (Soul).

Mandap. An open temporary structure, made with bamboo or other poles, with cloth roof and sides erected for festal occasions, for marriages, *kirtans,* etc.

Mantra. A text, prayer, hymn or verse, which possesses mystical or supernatural power.

Maya. This word is usually translated "Illusion," but this is not a satisfactory translation. Vedantic philosophy postulates that there is but one substance, called *Brahma,* or *paramatma,* or *atma.* This substance appears in the form of the universe, and to the various *forms* there are *names* (nama-rupa). These forms are temporary and changeable, and with the change of form the name disappears. It is due to Ignorance that these forms are supposed to be distinct from the One Substance. The reality of these forms is not denied, but that they are distinct from the One Substance is denied. That they are distinct, *i.e.,* that there is a duality, is the particular form of illusion which is indicated by the word *Maya.* In usage Maya becomes personified as the cause of the Ignorance (*adnyana*) which sees duality where is unity. One of the stock illustrations is that of gold in the form of various ornaments, each with its own name. That the gold appears in the form of various ornaments is not denied, but that ornamental forms are permanent and distinct from the gold is denied. The ornaments can be melted; they disappear as ornaments, but the gold remains unchanged. To think the ornaments were distinct from the gold would be through Ignorance (*adnyana*), and the cause of the ignorance, by a sort of personification is *maya.*

Modi. Is the cursive writing of the Marathi. The old Ashoka alphabet of the inscriptions, 250 B.C., gradually developed in time into the *Devanagari,* used in transcribing Sanskrit literature, as also Marathi literature. In business writing, however, haste being important, and the pen being lifted from the paper as little as possible, it led to a change in the form of the *Devanagari* letters, which to the casual observer seem a different character, but which can be most easily traced back to the *Devanagari origin.* The tradition that Modi was brought from the south, or that it was the invention of Hemachandra in the 13th century, may be due to the character of the southern cursive writing, and it could well be that Hemachandra adopted it as the form for official documents. There is no doubt, however, that the Modi has developed from the *Devanagari* simply by rapid writing, with the lifting of the pen from the paper as little as possible.

Moksha. Deliverance of the soul from the body, its exemption from further transmigration, with all its joys and sorrows, sins and good deeds, and its absorption into the divine essence.

Mukti. Exemption of the spirit from further migration and the reabsorption of it into its source the divine monad, Brahma, the substratum and substance of universal being. This deliverance from births and deaths, must be understood to include in the idea the deliverance from the sins and sorrows, even from the good deeds and joys of life, for each life is made up of these. The four forms of *mukti* are *sayujyata, salokata, samipata* and *sarupata,* (see *sayujyata*).

N

Namaskar. Worship, obeisance, reverential or respectful address or salutation. It is performed by joining the palms, inclining the head and pronouncing the word *namaskar.* A *sashtanga namaskar* is the prostration on the ground, so that eight parts (*ashta*) of the body touch the ground, and is the most profound method of showing reverence to God or man.

Nirguna. *Nir-guna.* Literally without a quality. *Brahma,* or *atma, paramatma* the one substance which appears to us as the universe, cannot be described in human words. It is indescribable (*avachya*). While the one substance cannot be described the forms in which it appears can be described, and their qualities determined. The forms with their names are, therefore, *saguna,* (Sa-guna) with quality. God, as a personal being, creator of the special form, in which the universe appears, is recognized as one of the forms in which the one eternal substance appears. God, therefore, is *saguna,* that is, he has qualities which can be described in human understandable words. *Brahma* is *nirguna;* God (*Ishvara*) is saguna. The gods, all *avatars,* idols, and the visions of God, are all *saguna* manifestations of the *Nirgun Brahma,* or *nirguna atma.* The *saguna ishvara,* being but the one of the many forms in which the *nirguna ishvara* appears, are, of course, to be identified as the golden bracelet is identified with the gold of which it consists. The poet-saints, therefore, in their hymns of praise, their invocations, their worship, and their prayers, make no distinction. They are addressed as well to the *nirguna* God as to the *saguna God.* This identity of the *saguna* and the *nirguna* is often asserted very definitely.

Nivritti. Cessation from worldly concerns and engagements; also Absorption into Brahma.

O

Ovi. A stanza of a particular metre of Marathi verse.

P

Pada. A variety of metrical compositions, used in hymns or anthems. Very many of the poet-saints have written in this metre. (See the *Padasangraha* in the *Kavyasangraha* Series for examples).

Paduka. An impression of a foot on stone, worshipped as the trace of some god or guru.

Pansupari. A roll of the Piper-betel leaf with Areca nut, cloves, lime, etc. (See *Vida*).

Pap. Sin in the abstract, or an evil deed. It is the exact negative correlative of the word *punya,* goodness or holiness in the abstract, or a good or holy deed. That *pap* and *punya,* evil and good deeds must receive a future reward of suffering or happiness is a part of Hindu philosophy, but this idea does not belong to the words themselves. Molesworth's Marathi English Dictionary of 1831, founded on the Marathi-Marathi Dictionary of 1829, rightly defines these words. I differ absolutely from the Notes on these words in Molesworth's Second Edition of 1857, and from its definition of the word *punya* as "merit," a meaning it never has had in Sanskrit, or in the whole course of Marathi literature, until influenced by Molesworth's second edition. See further discussion under *punya.*

Peth. A region or large division of a city. A manufacturing or a trading town. A market town. A ward of a city.

Pradakshina. Circumambulation of an object, keeping the right side towards it. These objects may be idols, sacred trees, the *tulsi* plant, a temple, even a sacred city. Keeping the object to the left would imply irreverence.

Prahar. An eighth part of the day of 24 hours. A *prahar* is, therefore, a period of three hours. The *prahars* begin at sunrise, at six, hence *Donprahar* (two-prahars) is noon.

Prakriti. In philosophy *prakriti* and *purusha* are words that denote the material and the immaterial universe. *Prakriti* (Nature, matter, phenomenon) conceived as female, and *Purusha* (male, the soul, life, activity) by their union make the whole universe, an anthropomorphic expression of the idea expressed in English as "matter and mind."

Prakrit. In the usage of the Maratha poet-saints the *Prakrit* language means the Marathi language. As distinguished from the Sanskrit (the polished language), it seems the common vernacular of the people. As may be seen from the lives of the poet-saints and their works, they had to encounter a certain amount of opposition against their Marathi, or *Prakrit* versions of the sacred Sanskrit texts. (See Eknath's life, *Bhaktalilamrita,* Chapter 21).

Prarabdha. Deeds in former births determined the course of one's life in the birth previous to this. Deeds in the previous life have determined the course of one's present life. Deeds in the present life will determine the life in the next birth. This is the law of *prarabdha.*

Prasad. 1. Favor, graciousness, propitiousness. 2. Any thing (a fruit, flower, rice, etc.) given by an idol, a guru, a saint, as a blessing or a mark of favor. 3. Food, etc., presented to an idol or a holy person to be distributed, thus honored, among worshippers, etc. 4. The sweetmeats and fruit distributed among the audience at the conclusion of a *katha, kirtan,* or puranic reading.

Punya. Goodness or holiness in the abstract, or a good or holy deed. Its negative is *pap,* or sin in the abstract or an evil deed. In the definition of this word as also in the definition of the word *pap* I differ absolutely from Molesworth's Marathi and English Dictionary, second edition of 1857. In a note it says, "The word bears not the feeblest implication of holiness, godliness or purity of spirit." On the contrary it implies all three. And by its using the definition of "merit" (not found in the edition of 1831) an idea foreign to the word has since then been attached to this noble word. "Merit", meaning a future reward of a good deed, is no part of the meaning of the word *Punya*, which is simply goodness or holiness in the abstract or a holy or good deed. The idea of merit belongs to Indian philosophy, but not to the word *punya*. Every *punya* will have its reward in the future, as will every *pap*, but this idea is not in the word itself.

The first edition of Molesworth of 1831, founded on the Pandits' Marathi-Marathi edition of 1829 has the correct definition. See also Monier-Williams' Sanskrit dictionary under *punya* and *pap*. The word *punya* twice used in the Rigveda, many times used in the Upanishads, and Bhagavadgita, and all through old Marathi literature, is the exact negative of *pap*. It, in no single instance, means "merit" as implying a future reward.

Puranpoli. A wheaten cake with stuffing of coarse sugar, pea flour, etc.

Puran. A particular class of Hindu sacred literature, generally regarded as eighteen in number. They deal with stories of the creation of the world, its destruction, its renewal, of gods, goddesses, and heroes. The eighteen are Brahma, Padma, Vishnu, Shiva, Linga, Garuda, Narada, Bhagvata, Agni, Skandha, Bhavishya, Brahmavaivarta, Markandeya, Vamana, Varaha, Matsya, Kurma and Vayu, but there are other lists of 18, slightly varying from this. Of the Purans the Bhagavata, giving the life and teachings of Krishna, has had the greatest influence on the thought and life of the Maratha poet-saints.

Puranik. A Brahman well read in the *Purans*. A public expounder of them. On account of the vast extent of

Sanskrit literature those who expound the sacred books have to specialize. There are those who make a specialty of expounding some Puran and are known as Puraniks.

Purusha. See Prakriti.

R

Ramayana. The great epic relating the exploits of Ram, ascribed to Valmiki as author.

S

Sadguru. Literally a true, or good guru (see Guru). While primarily the word applies to human teachers, or gurus, the poet-saints even applied it to God, for a *sadguru* is regarded as a manifestation of God. The Maratha poet-saints frequently refer to the high moral qualities, the sincerity, the unselfishness, the unhypocritical spirit, that marks a *sadguru,* as distinguished from a false guru.

Sadhana. The means employed to obtain deliverance from births and deaths and all that life implies in its sins and sorrows and even joys.

Saguna. See *Nirguna.*

Samsara. 1. The world, mundane existence, human life, man's mortal state. 2. The affairs of life; worldly business; the vocations and engagements, the cares and troubles of secularity.

Sannyasi. One who has cast off all worldly possessions, and carnal or natural affections; an ascetic. The poet-saints distinguish between the hypocritical, formal *Sannyasi,* who outwardly appears only to have given up all, and the true and sincere *sannyasi,* whose giving up of the world is genuine.

Santa. A saint, practically synonymous with *sadhu* (which see). He is one who has lost worldly desires and devotes himself to the worship of God. But whatever he may appear outwardly, no one is a *santa* without purity of heart and life. The appellation *Kavi-santa,* or poet-saints, designate those saints who were poets. The Maratha poet-saints begin with Dnyaneshvara, about A.D. 1290, so far as their works are known, and continue to the present day.

Satchidananda. Existence-intelligence-joy. Although *Brahma,* or the *paramatma* cannot be described in human words (avachya), yet because it is believed to *exist,* to be that which takes the form of *intelligent beings,* and to express itself in beings feeling *joy*—*Brahma* being the substratum of these—this definition of Brahma is very frequently employed. It should be noted that these three words, *existence, intelligence* and *joy* are not adjectives, but nouns. They do not connote that Brahma *exists,* is *intelligent* and *happy,* but that the one substance, *Brahma,* in taking form appears in the form of existing things, in the form of intelligent beings, and those possessing joy and goodness.

Sadhu. A holy man; a saint or sage; one of subdued passions and of contemplative habits. The poet-saints give the word a moral emphasis, hence a *sadhu* is a man of pure character, one truly devoted to God, a spiritually minded man; a good man. A man can appear hypocritically a *sadhu,* and not be a *sadhu,* for a *sadhu* must be pure in heart and life. The wandering professional *sadhu,* called such, may or may not be sincere, but he is not considered a true *sadhu* without purity of heart and life.

Sashtanga-namaskar. See *Namaskar.*

Sayujyata. The fourth of the four states in which *mukti* (final deliverance) is distinguished, *viz.,* absorption into the essence of Brahma. The four are *Sayujyata* (absorption into the essence of Brahma); *Salokata* (residence in the heaven of a particular deity); *Samipata* (Nearness to the Deity); and *Sarupata* (Bearing the likeness of God).

Savadhana. Literally attention, heed. At the moment of marriage, the priests in solemn tone repeat the words, "*Savadhanam, savadhanam,*" and at that moment the curtain between the bride and bridegroom is removed, and the marriage is complete.

Siddhi. A supernatural power or faculty supposed to be acquirable through the performance of certain magical, mystical or alchemical rites or processes. Eight are enumerated, *viz., anima, mahima, garima, laghima, prapti, prakamya, ishitva,* and *vashitva.* The powers or *siddhis* are personified as female beings or *siddhis,* who come and serve those who by their austerities or otherwise gain those powers.

Shraddha. A kind of funeral rite or ceremony in honor of the departed spirits of dead relatives, observed with great strictness at various fixed periods, especial honor being given to paternal and maternal ancestors.

Shudra. The fourth grand division of the Hindu body; also an individual of it. The four grand divisions are *Brahman,* (the priestly caste); *Kshatriya,* (the warrior, military, governing class); *Vaishya,* (agricul tural and mercantile class) and *Shudra* (the servile class, whose duty is to serve the upper three). The *atishudra* also called *anamik,* and *antyaja,* are those still lower than the Shudra, and outside of the four grand divisions. Hence they are *asprishya* (Untouchable) or *anamika* (Unmentionable).

Shanti. Peace. Unruffled mind.

Shloka. A verse, a stanza, a quantity of four lines. A particular metre; praise In the Marathi commentaries the *Shloka* commented on is the Sanskrit text.

Shruti. The Vedas severally or collectively. The word is from the Sanskrit, meaning "hearing."

Skandha. A section of a book, a book, a chapter.

Stotra. 1. Praise, panegyric, eulogium. 2. A book or writing in celebration of the praises; also a hymn.

Svami. A master or lord, the master or lord of, also the proprietor or owner of. Applied to the Deity, a god, a king, or prince, a spiritual preceptor, a husband, a holy personage, a learned Brahman, a *Gosavi-Sannyasi,* etc. It is used also as a title, Keshava-svami.

T

Tapa. Religious austerity, pious mortification of the body. It is especially connected with the *yoga* system, and the *yogis* carry it to its extreme limit. But it also has less austere usage, meaning the duties of life, the special duties of Brahmans, Kshatriyas, Vaishyas and Shudras. It is, therefore, the correlative of *japa, japa* signifying the inner spiritual life, and *tapa* the outer religious life. (See *Japa*).

Tilak. The spot or line made with coloured earths or unguents upon the forehead. It is considered either as an ornament or as a sectarial distinction.

Tirtha. 1. A holy or sacred place, any place of pilgrimage, but especially particular spots along the course of sacred streams or in the vicinity of sacred springs. 2. A holy stream, or water brought from one. Water in which a Brahman, sannyasi, etc., has dipped his foot, which has been poured over an idol; holy water.

Tulsi. A plant venerated by the Hindus, Holy Basil, Ocymum sanctum. It is usually grown in an earthen altar before the door of the house, or in the garden behind the house. Its leaf is used in offerings, in garlands, and its stalks also have sacred uses. Those worshipping the plant go around it, keeping it to the right (pradakshina) with palm to palm, repeating a *mantra*, or prayer.

U

Upanishad. The oldest philosophical literature.

Upasana. Worship or religious service.

V

Vaikuntha. The Heaven of Vishnu.

Vairagi. An ascetic or devotee; one who has subdued his worldly desires of passions. The word is also applied to a class of religious mendicants. The word is also pronounced *bairagi.* The poet-saints distinguish between the true and the hypocritical *vairagi.*

Vairagya. 1. Absence of worldly desire or passion. 2. Popularly, renunciation of all sensuous delight or gratification.

Vastu. The real as opposed to the unreal, Brahma. The Universe *Atma. Substance.* The substance of which the Universe consists, namely Brahma.

Vedas. The oldest of the Indian Scriptures. The four Vedas are, the Rigveda, the Yajurveda, the Samaveda, and the Atharvaveda.

Vida. A roll of the leaf of Piper-betel with Areca-nut, cloves, lime, etc. It is usually chewed after a meal. It is distributed to an audience after a *kirtan,* or any public assembly, and is the final act. It is believed to be a digestive, and also as purifying the mouth. It is generally called *pan-supari* (leaf supari nut). Many have the habit of chewing it constantly.

Videhi. Literally, one without a body (vi-deha). In usage, however, it implies a temporary or permanent absorption of the mind in a way to make one unconscious of the possession of a body, as when one is intensely listening to a *kirtan,* he is for the time being a *videhi.* Or when through a life of constant contemplation of the *atma,* or of God, the ascetic or devotee loses all thought of his body, or cold or heat, hunger or thirst, desires or passions, he is a *videhi.* A man is a *videhi* when the spiritual completely dominates the physical.

Viveka. Right-thinking. To the Vedantist right-thinking is the discrimination between reality and unreality.

W

Wada. 1. A stately or large edifice, a mansion or palace. 2. A division of a town, a quarter, a ward, as Brahmanwada, Maharwada. 3. An enclosed piece of meadowfield, or garden ground; an enclosure. 4. A cluster of huts of agriculturists, a hamlet.

Y

Yama. The god who rules over the spirits of the dead.

Yoga. Spiritual or abstract devotion; union with Brahma through abstract meditation, or contemplation; also the practice or exercise of this sort of worship.

Yogabhrashta. One who was interrupted in his preceding birth during the performance of Yoga (abstract meditation upon *Brahma*). As an example, a pious outcaste, devoted to Eknath, is called a *Yogabhrashta.* In the Autobiography of Bahinabai, a calf, because of its peculiar pious actions, is called a *yogabhrashta.* Indeed any pious person can be described as a *yogabhrashta,* as one whose pious life in a former birth was accidentally interrupted and has now a further opportunity.

Yogi. 1. A performer of the abstract meditation called *yoga.* 2. An ascetic or devotee in general. Popularly a *yogi* is supposed to be able to gain extraordinary powers through his practice of *yoga,* called *siddhis* (which see), and the ash-covered *yogi* is able to instil much fear in the minds of the ignorant. The poet-saints, of course, distinguish between the hypocritical *yogi* and the true *yogi* whose heart and life must be pure.

Yojana. A measure of distance equal to four *Kos,* roughly about eight miles.